GREENWOOD
G U I D E S

The Team

Simon Greenwood

Rachel Parsons

Oliver Needham

Jemila Twinch

First published in 2000 by Greenwood Guides,
46 Lillie Rd, London SW6 1TN, UK.

Third edition

Copyright (c) June 2004 Greenwood Guides

ISBN 0-9537980-6-2 printed in China.

THE GREENWOOD GUIDE TO
SOUTH AFRICA

special hand-picked accommodation

Including Phophonyane Lodge in Swaziland
and Malealea Lodge in Lesotho

third edition

www.greenwoodguides.com

Acknowledgements

Series editor Simon Greenwood

South African editor Oliver Needham

Writing collaboration and inspections Simon Greenwood, Oliver Needham, Rachel Parsons and Jemila Twinch

Maps created by InformAge, using ArcView GIS

Digital typographic contour and road data sourced from South African Chief Directorate: Surveys and Mapping

Production Jo Ekin

DTP and design Tory Gordon-Harris

Printing Colorcraft, Hong Kong

UK distribution Portfolio, London

SA distribution Quartet Sales and Marketing, Johannesburg

Cover image Jan Harmsgat Country House, entry 101

Incidental photographs
Title page and province intro pages all by Ollie Needham, except Western Cape (from Auberge Rozendal)

Symbols
and what they mean

 No credit cards accepted.

 Meals can be provided, often by prior arrangement.

 Stocked wild game can be seen. This does not include naturally occurring wild animals like springbok and waterbuck.

 Rooms all have TVs.

 Children are welcome without proviso.

 Working farm.

 Off-street car parking.

 Access only for wheelchairs.

 Full wheelchair facilities.

 Swimming available in pool, sea, dam or river.

 No smoking inside the buildings.

 Good hiking or walking direct from the house.

 They have their own horses for riding.

Contents

EASTERN CAPE

KWA-ZULU NATAL

Introduction

Just flicking through the photos in this book may give you that same uncomfortable feeling you can sometimes experience in restaurants where every single thing on the menu sounds unbearably delicious. You feel the pain of the things you didn't choose as much as the pleasure of the ones you did. I am sorry about that. You will just have to work your way through them slowly!

These places are not just telegenic posers however. That is not what we are about.

In general most places to stay do exactly what it says on the tin, BB&B: bed, breakfast and bill. As a result many people think of where they stay as incidental to their holiday, a convenient stopover between things they want to see.

Our approach is quite the opposite. We have found you places where the stay itself IS the holiday. Far more than just the skeleton of your trip, the places we have chosen will put the flesh on it, clothe it, put a hat on its head, wrap a scarf round its neck and pop a pipe in its mouth. We have sought and found accommodation that acts as destination. The owners in this guide will make sure that you experience the farm, the winery, the bush, the beach, the mountain, the city, the wildlife… often on private land. But vitally you will also meet extremely hospitable South Africans and go places other tourists will not find.

This book is full of people doing their own thing well.

EXPENSIVE DOES NOT MEAN GOOD

There are essentially three types of place to stay. There are those that fulfil their obligations in a commercial way and leave you feeling throughout your stay like the paying customer that you are. There are those few great places where you are welcomed in and treated as a friend, cliché though this may now have become, and where paying at the end of your visit is a pleasurable surprise. And of course there is a third category where paying for your stay is a disagreeable inevitability!

It is a particular irony of the accommodation world that no price is ever put on the essential qualities of a place – people, atmosphere, charm. These terms are too woolly, perhaps, to quantify, but this is where one's real enjoyment of a place to stay stems from. You are asked to pay instead for tangible facilities like marble bathrooms and en-suite showers.

This is a fallacy that we try to dismantle in all our guides, which is why you will find places at all reasonable price levels. Expensive does not mean good. And nor does cheap (however appealing the word may sound!). If a place costs plenty then it will probably offer facilities in keeping with the price. But that does not mean you will have any fun. Some very expensive places forget that they are providing a service and look down their noses at their own guests. At the other end of the spectrum, the very cheapest places are often cheap for good reasons. Sometimes for spectacular reasons!

Character and genuine hospitality, the extra qualities we search for, are found spaced evenly across the price spectrum. Nowhere in this guide cuts corners at the risk of your displeasure. We give equal billing to each place we choose, no matter if it is a gorgeous lodge or a home-spun B&B.

At the top end, the most jewel-encrusted, nay 'boutique' places may drip with luxurious trimmings, but have retained their sense of atmosphere and humour, are friendly and informal and nearly all are still owned and managed by the same people. ('Boutique' always used to mean a 'small clothes shop in France', but it has sneaked into accommodation vocab somewhere along the line.)

Equally, there are places in the book that do not have much in the way of luxury, but easily compensate with unique settings, wonderful views and charming hosts.

It is the quality of experience that draws us in and this is not determined by how much you pay. In the end I know that you will really like the owners in this book, many of whom we now count as friends. And you will certainly make friends yourselves if you stick to the Greenwood trail.

DRIVING
There is nowhere in this book that would make a 4-wheel drive a necessity.

CAR HIRE
Make sure that you have considered the amount of daily mileage your car hire company gives you. 100km or even 200km a day is virtually nothing and the final cost can be far higher than you estimated. Try and work out roughly what distances you will be covering and ask for the correct daily allowance.

MOBILE/CELL PHONES
Airports all have shops that provide mobile phones. They are invaluable and we recommend that you get one. You can buy a cheap handset and then pay for calls as you go with recharge cards. You don't need to get locked into year-long contracts.

TELEPHONE NUMBERS

To call South Africa from the UK dial 0027 then drop the 0 from the local code. To call the UK from South Africa dial 0944 the drop the 0 from the local code. The numbers printed in this book are all from within South Africa.

TORTOISES

Look out for tortoises. They are slow, but seem to spend a lot of time, completely against the tide of advice put forward for their benefit, crossing roads.

TIPPING

* In restaurants we tend to give 15%.

* At a petrol station my policy is to give no tip for just filling up, 3 rand for cleaning the windows, and 5 rand for cleaning the windows and checking oil and water. If you really don't want the attendant to clean your windows you need to make this a statement when you ask for the petrol… or they will often do it anyway.

* At a guest-house I would typically give R15 per person staying for up to two nights. If you are staying longer than two nights then you might feel like adding more. If there is obviously one maid to whom the tip will go then give it to her direct. If there are many staff members who will be sharing the tip then give it to your host.

TIME OF YEAR

I got in a bit of a tangle in the first edition trying neatly to package up what is really quite complicated. So I will limit myself to one observation. It seems to me that most Europeans come to South Africa in January, February and March to avoid their own miserable weather and write taunting postcards home from a sunny Cape. I've been doing this myself for the last few years.

However, the very best time of year to visit the Northern Cape, Mpumalanga, Limpopo, North-West Province, KwaZulu Natal and the Karoo, i.e. the whole country except the southern Cape, is from May to October. The air is dry and warm, game viewing is at its best and there are fewer tourists keeping the prices higher. It's worth mentioning.

WHERE TO GO

I just wanted to make a case for those areas of SA not frequented by overseas tourists, which as a result offer a really exciting and often much better value holiday in terms of cost and experience. Hardly anyone makes it to the Free State, the Northern Cape or the parts of the Eastern Cape on the other side of Addo. All these areas are highly recommended.

PAY FOR ENTRY

We could not afford to research and publish this guide in the way we do without the financial support of those we feature. Each place that we have chosen has paid an entry fee for which we make no apology. It has not influenced our decision-making about who is right or wrong for the guide and we turn down many more than we accept. The proof of this is in the proverbial pudding. Use the book and see for yourself. It is also very hard for us to write up a place that we are not enthusiastic about.

THE MAPS SECTION

The maps at the front of the book are designed to show you where in the country each place is positioned, and should not be used as a road map. There are many minor and dirt roads missing and we recommend that you buy a proper companion road atlas.

Each place is flagged with a number that corresponds to the page number below each entry.

Some have complained that it is hard to find detailed road maps of South Africa in the UK, so I suggest you buy one at the airport when you arrive in SA.

CANCELLATION

Most places have some form of cancellation charge. Do make sure that you are aware what this is if you book in advance. Owners need to protect themselves against no-shows and will often demand a deposit for advance booking.

PRICES

The prices quoted are per person sharing per night, unless specifically stated otherwise. Every now and then complications have meant we quote the full room rate. Single rates are also given.

We have usually put in a range within which the actual price will fall. This may be because of fluctuating prices at different times of year, but also we have tried to predict the anticipated rise in prices over the book's shelf life. Obviously we cannot know what will happen to the value of the rand and prices might fall outside the quoted range.

Most game lodges quote an all-in package including meals and game activities.

CHILDREN

We have only given the child-friendly symbol to those places that are unconditionally accepting of the little fellows. This does not necessarily mean that if there is no symbol children are barred. But it may mean chatting with your hosts about their ages, their temperaments and how suitable a time and place it will be. Most owners are concerned about how their other guests will take to kids running wild when they are trying to relax on a long-anticipated holiday… from their own children.

RIDING
We have only given this symbol to places with their own horses. Many places can organise riding nearby.

DISCLAIMER
We make no claims to god-like objectivity in assessing what is or is not special about the places we feature. They are there because we like them. Our opinions and tastes are mortal and ours alone. We have done our utmost to get the facts right, but apologize for any mistakes that may have slipped through the net. Some things change which are outside our control: people sell up, prices increase, exchange rates fluctuate, unfortunate extensions are added, marriages break up and even acts of God can rain down destruction. We would be grateful to be told about any errors or changes, however great or small. We can always make these editions on the web version of this book.

DON'T TRY AND DO TOO MUCH. PLEASE.
It is the most common way to spoil your own holiday. South Africa is a huge country and you cannot expect to see too much of it on one trip. Don't over-extend yourself. Stay everywhere for at least two nights and make sure that you aren't spending your hard-earned holiday fiddling with the radio and admiring the dashboard of your hire car.

PLEASE WRITE TO US
Our email address is simon@greenwoodguides.com for all comments. Although we visit each place each edition many of the places featured here are small, personal and owner-run. This means that their enjoyability depends largely on the happiness, health and energy of the hosts. This can evaporate in double-quick time for any number of reasons and standards plummet before we have had a chance to re-evaluate the place. So we are also very grateful to travellers who keep us up to date with how things are going. We are always most concerned to hear that the hosting has been inattentive.

We also have guides to Australia, New Zealand and Canada. These books are available in bookshops or by emailing us direct.

THE CAPE SALMON (REPRISE)
About the so-called Cape salmon…. Any who bought either of the first two editions will know that I have been floundering around (the right word I think) wondering whether this fish was really a salmon at all. In the second edition I

suggested, after due thought and prayer, that in fact I believed that it was a salmon. Then I received this enlightening email from Nick Cooling, which I hope puts the seal on the whole affair:

"Simon, I'm sure you will not wish to become involved in "fishy" controversy but reference to Professor J.L.B. Smith's weighty tome The Sea Fishes of South Africa will show that the so-called Cape salmon is elops saurus of the family elopidae. Common names include Cape salmon, wildevis and skipjack in South Africa and tenpounder, bonyfish, etc. (America). "It is a large predatory fish of tropical seas which does enter tidal rivers almost to fresh water, possibly to spawn." (Smith). "The flesh is disappointing, being insipid and full of bones." (Smith)

Atlantic and Pacific salmon belong to the family salmonidae, the Atlantic salmon being salmo salar. It seems that the several species of true salmon spring from a common ancestor and most members are unable to breed in salt water - hence the well-known runs of both the Atlantic and Pacific salmon back into their rivers of origin.

In short, I believe you were right in the first edition. Anyone who has caught both will know from the colour and quality of the flesh and other characteristics that they are quite different - without need for scientific identification!

Regards and best wishes. Nick Cooling."

It is hard to argue with such a coherent and well-researched argument. But if you do have an issue with what he says get in touch! Our email doors are always open.

TRAVELLER TALES

I want to start a GG travellers' tales bit. So if any of you want to write to me about your travels in South Africa, I will cherry-pick anything particularly interesting or humorous and create a section in the next (4th) edition. Again emails to simon@greenwoodguides.com.

So that's about it for another year. My thanks to Ollie, Rachel and Jemila for their driving legs, their sunny personalities and their dedication to unearthing new gems.

And I wish all of you who use the guide a wonderful time. I hope the Greenwood Guide will be seen as the main reason why you enjoyed your holiday as much as you did.

Simon.

General Map

Approximate scale 1 : 9.2 million

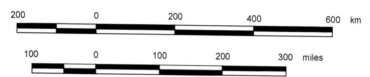

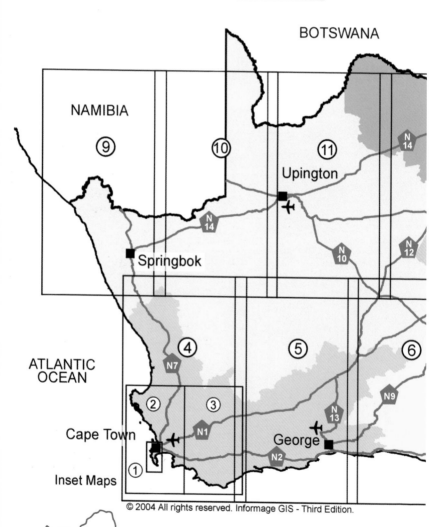

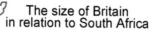

The size of Britain
in relation to South Africa

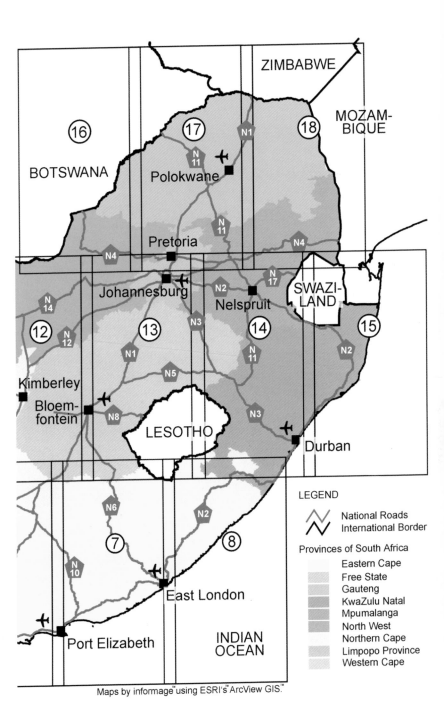

ZIMBABWE

MOZAM-
BIQUE

⑯

BOTSWANA

⑰ N1

N11
Polokwane

N11

N4 Pretoria

N14

N4

N17
Johannesburg SWAZI-
LAND
N2
Nelspruit
⑫ N12 ⑬ N3 ⑭ ⑮

N1 N11 N2

Kimberley N5

Bloem- N8
fontein

LESOTHO

N3
Durban

N6 N2

⑦ ⑧

N10

East London

Port Elizabeth INDIAN
OCEAN

LEGEND

National Roads
International Border

Provinces of South Africa

Eastern Cape
Free State
Gauteng
KwaZulu Natal
Mpumalanga
North West
Northern Cape
Limpopo Province
Western Cape

Maps by informage™ using ESRI's™ ArcView GIS™.

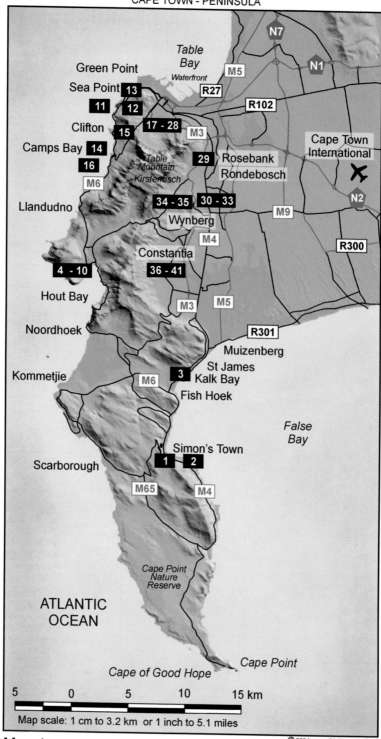

CAPE TOWN - PENINSULA

Map 1

© 2004 emap@informage.co.za

Map scale: 1 cm to 3.2 km or 1 inch to 5.1 miles

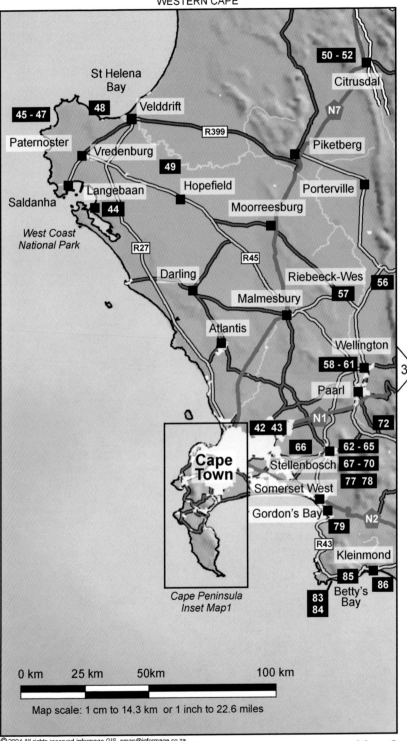

St Helena
Bay

45 - 47

48 Velddrift

Paternoster

Vredenburg

49

Hopefield

Saldanha

Langebaan

44

West Coast
National Park

Citrusdal

N7

R399

Piketberg

Porterville

Moorreesburg

Darling

R27

R45

Riebeeck-Wes

56

Malmesbury

57

Atlantis

Wellington

58 - 61

3

Paarl

72

42 43

N1

66

62 - 65

Cape
Town

Stellenbosch

67 - 70

77 78

Somerset West

Gordon's Bay

N2

79

R43

Kleinmond

85

86

Cape Peninsula
Inset Map1

**83
84**

Betty's
Bay

0 km   25 km   50km   100 km

Map scale: 1 cm to 14.3 km or 1 inch to 22.6 miles

Map 2

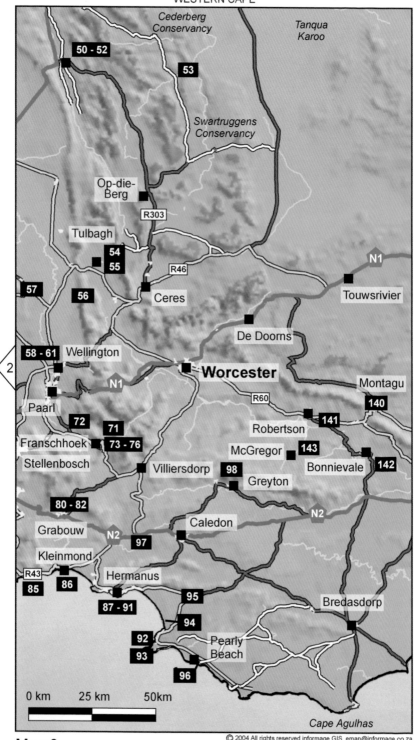

Map 3

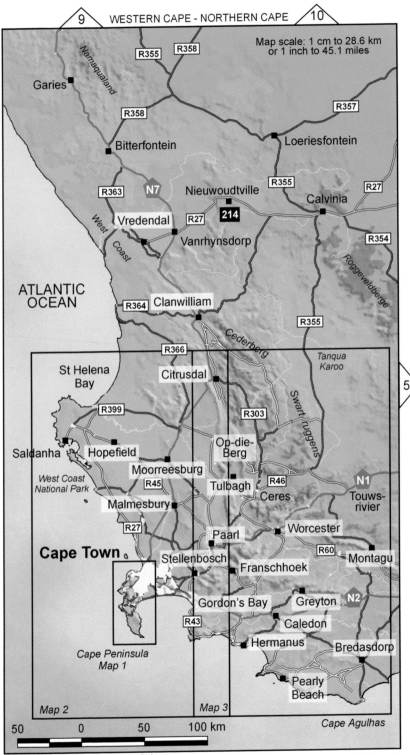

Map scale: 1 cm to 28.6 km
or 1 inch to 45.1 miles

R355 R358

Garies

Namaqualand

R358

Bitterfontein

R357

Loeriesfontein

R363   N7   Nieuwoudtville   R355   Calvinia   R27

Vredendal   R27   **214**

Vanrhynsdorp   R354

West Coast

Roggeveldberge

ATLANTIC
OCEAN

R364   Clanwilliam

R355

Cederberg

R366   *Tanqua Karoo*

St Helena Bay   Citrusdal   5

R399   R303   *Swartruggens*

Saldanha   Op-die-Berg

Hopefield

West Coast National Park   Moorreesburg   Tulbagh   R46   N1   Touws-rivier

R45   Ceres

Malmesbury

R27   Paarl   Worcester

Cape Town   Stellenbosch   R60   Montagu

Franschhoek

Gordon's Bay   Greyton   N2

R43   Caledon

Cape Peninsula Map 1   Hermanus   Bredasdorp

Map 2   *Map 3*   Pearly Beach

50   0   50   100 km   *Cape Agulhas*

Map 4

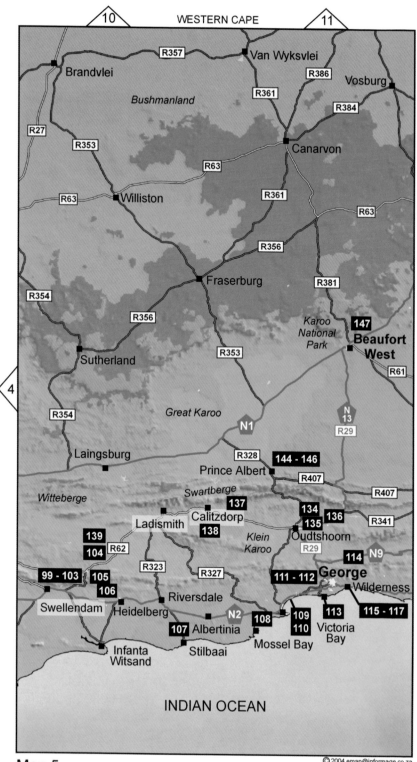

Map 5

© 2004 emap@informage.co.za

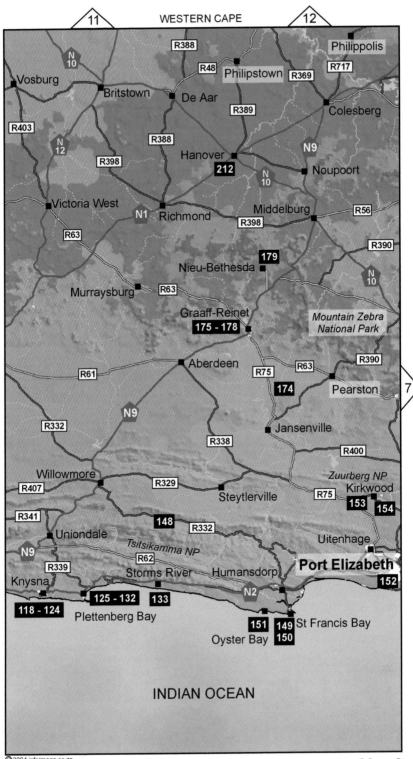

Philippolis

N10

Vosburg

Britstown

De Aar

R388

R48

Philipstown

R369

R717

R389

Colesberg

R403

N12

R388

Hanover

212

N9

Noupoort

R398

N10

Victoria West

N1

Richmond

Middelburg

R56

R398

R63

R390

R179

Nieu-Bethesda

N10

Murraysburg

R63

Graaff-Reinet

175 - 178

Mountain Zebra National Park

Aberdeen

R75

R63

R390

R61

174

Pearston

7

N9

Jansenville

R332

R338

R400

Willowmore

R329

Zuurberg NP

R75

Kirkwood

R407

Steytlerville

153

154

R341

148

R332

Uniondale

Tsitsikamma NP

Uitenhage

N9

R62

Port Elizabeth

R339

Storms River

Humansdorp

N2

152

Knysna

125 - 132

133

118 - 124

Plettenberg Bay

151

149

150

Oyster Bay

St Francis Bay

INDIAN OCEAN

©2004 informage.co.za

Map 6

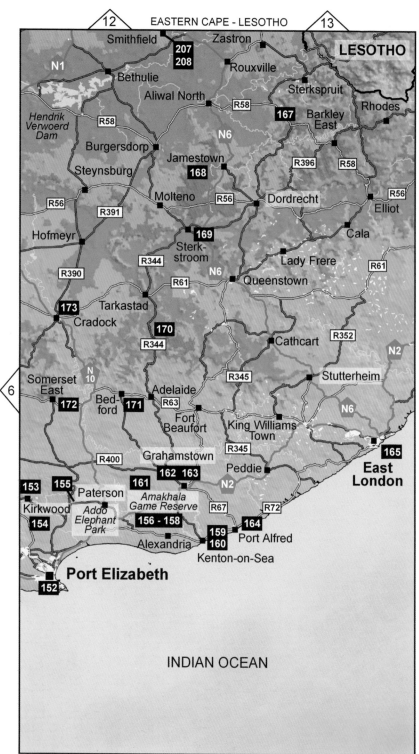

Map 7

© 2004 informage.co.za

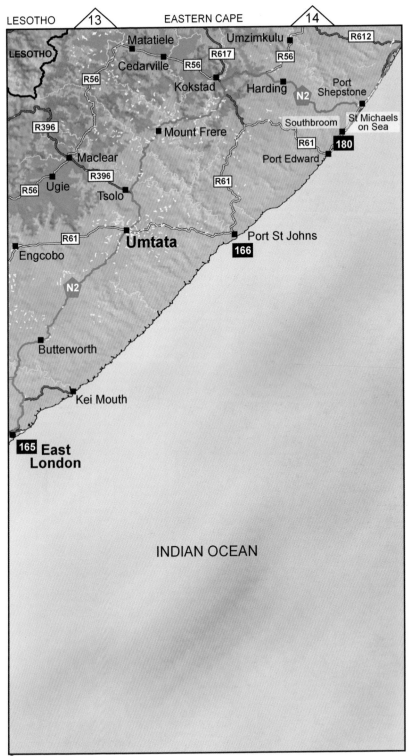

LESOTHO

Matatiele

Cedarville

R617

R56

R56

R612

R56

Umzimkulu

Harding

N2

Port Shepstone

Kokstad

R396

Mount Frere

Southbroom

St Michaels on Sea

Maclear

R396

R61

180

Port Edward

Ugie

R56

Tsolo

R61

R61

Engcobo

Umtata

Port St Johns

166

N2

Butterworth

Kei Mouth

165 East London

INDIAN OCEAN

Map 8

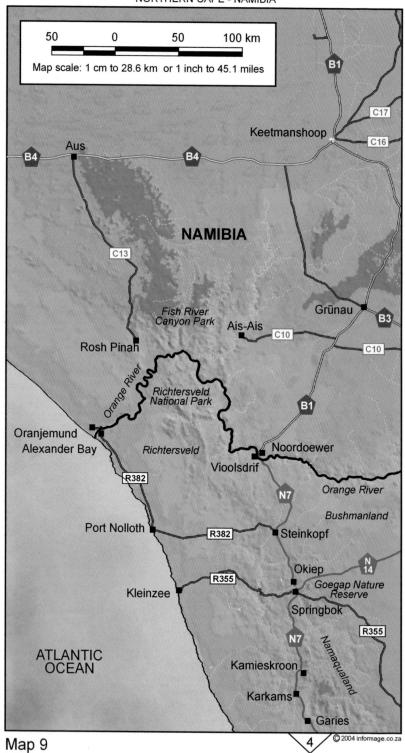

Map 9

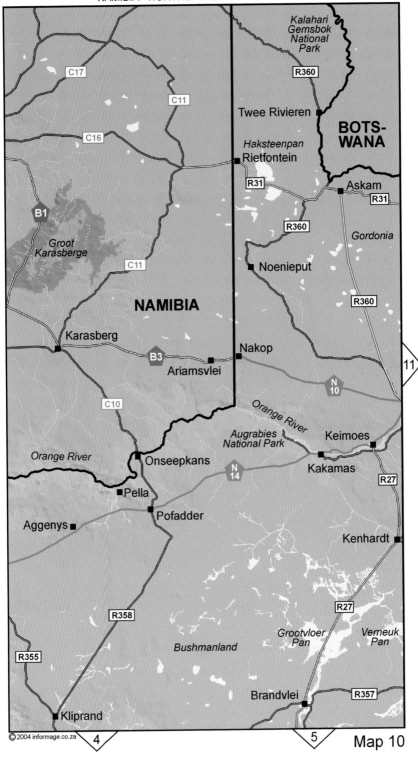

Map 10

© 2004 informage.co.za

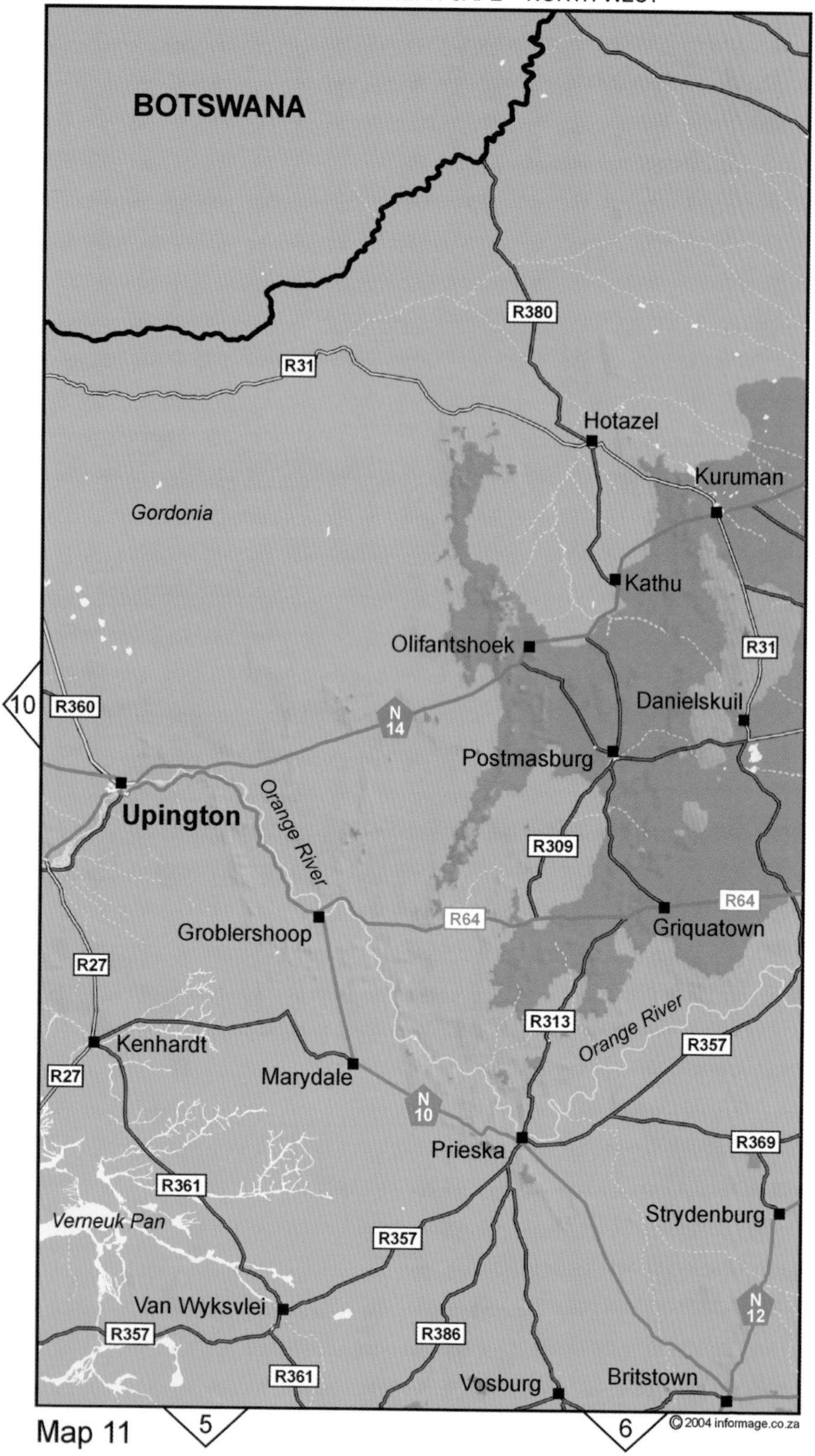

BOTSWANA

Gordonia

R380

R31

■ Hotazel

Kuruman ■

■ Kathu

R31

Olifantshoek ■

Danielskuil ■

10 R360

N 14

Postmasburg ■

Upington ■

Orange River

R309

R64

R64

Groblershoop ■

Griquatown ■

R27

R313

Orange River

R357

Kenhardt ■

R27

Marydale ■

N 10

R369

Prieska ■

Verneuk Pan

R361

Strydenburg ■

R357

N 12

Van Wyksvlei ■

R357

R386

R361

Vosburg ■

Britstown ■

Map 11   5   6   © 2004 informage.co.za

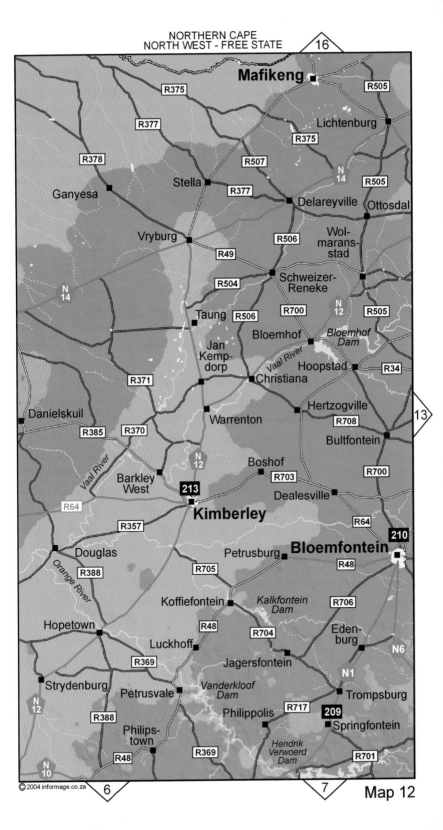

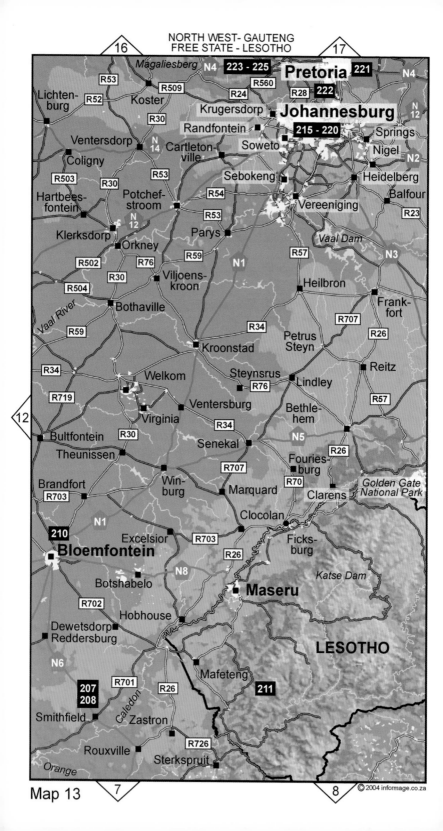

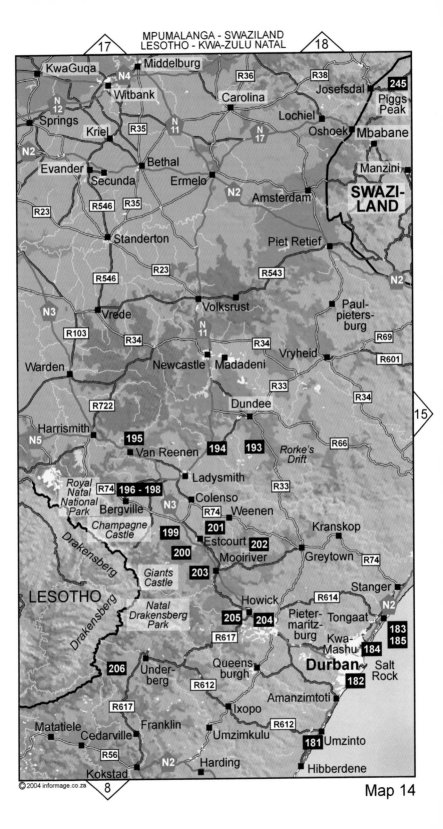

KwaGuqa
Middelburg
R36   R38
Josefsdal
245
Piggs
Peak
Witbank
Carolina
N4
N12
Springs
Lochiel
Oshoek
Mbabane
Kriel
R35
N11
N17
Bethal
Manzini
Evander
Secunda
Ermelo
SWAZI-
LAND
R23
R546
R35
N2
Amsterdam
Standerton
Piet Retief
N2
R546
R23
Paul-
pieters-
burg
N3
Vrede
Volksrust
R103
R34
N11
R34
R69
Warden
Newcastle
Madadeni
Vryheid
R601
R722
R33
R34
Harrismith
Dundee
15
N5
195
Van Reenen
194   193
Rorke's
Drift
R66
Ladysmith
Royal
Natal
National
Park
R74   196 - 198
Colenso
R33
Bergville
N3
R74   Weenen
Champagne
Castle
199
201
Kranskop
200
Estcourt   202
Giants
Castle
203
Mooiriver
Greytown   R74
LESOTHO
Natal
Drakensberg
Park
Stanger
Howick
R614
Drakensberg
205   204
Pieter-
maritz-
burg
Tongaat
N2
183
185
Kwa-
Mashu
184
206
Underberg
Queens-
burgh
Durban
Salt
Rock
182
R617
R612
Matatiele
Cedarville
Franklin
Amanzimtoti
R612
R617
Ixopo
181
Umzinto
R56
Umzimkulu
N2
Kokstad
Harding
Hibberdene
8

© 2004 informage.co.za

Map 14

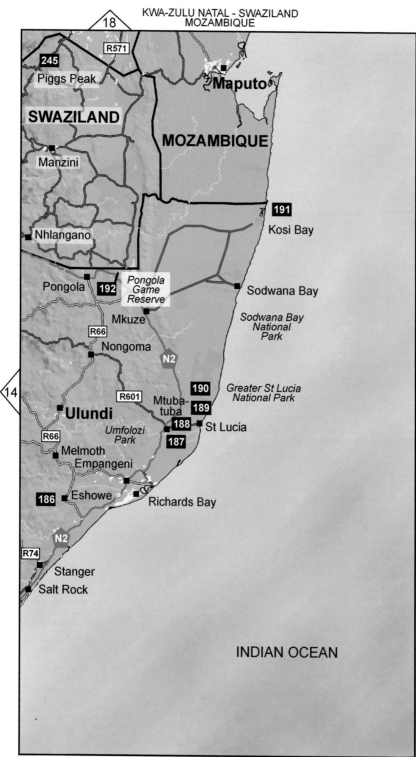

Map 15

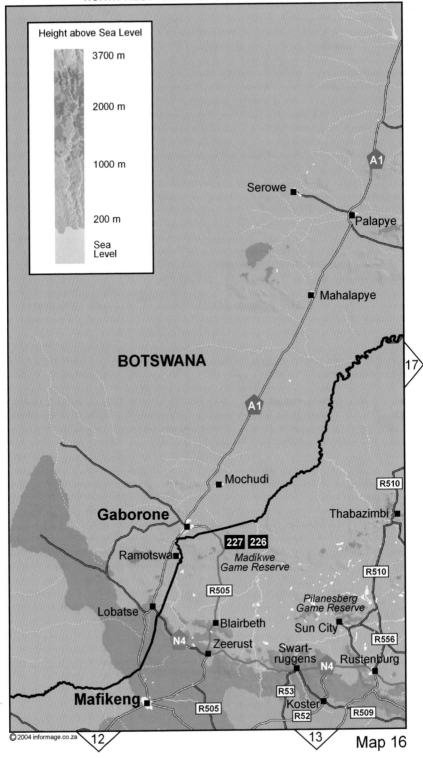

Map 16

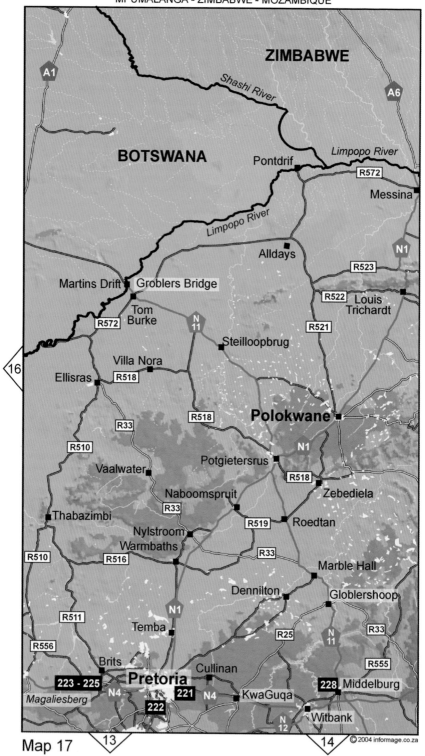

ZIMBABWE

Shashi River

A1

A6

BOTSWANA

Limpopo River

Pontdrif

R572

Messina

Limpopo River

Alldays

N1

R523

Martins Drift

Groblers Bridge

R522

Louis Trichardt

Tom Burke

R572

N11

R521

Steilloopbrug

16

Villa Nora

R518

Ellisras

Polokwane

R518

R33

R510

Vaalwater

Potgietersrus

N1

R518

Naboomspruit

R33

Zebediela

Thabazimbi

R519

Roedtan

Nylstroom

Warmbaths

R510

R516

R33

Marble Hall

R511

Dennilton

Globlershoop

Temba

N1

R25

N11

R33

R556

Brits

R555

223 - 225

Cullinan

228

Middelburg

Pretoria

221

Magaliesberg

N4

N4

KwaGuqa

222

N12

Witbank

Map 17

13

14

© 2004 informage.co.za

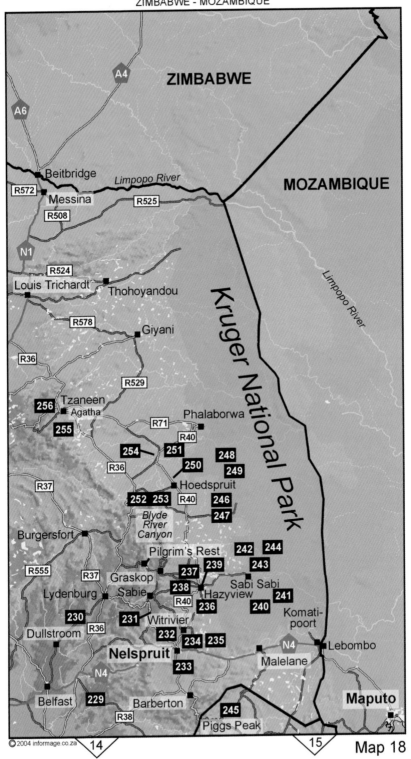

Western Cape

Boulders Beach Lodge

Frans Hollenbach

4 Boulders Place, Boulders
Beach, Simon's Town 7995
Tel: 021-786-1758
Fax: 021-786-1825
Email: boulders@iafrica.com
Web:
www.bouldersbeach.co.za

I screeched to a halt at the sight of three penguins sitting unperturbed on a garden wall. I excitedly snapped shots, delighted at their tame nature and vanity poses, until some passing tourists suggested that I save my film and look around the corner. Here on the beach front, with Boulders Beach Lodge on one side and the ocean on the other, was an entire colony of plumed p-p-p-penguins, some in their natural habitat on the boulders and sandy beach, and others, wherefore I know not, waddling along the streets. In the limited time I was here I ate wonderfully fresh king prawns at the in-house restaurant, sipped complimentary cream liqueur in my enormous bath and experienced the forget-everything feeling of the flotation tank (the on-site wellness centre also has a massage room). Bedrooms all have wrought-iron beds and are decorated with wooden carved sculptures of microscopic sea life. But time spent in your room will be limited by the multitude of activities on your doorstep: safe bathing from the penguin beach, kayaking in False Bay, beach walks with views of the distant Hottentots Holland mountain range, mountain hikes above Simon's Town, mountain-biking, practising your golf swing at the next-door golf course, sailing at the yacht club, fishing, scuba diving and whale-watching. Phew. I suggest you stay at least three nights to take full advantage of this superb location.

Rooms: 14: 9 doubles, 2 twins, 1 triple, all with en-suite bath and shower or bath with shower
overhead. 2 self-catering suites for 6, 1 double and 4 bunks.
Price: In winter prices include a set-menu dinner.
Meals: A choice of breakfasts is included. In-house restaurant for lunch and dinner.
Directions: Emailed or faxed.

Map Number: 1

Water's Edge

David Sloan
7 Kleintuin Rd, Simon's Town 7975
Tel: 021-701-9343
Email: sloandaj@kingsley.co.za

If you've never lain awake and listened to the noise of whales breathing not ten metres from your very bed, then you should come to Water's Edge during the season (August to November). The Browne family retreat (and GG hot spot) is a dreamy far-away place, so relaxed and in such a beautiful location that you may have to pinch yourself as a reality check. It's not really that glam inside - think clean and comfy. There is a big proper kitchen and a cavernous dormitory bedroom that can lose six kids easily. Downstairs the seaside rooms are the best. But best place of all has to be the open-fronted stoep. A table on one side and a sofa on the other channel the eyes out to sea. Locals make use of the beach during summer and Easter school holidays, but always go home in the evening. Otherwise it's all yours. On both ends of the crescent of sand, huge smooth boulders are perfect for rock hopping, fishing, reading and watching for sea mammals. Adults and children alike will spend hours poking around in rock pools, barbecueing on the beach, building sand-castles and watching the sun set. Kids can also go off finding fairies in the garden or making dens under up-turned dinghies. *Kids' holiday and day care at the primary school next door. Canoe is thrown in for you.*

Rooms: 5: 2 doubles and 2 twins with shared bathroom and shower room; 1 room with 5 singles and 1 double upstairs.
Price: Dec-April: R3,150 per day. May-November: R2,000 per day. Min stay 1 week. To secure booking 25% of total rent at time of booking.
Meals: Self-catering. Restaurants nearby. Catering can be organised.
Directions: Take M3 south towards Muizenberg and once in Simon's Town pass the naval base. Seaforth Rd is signed to your left. Pass the car park, turn right into Kleintuin Rd and follow brick wall to end. No. 7 beachside.

Lou's Place

Conal and Louise Gain

9 Hillrise Rd, St James 7945
Tel: 021-788-6282 Fax: 021-788-6282
Email: gain@global.co.za Web: www.lousplace.co.za
Cell: 083-625-9288

Conal only managed to put a stopper on my excited babble by showing me the view, at which point I forgot that I was supposed to be a GG guidette and stood jaw-on-the-floor speechless. He is also a guide (game in Africa and birds around the world) and filled me in on what I was watching. Whales! Big ones! Five whole pods out in the wide bay, doing whaleish things like breaching, lobtailing and spouting. They had me entranced. Back to business though. There are two lovely apartments here and both make the most of the amazing view. The lower one is simple, mainly white, with a kitchenette and a sea view from the main bed. Sit out on your own deck under the leafy hibiscus and roses to watch iridescent flycatchers, sunbirds and, of course, the whales. If upstairs is your go, you'll be lofting it. The conversion is suave with lime-washed, vaulted ceiling panels and polished floorboards that reflect the light around you. It's furnished with a few antiques, a smart kitchenette, his and hers marble sinks and a giant bath. Your deck looks out over the pretty fishing village, tidal swimming pool, restaurants, ocean and spectacular mountains either side. Conal kayaks and brings home crayfish. If you order breakfast, Louise will leave provisions in a basket outside your room.

Rooms: 2: 1 king with bath and shower, cot and sofa bed also in apartment. In loft: 1 king, also with sofa bed and en-suite bath and shower.
Price: Lou's Place: R200 – R250 pp. Lou's Loft: R300 – R350 pp.
Meals: Breakfast is DIY and extra at R40 pp.
Directions: Take M3 toward Muizenberg. Keep heading towards Simon's Town. In St James pass the train station. Then 4 streets after on right. No 9 is right at the top on the left.

Amblewood Guest House

June and Trevor Kruger

43 Skaife St, Hout Bay 7806
Tel: 021-790-1570
Fax: 021-790-1571
Email: info@amblewood.co.za
Web: www.amblewood.co.za
Cell: 082-881-5430

One of the more unusual sights in Hout Bay is the A-team van that patrols the streets, a wild-haired Murdoch at the wheel. Such a fellow is surely a man of distinction, quite possibly with the temperament to run a B&B, so I resolved to track him down. How lucky then, that on a visit to Amblewood, I should discover both van and man. I love it when a plan comes together! Trevor fixed me a G&T, and amidst heavy beams and family antiques we chatted away until the rains came, and guests wearing borrowed woollies and waterproofs returned, and Trevor raced out with a brolly for June. This softly-spoken duo love doing what they do. They share an eye for detail and an enthusiasm that will have you feeling right at home. I browsed the library and admired the bay from my balcony, which I shared with two turtle doves. Friday is braai day, but tonight we headed to a steakhouse, where everybody knew the Krugers. At breakfast, a humble, hair-netted Trevor claimed that guests' plates were left spotless because the dog had been at them. I'm not so sure – I for one licked mine clean and blamed Doc. I enjoyed myself so much that I think they wondered whether I was doing a job at all. But I wasn't alone – as I left, wise guests were extending their stay.

Rooms: 4: 2 doubles, 1 with en-suite shower, 1 with en-suite shower and bath; 2 twins with en/s shower and bath.
Price: R240 – R400 pp sharing. Singles rate R360 – R525.
Meals: Full cooked breakfast included.
Directions: Faxed or emailed on booking.

Map Number: 1

Frogg's Leap

Jôke Glauser
15 Baviaanskloof Rd, Hout Bay 7806
Tel: 021-790-2590 Fax: 021-790-2590
Email: info@froggsleap.co.za Web: www.froggsleap.co.za
Cell: 082-493-4403

The huge Frogg's Leap verandah, with its impressive views of the Hout Bay mountains and sea seems to be the focal point of life here. At breakfast the house springs to life with Jôke (pronounced *yokie*) and Stewart engaging in easy banter with all who emerge, and chiding guests for sitting at the long wooden table inside when the parasol-shaded tables outside are so enticing. Then in the evening, with the sea breeze swinging the hammocks and a sundowner in your hand, it is not hard to get to grips with being lazy and on holiday. I can't remember a place where guests made themselves so at home. Jôke and Stewart used to run charter boats in the West Indies and Frogg's Leap has a breezy Caribbean feel with many open French doors and windows. Bedrooms are cool ensembles of natural materials: painted floors, seagrass matting, palms, natural stone in bathrooms, lazy wicker chairs, reed ceilings, thick cotton percale linen and old wooden furniture. Hout Bay itself is a fishing harbour enclosed by mountains and is within minutes of beaches and hiking trails. Jôke and Stewart keep a 26-ft catamaran there and, when the spirit moves them and weather permits, will take guests cray-fishing, or whale-watching when whales are in town. This is a place that has been consistently recommended both before and since the first edition and it is a continued pleasure to recommend it myself. *Guest telephone 021-790-6260.*

Rooms: 6: 5 doubles/twins and 1 double, all with en-suite bathrooms; 3 with shower, 3 with bath and shower. Plus extra single room.
Price: R250 – R350 pp sharing. Singles on request.
Meals: Full breakfast included and served until 10am. There are 20 restaurants nearby for other meals.
Directions: A map will be faxed to you on confirmation of booking.

Harbour Lodge

Kristian Collard and Lou Trost
14 Albert Rd, Hout Bay 7806
Tel: 021-790-0657 Fax: 021-790-5115
Email: info@harbourlodge.co.za Web: www.harbourlodge.co.za
Cell: 082-640-0624

Harbour Lodge is the sort of place that particularly excites us, an ordinary-looking house that from the outside gives no hint of the treasure within. Kristian and Lou have taken the tired cottage behind their home, waved the magic wand and hey presto, one metamorphosis later... Manhattan loft meets Limpopo lodge. Vast black-framed mirrors, coarse carpet and dark chairs dressed in white cotton set the tone for the main room. Luminous lemons are magnified in vast glass vases atop black-lacquered tables, and arrangements of ostrich eggs, zebra skins and bottles of Dutch courage are guarded by two delicate carved figures. On the walls are stunning sepia prints of African wildlife, some lifted straight from guests' photo albums. Beds are found under piles of pillows, folds of blankets in brown, beige and grey and wicker baskets proffer towels and gowns to use in the bathrooms. On the secluded patio, blood-red bottlebrushes attract hummingbirds and potted pastel aloes laze by a bijou pool, where breakfast is served. You'll be in no hurry to explore the vineyards, beaches, walking trails or harbour. I didn't stay for nearly as long as I'd have liked, but by the time I left I felt that I'd made two new friends. You really can't ask for much more than that.

Rooms: 5: 1 king, 2 doubles and 1 twin all with en-suite shower and 1 queen (room 2) with en-suite bath.
Price: R175 – R300 pp sharing. Singles rate from R300.
Meals: Full breakfast included. Variety of restaurants nearby, Butcher's Grill, Mariner's Wharf and even a KFC!
Directions: From Cape Town follow coastal M6 to Hout Bay. At "robots", continue straight (to harbour). First right after mini-roundabout, then left into Albert Rd. Harbour Lodge on left.

Hattons Hout Bay

Liz and Kevin Davis

2 Harold Close, Oakhurst Estate, Hout Bay 7806
Tel: 021-790-0848 Fax: 021-790-3050
Email: liz@hattons.co.za Web: www.hattons.co.za
Cell: 082-760-2624

Nature has run its course at Hattons since the last edition: the vine arbour has gone, leaving Liz and Kevin an uninterrupted mountain view, and their son Connor is a wee bairn no more. The approach, however, remains perfectly unassuming. Only once you're inside do the building's true dimensions reveal themselves, a great surprise with breezy open spaces and a cavernous sitting room with pole beams and steepling thatched roof. Doors open on both sides, one leading to the pool, the other out to the view over the back of Table Mountain and their own garden. This is immaculately laid out with paths that wind past tropical blooms, riotous colours against white-washed walls… and where the rooms, named after trees – strelitzia, mimosa, kumassi – are kept. Not so much rooms as little cottages, with their own doors to the garden and fully-equipped kitchenettes. The most popular has an unusual gallery bedroom, which looks down on its own sitting room from a great height. Kevin and Liz are a young couple dedicated to their guests, and they'll welcome you in with wine, OJ or coffee. They often have a braai for guests who stay a little longer and now they can drive you in their vintage 1969 Rolls Royce Silver Shadow for sunset picnics or tours of the Peninsula. Nearby, enjoy a coffee at the local farm stall or a sunset concert at Kirstenbosch, and listen carefully when they are spilling the beans about the best spots on the Garden Route!

Rooms: 4: 3 apartments (self-catering or B&B) with en-s shower & bath and 1 B&B dble with en-s sh'r.
Price: R250 – R350 pp sharing. Singles R350 – R450. Less R40 if you don't have breakfast.
Meals: Self-catering possible. Breakfast served on the terrace or a breakfast basket can be delivered to your door.
Directions: Emailed or faxed on booking.

Map Number: 1

Houtbay Manor Hotel

Fiona McIntosh

Baviaanskloof Rd, off Main Rd, Hout Bay 7872
Tel: 021-790-0116 Fax: 021 -790-0118
Email: greenwood@houtbaymanor.co.za Web: www.houtbaymanor.co.za

There's an undeniable grandeur to Hout Bay Manor, befitting of a Cape Peninsula landmark. At the end of a drive that encircles a fountain, the timeless Cape Colonial building, its solid white walls punctuated by long, green-trimmed sash windows, forms an L-shape around a paved courtyard shaded by century-old oaks. The formal dining room spills out here and the tiled lobby is accessed via a stout doorway and leads into a spectacular lounge. Running the length of the hotel, it's a composition of dark timber ceiling and painted beams, terracotta tiles, mahogany antiques, floral arrangements, richly-coloured sofas and an attentive service that's become a hallmark. A hotel since 1871, it's now owned and run by the McIntoshes, who've left their subtle imprint throughout. Hallways make a feature of exposed stonework and plaster architraves, leading to rooms individually decorated by Fiona's mother. Downstairs, the bedrooms have smooth wood floors and French windows to the rear; upstairs there's the blue honeymoon suite, with wrought-iron four-poster. All rooms have large bathrooms and mod cons. What differs is the size: the bigger the room, the more windows it has and the better you can enjoy the views of pool, patio or mountain. If you need further proof that this is a special place, consider this: when fire threatened to destroy the building, guests used their beer to dowse the flames. Considering they were South Africans, that's saying something!

Rooms: 20: mix of standard, deluxe and premiere rooms, all with en-suite bath and shower.
Price: R575 – R875 pp sharing. Singles R725 – R1,650. Children R250.
Meals: Full breakfast included. Light lunches and afternoon tea available daily, plus traditional roast Sunday lunch and à la carte dinner on Fridays.
Directions: From Cape Town turn right off M3 into Rhodes Drive and follow signs to Hout Bay. At Constantia Nek roundabout straight ahead into Hout Bay. Turn left under "Hout Bay Manor" archway. Hotel 500 metres on the left.

Map Number: 1

Thandekayo Guest House

Kiki and Erwin van der Weerd
14 Luisa Way, Hout Bay 7806
Tel: 021-791-0020 Fax: 021-791-0022
Email: info@thandekayo.co.za Web: www.thandekayo.co.za
Cell: 072-447-8293

Erwin's thirst for light, open space and modernity saw him knocking through walls and creating the sunshine-permeable, multi-squared windows and glass doors that now lead out onto the Thandekayo balcony. The sea view from here stretches from Chapman's Peak to the Twelve Apostles. I could see the valley channelling the Disa River into Hout Bay, the studs on the stud farm and, more immediately, the all-important braai area in the trim garden below. Open-plan is also the theme for the bedrooms, where doors do not divide sleeping and washing zones. In the first room, with Mediterranean orange walls, a large oval bath made of crushed and re-set marble faces the bed, slightly Flake-advert-esque, but with a modern touch. Each bathroom has an innovative layout, but all require you to be totally at ease with your room partner. The baths are family-sized, the rooms are individually designed (Erwin, I forgot to mention, is an architect) and the house displays a modest collection of contemporary art, including some of Erwin's mother's paintings. Stencils of elephants accompany you up the stairs and crayons are used for guest book entries. Thandekayo means 'warm welcome in our home', and Erwin and Kiki share with their guests all the enthusiasm they have for South Africa, happy to help with day plans and bookings.

Rooms: 5: 2 queens, 1 king, 2 twins. 1 twin has en-suite shower, others have en-suite bath and shower.
Price: R260 – R435 pp sharing. Singles + 50%.
Meals: Full breakfast included.
Directions: Emailed or faxed.

The Hout Bay Hideaway

Niels van Reenen
37 Skaife St, Hout Bay 7806
Tel: 021-790-8040 Fax: 021-790-8114
Email: info@houtbay-hideaway.com Web: www.houtbay-hideaway.com
Cell: 082-332-7853

Greenwood Guides appraisal forms, while brilliantly designed, do not easily cater for the varied delights of houses such as The Hout Bay Hideaway. By the time I left Niels's magical kingdom I was all but writing on my trousers in an effort to record everything I had seen and heard. Art Deco furniture – lights, *chaise longue*, Bakelite ashtrays, armchairs et al – is the defining motif, but competes for attention with the stunning garden, bay views, fireplaces, paintings and Niels, one of Holland's finest. There are three suites and two apartments all abounding in character. Honeymooners will love the double-headed shower of the Garden Apartment, while older-school romantics can fight over the views of the mountains from the aptly-named Skylight Suite. My favourite was the Deco Apartment, with furniture from the Amsterdam school, Zambian sculptures, jacuzzi and a discreet outdoor shower where you can munch grapes hanging off the trellis. The house melts into its surroundings because its colour, which attracts strangers in off the street, derives from the garden's eucalyptus tree. Niels does not do things by halves! Want to cool off outside? Choose between pool and fully-plumbed Victorian bath. Need a drink? Enjoy the open bar in its 230-year old cupboard. Fancy a drive? Then hire one of the vintage Jaguars. I could go on for hours. *House can be hired in its entirety, children 12+ welcome, free ADSL internet connection in every room.*

Rooms: 5: 2 x 2-room apartments (sleeping up to 3); 3 suites sleeping 2. Or this can be converted to a "penthouse" sleeping 6. Or take the entire villa: sleeps 10 – 12.
Price: Suites and apartments: R295 – R650 pp sharing. Singles on request. If you take the entire villa (sleeps 10-12) it costs from R3,950 per day.
Meals: Breakfast included and served in rooms for individual bookings. Other meals by arrangement, but excellent restaurants in Hout Bay.
Directions: Emailed or faxed on booking. Car rental company can pick up from and deliver to the airport or Niels will fetch you in one of the vintage Jags.

Map Number: 1

Blackheath Lodge

Rick Meyer and Roland Jolink

6 Blackheath Rd, Sea Point
8005
Tel: 021-439-2541
Fax: 021-439-9776
Email:
blackheathlodge@iafrica.com
Web:
www.blackheathlodge.co.za
Cell: 082-772-6606

A teetering carving of the daintiest hippo, a blossoming chandelier, golden elephant tie-backs and a dresser's dummy, legacies from Rick's past life as an antique dealer, are the sort of things that make Blackheath so personable. Inside this bright 1890s Victorian villa, a rouged hallway with a double-height ceiling leads to the breakfast and sitting rooms. In this latter, an ornate mirror hangs above a marble fireplace, the focal point for sensuous chairs and deep sofas. Stairs climb into the eaves, to two bedrooms, beds tucked under a slanting timber roof with sea views. Other rooms are less elevated, but just as good. One is fitted out with buck-skin mat, leopard-print duvet and a collection of African faces, figures and felines. Another is full of fabulous furniture and beyond its floor-to-ceiling curtains lies the shaded verandah. Out here, plants and people congregate to admire the garden with its swimming pool, around which sun-lovers, like the hibiscus, bask. Other more practical paraphernalia for guests include European TV with MNET, telephones, power-plugs, a fax-machine, a computer and air-conditioning for the rooms in the roof. Rick and Roland cook breakfast themselves (fresh juices, coffees and breads) and if you're a "cholesterol-junkie" you might get a disparaging look, but you'll be presented with the breakfast of your dreams!

Rooms: 7: 3 queens, 2 with en-suite shower, 1 with en-suite bath; 4 twins with en/s showers.
Price: R250 – R350 pp sharing. Singles rate R350 – R550. Special winter rates are available.
Meals: Full breakfast included. Minutes from the city centre, Bo-Kaap and the V&A Waterfront, where you'll find plenty of restaurants and bars.
Directions: Faxed or emailed on booking.

Map Number: 1

Brenda's Guest House

Brenda Furman
14 Pine Rd, Green Point 8005
Tel: 021-434-0902 Fax: 021-434-0109
Email: brendas@mweb.co.za Web: www.brendas.co.za
Cell: 083-627-5583

From the green brick garden terrace this early 1900s house juts forward like the prow of a ship and Brenda has done nothing to dispel the image. Life-saving buoys, fishing nets and oars cling to the surrounding walls. Guests sit out here for alfresco evening drinks round the pool from the 'honesty' bar (sherry and port are on the house, by the way). Rooms inside are bright and cheerful in wicker, tiles and wood, while quilts, sunflowers and oil paintings add plenty of vivid colour. The rest of the interior space is open-plan: a sitting room with white sofas and glass coffee table, and the dining table where breakfasts are taken all together (breakfast also makes its appearance outside on fine mornings). Brenda makes the breakfast herself (including specials), serving through a marble-topped hatch, so she can spend at least some of the day helping you out with things to do. She patrols the Cape countryside on her huge motorbike gaining first-hand knowledge of where to go and what to do. A very friendly base indeed... Purdy, Brenda's minuscule dog, has not grown much since I last saw her. *Golf, the Waterfront shopping complex and the city centre are all close by.*

Rooms: 5: 1 twin in outside cottage, 2 doubles and 2 twins in the house; all with en-suite shower or bath and shower.
Price: R340 – R390 pp sharing. Singles rate from R480.
Meals: Continental breakfast included.
Directions: Ask Brenda to fax her map when booking.

Map Number: 1

Cedric's Lodge

Jutta Frensch and Inge Niklaus

90 Waterkant Street and 39
Dixon Street, Green Point
("De Waterkant") 8001
Tel: 021-422-4868
Fax: 021-422-4868 Email:
cedrics.lodges@global.co.za
Web: www.newsinafrica.co.za
Cell: 083-327-3203

Once Cape Muslim slave-quarters, De Waterkant's brightly-coloured, cobbled hill-side streets are amongst the most cosmopolitan in Cape Town, full of fashion labels, interior design showrooms, art galleries and trendy bars. The city's heart beats fast here and Inge and her architect sister Jutta have their finger on the pulse. They metamorphosed a 17th-century slave-house into Cedric's, a washed-grey, contemporary town house. Downstairs is given over to an open-plan living space with steel-and-chrome kitchen, sleek dining table and grey suede sofas arranged around a concrete fireplace. There's glass, polished floorboards and colourful prints throughout and, upstairs, beds have dark headboards and chinoiserie fabrics. My room also had Indian chairs, slate bath and balcony, a blissful spot in the thrall of Table Mountain for this cold-blooded European to bake. Inge and Jutta will take you up there or up Signal Hill for champagne as the sun dissolves into the Atlantic. They'll just as likely drag you off to a concert or they might invite you to join them for lunch with friends in the Cape Flats. Inge edits the village rag and is an inspirational source of what's hot in the Mother City. Spend a lazy breakfast in one of the corner cafés and meander round this forward-looking historic area and you'll be hooked. As the Eagles (almost) said: "You can check out any time you like, but you can never (really) leave." *5 minutes' walk to Convention Center.*

Rooms: 4: all doubles with en-suite bath or shower.
Price: R800 – R1,100 per room. The whole house can be let from R3,200 – R4,400 per night.
Meals: Rate includes vouchers for breakfast at next-door cafés. Cape Town's most fashionable restaurant on the doorstep.
Directions: Directions faxed or emailed on booking.

Cramond House

Gail Voigt
Cramond Rd, Camps Bay 8005
Tel: 083-457-1947 Fax: 083-118-457-1947
Email: gailvoigt@mweb.co.za
Cell: 083-457-1947

Easily stylish enough to keep the smart crowd calm, Cramond House is yet as walk-in-and-make-yourself-at-home as you'll find anywhere. Set high up, dandled on the knees of the Twelve Apostles, wall-to-wall windows along the ocean-facing front look down over Camps Bay's palm-fringed crescent of white sand. The glorious view is unavoidable, from the bedrooms, from the pool, from the wide sundeck. Will you get out of the house at all, I wonder! This is a dreamy place, the epitome of understated easy living, big on simplicity, space and light and small on clutter. My suite was huge and super-swish, with a cavernous walk-in wardrobe, deep spa and a sundeck… but all the rooms are special. There is a sandpit, a pool, a stunning garden, a family of tortoises…. Delicious things to eat and drink spill from the fridge, the bar and cupboards. Gail will come to settle you in, introduce you to the permanent house staff (Gerald, Jan and Beauty). Here's part of an email from her that sets the scene rather well: *My husband is a very keen hiker and would gladly take visitors on hikes… we are so close to so much in CT. Walt, my son takes folk on wine routes etc... and I am always available with my microbus for shopping expeditions, sightseeing etc. We love people and I am from the Eastern Cape originally where one's life is.... people!* Luxury at Cramond House is only half the story.

Rooms: 3: 1 double with en-suite shower and sleeper couch. 2 queens both with bath and shower.
Price: For the house: May – July per night R2,000. Dec R4,000. All other times R3,000. Discounts for 1 couple only, ask Gail.
Meals: By arrangement.
Directions: From the CBD take the Strand around the coast to Camps Bay. At traffic lights turn left into Geneva Rd. Then left to Woodford Ave. Cramond Avenue is 2nd left.

Huijs Haerlem

Johan du Preez and Kees Burgers
25 Main Drive, Sea Point 8005
Tel: 021-434-6434 Fax: 021-439-2506
Email: haerlem@iafrica.com Web: www.huijshaerlem.co.za

Don't even try and pronounce it! Imagine, it used to be called 't Huijs Haerlem, so small thanks for small mercies! But what a great place: a secret garden, perched high on the hill above Sea Point, enclosed behind walls and gates, abloom with tropical flowers in beds and earthenware pots, with suntrap lawns, a pool (salt-water, solar-heated) and views over Table Bay. The verandah frame is snaked about with vine and small trees provide the shade. Johan and Kees have a lovely, caring approach to their guests and look after you royally. There's no formal reception area, the bar is based on honesty, all their fine Dutch and South African antiques are not hidden away for fear of breakage. In fact both of them suffer from magpie-itis and walls and surfaces teem with eye-arresting objects: a tailor's mannequin, cabinet-making tools, old linen presses. Of course breakfast is enormous with fresh breads, rolls and croissants, fruits, cheeses, cold meats and the full cooked bonanza. This is Johan's domain, a chance for him to banter with guests and make a few suggestions. All the bedrooms are different, but all have their advantage, some with private terraces, some great views, one a four-poster. Whichever room you are in you will feel part of the whole.

Rooms: 8: 5 twins and 3 doubles; all en-suite, 2 with separate bath and shower, the rest with shower over bath.
Price: R390 – R600 pp sharing. Singles plus 35%.
Meals: Full breakfast included.
Directions: Faxed or emailed on booking.

Map Number: 1

Ocean View House

Mark Goveia
33 Victoria Rd, Bakoven 8005
Tel: 021-438-1982 Fax: 021-438-2287
Email: oceanv@mweb.co.za Web: www.oceanview-house.com

There's no end to Ocean View's eccentric delights – Russian marble, Malawian fish, award-winning gardens. Everyone has either a balcony or a terrace with fabulous views of both the sea and the Twelve Apostles that line up behind the hotel. It is a hotel I suppose, but such a personal one. The unobtrusive style endures, so too the humour noted in our last edition. The zebra room is kitsch-but-fun, though sadly the two-ton wooden elephant that wallowed in the water fantasia garden, amongst 200-year-old milkwood trees, got worms and was removed. Of course there's a great pool and how many hotels run an honesty bar? To cap it all, Ocean View has its own nature reserve, a tropical garden that ushers an idyllic river from the mountains to the sea. They have placed tables and sun-loungers on the grassy river banks, a sort of exotic *Wind in the Willows* scenario with rocks, ferns, trees, tropical birds and butterflies. If you ever feel like leaving Ocean View, Camps Bay beach is a stroll away with its string of outdoor restaurants and zesty atmosphere. It's a good place to watch trendy Capetonians-at-play. Tired out long before they were, I walked back to the hotel. The nightwatchman was expecting me and escorted me to my room, which was also expecting me, tomorrow's weather report by my bed.

Rooms: 14: 1 Presidential Suite, 1 Milkwood Suite, 4 Royal Suites, 7 Luxury Rooms (all sea-facing). 13 have showers, 1 with bath & sh. 1 self-catering villa for families.
Price: R400 – R800 pp sharing. Singles rate available off-season. 3-bed villa R4,000 – R6,000 per day.
Meals: Full breakfast is included and served until 10.00 am.
Directions: On the coast road a mile out of Camps Bay towards Hout Bay.

Map Number: 1

Acorn House

Bernd Schlieper and Beate Lietz

1 Montrose Avenue, Oranjezicht 8001
Tel: 021-461-1782 Fax: 021-461-1768
Email: welcome@acornhouse.co.za
Web: www.acornhouse.co.za

Bernd and Beate can barely contain the happiness they derive from Acorn House, and their enthusiasm rubs off quickly on all but the stoniest of their visitors. I was a pushover. The listed building, designed by busy Sir Herbert Baker in 1904, sits on the sunny, sea-facing slopes of Table Mountain with tip-top views to Table Bay. The house is typical Sir Herbert, timber colonnade, broad verandah et al, and there is an immaculate garden with black-slate swimming pool and a sun-lounging lawn, cleanly demarcated by agapanthus and lavender bushes. Breakfast, often served by the pool, is a no-holds-barred display of meats, cheeses, eggs and freshly-squeezed fruit juices; "probably the second-best breakfast in Cape Town" is Beate's carefully-worded claim! Upstairs, in your wood-floored bedroom you will find notes of welcome or farewell, chocolates and sprigs of lavender. Wine-lovers are also well served: Bernd is *pazzo* for the stuff, and regularly visits local vineyards to ensure that his house wines are up-to-the-moment (just for his guests' benefit, of course). Bernd and Beate have only been living in South Africa since October 2000 and are awash with excitement about their new surroundings. A stay in Acorn House will leave you feeling much the same.

Rooms: 8: 1 king, 3 twins and 3 doubles, all with en-suite bath; 1 family suite with twin.
Price: R390 – R490 pp sharing. Singles R590 – R690. Family suite as double R780 – R980 + R200 for up to 2 kids.
Meals: Full breakfast included.
Directions: See web site or ask for fax.

Cape Heritage Hotel

Nick Garsten
90 Bree Street, 8001
Tel: 021-424-4646 Fax: 021-424-4949
Email: info@capeheritage.co.za Web: www.capeheritage.co.za

Wham-bam in the city centre, on the fringe of Cape Town's historic Bo-Kaap area, the small, intimate and innovative Cape Heritage Hotel has a delightfully informal, sociable guest-house feel. Central to the breakfast room is a communal table bordered by large grapefruit and pomegranate paintings and cocoon-like lampshades hanging over the coffee bar. Architects and archaeologists have played their roles in the reconstruction of the building which dates back to 1771. I admired the black-and-white photos and line drawings in the hallways depicting the building's history, amongst other old photos of Cape Town. Throughout the building patches of murals and exposed walls have been left untouched to showcase the original architecture and workmanship. High-beamed ceilings and burnished wooden floors line the rooms, and each of the bedrooms has been individually styled with antiques: sleigh beds or four-posters and rooms in Malay, African, Zulu and Japanese style. I particularly liked the Pakhuis (pack house) historic room. A major attraction is the choice of restaurants on your doostep and, come evening, in the courtyard there is a thriving atmosphere, even live music... and, as it happens, the oldest known living grapevine in South Africa. Heritage Square also houses a virtual museum of the oldest operational blacksmith in SA, a health club and a resident masseuse.

Rooms: 14: 6 luxury, 2 suites and 6 superior, all with en-suite bath and shower.
Price: Seasonal. Superior R385 – R500, Luxury R420 – R600, Suites R660 – R800 pp sharing. Single supplement + 50%.
Meals: Breakfast an extra R60.
Directions: From airport take N2, turn off at Strand St exit. At 8th set of lights turn left into Bree St. At 2nd set of lights hotel is on your right.

Floreal House

Patti Rutherford

26 Upper Orange St, Oranjezicht 8001
Tel: 021-465-6259 Fax: 021-461-1365
Email: floreal@mweb.co.za Web: www.florealhouse.com

Since GG mark one Floreal has had a total revamp, thus multiplying the charms of this already alluring 1920s mansion. At the helm is Patti, a wonderful lady and committed hostess whose mission is apparently to cater to her guests' every whim. On the skirts of Table Mountain and separated from the neighbours by a verdant, bird-filled garden it is easy to forget your urban surroundings once within Floreal's secure gates. Wooden pool-loungers wait expectantly on the decking, inviting you to kick back with a cool drink, and a patio with canvas umbrellas provides a shady spot for breakfasting on. Rooms are varied and you can choose from a tropical '80s theme (Tom Cruise in *Cocktail* springs to mind), the timber-shed 'cottage' or the more traditional colonial affairs. All have safes, gleaming bathrooms and technological luxuries such as DSTV. Soaking in bubbles and watching your favourite movie is never a bad option as far as I'm concerned. The food is another bonus and you'll find recipes from Germany, France, Holland… and some favourites from Mpumalanga too. Calories can always be disposed of on your walk up Table Mountain… I trust you're not thinking of taking the cable car. *Floreal is very close to the Castle, the cable car and all the restaurants on Kloof Street.*

Rooms: 10 king/twins, all with en-suite bath, shower or both. Downstairs apartment is sound-proofed (cot available) and has a sofa-bed in sitting room.
Price: R350 – R780 pp sharing. Ask about singles.
Meals: Full breakfast included. Dinners by request but there are 32 restaurants locally to choose from.
Directions: Ask when booking.

Map Number: 1

Guesthouse de Tafelberg

Ann and Kris van Cappellen
68 Molteno Rd, Oranjezicht 8001
Tel: 021-424-9159 Fax: 021-424-9157
Email: info@detafelberg.com Web: www.detafelberg.com

We strolled across the marble floor and through the sunlight-infused room, our passage reflected in a wall of mirrors. Two wide French doors open out to the breakfast balcony and a beautiful view. Pool just below, skyscrapers next and the glittering ocean beyond. But if you actually want to see Cape Town, don't stay here since it's likely that you won't make it outside once you've settled in. I visited mid-morning and guests were still enjoying piles of warm croissants, fruits, organic yoghurts and scrambled eggs with bacon and tomatoes aside six-seed bread. The only thing they were going to shift for was to test the depth of the pads on the pool loungers, the jacuzzi or maybe reading the papers in the outside sitting room. Why they even came out of their rooms to eat beats me. Decorated in neutrals, reds and monochrome they vary in size and view. "Table Mountain or sea?" The main one is surely only free when Bond isn't in town. The statuesque bed is mounted on a plinth, the spa bath is surrounded with wall-to-wall mirrors… for your eyes only perhaps. You could hide a gondola in the arched double shower. Your hosts are relaxed and friendly people who exchanged vintage wines for the living delights of Cape Town and busied themselves creating a hotel/home for media types who needed a base in town.

Rooms: 8: 2 suites with en/s bath and shower; 2 queens with en/s shower; 2 queens with en/s bath and shower; 2 twins with en/s shower.
Price: From R440 pp – R750 pp.
Meals: Full breakfast included.
Directions: Emailed and faxed on booking.

Hillcrest Manor

Gerda and Gerhard Swanepoel

18 Brownlow Rd,
Tamboerskloof 8001
Tel: 021-423-7459
Fax: 021-426-1260
Email: hilcres@mweb.co.za
Web:
www.hillcrestmanor.co.za
Cell: 082-700-5760

Step inside my fantasy world for a moment: the real politik of real estate doesn't exist and you can choose anywhere in Cape Town to build your new home. You'd probably end up precisely where I am now. Sadly, you're a hundred years too late and Gerda and Gerhard already live here. Happily, however, they've opened their home to guests and you'll be assured a warm welcome. Situated at the foot of Lion's Head in a leafy hillside suburb, their Victorian town house looms above the street and faces the most stunning view of Cape Town. From pool, balcony or bed you can see all the detail of the city and waterfront and Table Mountain's acclaimed acclivity clearly. This elegant house, its tall windows and wooden shutters set atop an elevated blue-stone foundation, is where Gerhard grew up. Nowadays the whitewashed steps lead up past a sunny lawn, patio and pool to a sitting room with original pressed-metal ceiling and a bright breakfast room, where the local artwork is for sale. Upstairs the bedrooms are designed to give respite from the long hot summer. Floors are a mix of polished timber and seagrass, beds are pine, furniture wicker. Ceiling-fans loll lazily and curtains billow in the breeze. One bedroom is pure C. S. Lewis, though here the wardrobe leads not to Narnia, but to your own claw-foot bath.

Rooms: 7: all doubles with en-suite shower, one with bath too.
Price: R260 – R400 pp sharing. Single supplement R100.
Meals: Full breakfast included. Meals for groups by prior arrangement. 3-course dinner R45, wine not included.
Directions: Faxed or emailed on booking.

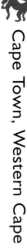

Lézard Bleu Guest House

Chris and Niki Neumann
30 Upper Orange St, Oranjezicht 8001
Tel: 021-461-4601 Fax: 021-461-4657
Email: welcome@lezardbleu.co.za Web: www.lezardbleu.co.za
Cell: 072-234-4448

It's going to be hard to book the tree house, particularly when word gets round, but you have got to try! Surely the most wonderful bedroom in Cape Town. The trunks of two giant palm trees spear through a wooden deck at vertiginous heights and a tiny balcony is in among the topmost fronds and spikes. Lézard Bleu was just about the best guest house in Cape Town anyway, so this latest extravagant addition represents one great big cherry on a mouthwatering cake. Niki is an actress and Chris is a chef, although he has hung up his hat now… no, don't even ask! They are still young and humorous and the house remains sleek and modern with solid maplewood bedframes, white pure cotton, sandy shades and tones, bright splashes of local and modern art on the walls. Breakfast is the best beanfeast in Cape Town (and that's the opinion of other guest house owners). The Blue Lizard snakes pleasingly from area to area, each room with its own doors out to a patio and to the large pool, where deck loungers take it easy on a surrounding timber deck. There are real fires in winter, an honesty bar, free ADSL internet access – mere details, but typical. Individual, creative, very comfortable, but most importantly this is somewhere really natural and friendly.

Rooms: 7: 1 family room; 5 doubles/twins; 4 with en/s bath and shower; 1 with en/s shr; 1 tree house double en/s b and shr.
Price: R350 – R600 pp sharing. Singles +50%.
Meals: Full (enormous!) breakfast included and served till 10.30 am.
Directions: Ask for directions when booking.

Map Number:

Liberty Lodge

Jimmy van Tonder

33 De Lorentz St, Tamboerskloof 8001
Tel: 021-423-2264 Fax: 021-423-2274
Email: liberty@capetowncity.co.za Web: www.capetowncity.co.za
Cell: 082-920-5508

Liberty Lodge is an African colonial town house alright, built in 1894 as a bachelor pad… but it is original in more ways than one, and any gravitas associated with the Victorian era is gently undermined. Co-host Louis, who earns his keep (and keeps his day job as an interior designer), has senses of colour and humour that are equally deft. Jimmy your gentleman host implicitly knows when to be there and when not to be. Inside the cool house the atmosphere is relaxed and easy and the bedrooms are destinations in themselves. Bathrooms are sometimes small, but use limited space inventively. New and nearby is another yet more African town house where the interiors have been inspired by your Xhosa host Tandi's tribal colours. The chimney wall is in red and brown geometric patterns and huge red tribal wedding hats hang in the sitting room. There is less bustle here and Jimmy tells me it's a favourite for the cufflinks and high-heels brigade that come for R&R weekends. Outside Mediterranean-feeling, enclosed breakfast terraces at both houses will tempt you to lay back and tease breakfast out till sunset. Nearby there are also six bigger, just-as-swish apartments. Who needs Cape Town, even if it's only down the street! Buckets of character and comfort at Liberty Lodge. *TV (MNET) and personal telephones in bedrooms. Airport transfer can be arranged.*

Rooms: 13: Liberty Lodge: 4 doubles (3 en/s shower, 1 en/s bath). African Lodge: 4 (2 en/s bath, 2 en/s shower). 5 self-catering apartment suites, all en/s b and sh.
Price: From R575 – R750 double in lodges (10% off over winter) to R1,000 for Penthouse Suite in summer.
Meals: Restaurants within 3 minutes' walk.
Directions: Faxed or emailed on booking.

Map Number: 1

Parker Cottage

Izak Holtzhausen and Dawie du Toit
3 Carstens St, Tamboerskloof 8001
Tel: 021-424-6445 Fax: 021-424-6445
Email: info@parkercottage.co.za Web: www.parkercottage.co.za
Cell: 083-702-5743

I knew this was one for us in a single shake of a cat's tail. This is a true home stay – Izak and Dawie live here too – but Parker Cottage has all the style and panache of a chic city hotel. Two Victorian town houses have been merged. Covered verandahs on both sides mean it's shady inside, made darker by deep wall colours, but gloomy it certainly is not! Dawie's hand-made stencils, specially designed for each room, echo the colours of the exquisite soft furnishings. If rooms could smile – well, these would! The red bathroom has sheet music papered under the dado, the blue room is a riot of colour, one luxurious bed pays homage to a church pulpit and the downstairs bathroom has a curtain-less wall of glass looking outside to a private garden. In fact guests can check out and leave bags here, returning to use that shower en-route to the airport. Breakfast is no less of a glory. Mine looked too serene to disturb. But then it also smelled out of this world, so I hoed into it like there was no tomorrow! To look at it, you'd think you'd walked onto a fashion shoot. But at Parker Cottage life is for living, sofas are for curling up on, showers are for dancing around in and seriousness is for somewhere else altogether. I defy you not to love it.

Rooms: 8: 3 queens, 3 doubles and 2 twins, all en-suite with bath and/or shower.
Price: From R300 – R400 pp sharing. Single R475 – R550.
Meals: Full breakfast included. Health and Cooked on alternate days.
Directions: Both N1 and N2 feed into one way Buitengragt St, which turns into New Church St. At Burnside Rd U-turn back into Upper Buitengragt St and then second street left is Carstens St.

Map Number: 1

Redbourne Hilldrop

Jonny and Sharon Levin
12 Roseberry Avenue, Oranjezicht 8001
Tel: 021-461-1394 Fax: 021-465-1006
Email: info@redbourne.co.za Web: www.redbourne.co.za

One of the happiest and most humorous guest houses in Cape Town, so it always seems to me. Many of Jonny and Sharon's guests refuse to stay elsewhere and gifts arrive daily from overseas… well almost. One day you may be surprised to find yourself packing up toys for their kids. It's a small, intimate place and you are spoiled: free-standing baths, fluffy duvets, big white pillows, unflowery good taste in mirrors and wood floors, magazines, African artefacts, great showers. One room has a spiral staircase down to its bathroom. You eat breakfast at a diner-style bar stretched along a wall of pretty windows with incredible city views. Guests are treated as far as possible as friends and each time I visit I notice the easy rapport that Jonny and Sharon have generated with their guests – probably overnight. Last edition I said that a wall-enclosed pool would be ready for this edition, but I didn't really believe it. "It wouldn't matter if it wasn't," I said, hedging my bets. Well, lo and behold, there it is, with Table Mountain looming above as suggested it might!

Rooms: 4: 2 doubles and 1 twin; 2 with en/s bath and shower, 1 with en/s sh. And 1 family room with sunroom (pictured above).
Price: R295 – R425 pp sharing. Singles on request.
Meals: Full breakfast included. Dinners by prior arrangement. Restaurants nearby.
Directions: Ask when booking.

Map Number: 1

Trevoyan Guest House

Philip Lamb and Max Bowyer

12 Gilmour Hill Rd, Tamboerskloof 8001
Tel: 021-424-4407 Fax: 021-423-0556
Email: trevoyan@iafrica.com Web: www.trevoyan.co.za

Max and Phil visited in 2001 and didn't even get past the brick terrace and the front step before they had decided to buy Trevoyan. Bit rash you might think? Not once you've seen it. There's something cool and sequestered about the place that cossets you from the noise and heat of the surrounding city. It faces Table Mountain and from seats set out on the long brick terrace you can see those forbidding cliffs through the branches of the massive oak that lords it over both house and garden. It's an under-canopy kingdom, complete with glamorous swimming pool, a perfect lawn bordered by leafy perimeter hedge and a recently added eight-seat jacuzzi, a spiral staircase and rooftop sun deck. The main building was built for entertaining military types visiting the Cape in the early 1900s. Rooms are indulgent now, furnished in soft pashmina tones – mint, cadmium yellow and sailor's blue – with many extras like big TVs, cream sofas, mini-bars and safes. The main bedroom is the most indulgent of all, with its enormous double shower, and state-o'-art entertainment system. Take breakfast on the back arched terrace in summer or the sunny dining room in winter. Max and Phil share a warm sense of humour and are natural hosts.

Rooms: 7: 2 kings and 2 queens all with en-suite bath and shower. 1 king with twin showers only. 2 twins with en/s bath and shower.
Price: R650 – R800 double occupancy. Singles R475 – R600. Garden Suites R750 – R1,000.
Meals: Full breakfast included. Restaurants 5 minutes' walk.
Directions: From city centre take Buitengracht Rd towards Table Mountain until it becomes Kloof Nek Rd. Take 2nd right into Gilmour Hill Rd. 100 metres, on right before stop sign.

Map Number: 1

Villa Christina

Markus and Simone Brabetz

2 Rocklands Avenue,
Highlands Estate, Cape Town
8001
Tel: 021-461-9288
Fax: 021-461-9283
Email: christina@new.co.za
Web: www.villachristina.co.za
Cell: 082-335-4093

There's something of the Sound of Music about Villa Christina – a happy concert of mountains, music and family. Maybe it's the faintly alpine air. The house sits so close to Table Mountain that the tassels of the 'tablecloth' tickle its tiles. On my visit Simone, an accomplished violinist, was ushering the kids to music class, while Markus handled a steady stream of visitors with trademark courtesy (and without breaking into song!). His delight in providing for his guests is obvious, booking the must-see theatre, making that dental appointment or simply rustling up a bottle of merlot. As he says, "'n Boer maak 'n plan." Here in the heart of the rainbow nation I found a few of my favourite things – the freshest of breakfast plates (think paw-paw, passion fruit and mangoes on colourful crockery), the bloom of the morning flower market, the be-bop of the brightly-painted Bo-Kaap quarter… Villa Christina is a grand Italianate affair, daubed in yellow with large white-trimmed windows. The Crete-stone bedrooms are arranged on the ground floor, their French doors overlooking a manicured garden lined with lime trees, cacti and pines harbouring Egyptian geese. From the pool you can count the creeping cable cars and contemplate climbing every mountain. It's all "just-so", until you discover the charming quirks, like the garden trampoline, used by young and old alike. A drop of golden sun.

Rooms: 5: all doubles with en-suite showers.
Price: R295 – R325 pp sharing. Singles rate R450 – R500.
Meals: Full cooked breakfast included. Some of Cape Town's finest restaurants only moments away. Picnic baskets can be arranged.
Directions: Faxed or emailed on booking.

Welgelegen Guest House

Lanie van Reenen
6 Stephen St, Gardens 8001
Tel: 021-426-2373 Fax: 021-426-2375
Email: lanie@city-bowl.co.za Web: www.welgelegen.co.za
Cell: 082-927-5306

As I passed through the entrance door, lured by the beaded lampshades of a circular light pendulum, I could already tell that Welgelegen was a gem. Lanie's background is in interior decorating and it shows. The house displays the sort of style and elegance that you see in magazines and dream of reconstructing at home, but are too messy or inept to achieve. I found the unique hand-made lampshades throughout the house particularly appealing. I dug the funky chunky mirrors, the stripy duvets, the wall colours, the modern mosaic tiles in the bathrooms, the sink-in-me sofas of the sitting room... and the air-conditioning is a plus too! In the hallway is an art exhibition displaying for-sale-able paintings and in the breakfast room are Mokonde body masks from Tanzania. I ate a wonderful breakfast listening to mellow jazz, watched by an elongated Giacometti-style African statue. The breakfast room leads onto an enclosed courtyard with a plunge pool; then comes the other section of the guest house, with tabletop mountain views, that used to be Lanie's home. The evidence is in the pencil marks of children's height measurements on the wall. Restaurants and nightlife are only up the road in Kloof St, although the tranquillity of the neighbourhood makes this hard to believe. Lanie and her friendly staff are always on hand and the hosting is extremely attentive and personalised.

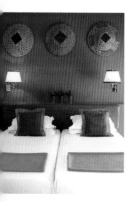

Rooms: 13: 11 superior, 1 standard, 1 budget room. Most with en-suite bath and shower.
Price: Seasonal: luxury rooms R490 – R750 pp sharing, standard R325 – R450 pp sharing, budget R225 – R300 pp sharing. Single supplement on request.
Meals: Full breakfast included.
Directions: Map faxed or emailed.

Medindi Manor

Geoffrey Bowman, Leshira and Basetsana Mosaka

4 Thicket Road, Rosebank 7700
Tel: 021-686-3563 Fax: 021-686-3563
Email: manor@medindi.co.za Web: www.medindi.co.za
Cell: 082-480-0103

Medindi is a secluded Edwardian manor of grand dimensions, banded by ground and first-floor verandahs with a garden and swimming pool tucked away behind tall hedges and bushes. Some of the rooms have their own doors out onto the stoep and the main building has been renovated with panache and a sensitive feel for the period. Although well-stocked with bar fridges, telephones, TVs etc, Medindi avoids like the plague any h(ot)ellish homogeneity in its décor and design. The Oregon pine floors, bay windows, intricate ceilings and marble fireplaces are original and there are unique, antique touches everywhere, such as Edwardian designs for stately marble and slate floors. Bathrooms have free-standing baths, Victorian 'plate' shower heads, brass fittings and a small antique cabinet has been found for each. There is modernity too, in bright wall colours (yellows and blues), and splashes of modern art – from the turn of one century to the turn of the next. Music is an important ingredient for Geoffrey, Medindi's owner. He plays the piano (there was and will be again a grand in the huge breakfast room). A freewheeling, relaxed and youthful place. Since the last edition Leshira and Basetsana have taken over the day-to-day management of Medindi and six new rooms have been created from a converted outbuilding – the smaller rooms are cheaper.

Rooms: 13: in the house: 4 dbles + 2 twns with en/s bathrooms, 3 with bath + shower, 3 with shower. Plus 6 more rooms in converted outbuilding. Plus 1 self-c cottage.
Price: R295 – R495 pp sharing. Singles R350 – R695.
Meals: Buffet breakfast included, cooked breakfast extra: R27.50. Dinner by prior arrangement. Local African food a speciality. Restaurants nearby.
Directions: From CBD + Waterfront take N2 towards airport. Take Lisbeek Parkway off-ramp. At 2nd lights left into Durban Rd. Cross Raapemberg Rd and immediately first right, then 1st left.

Map Number: 1

Knightsbury

Tom and Enid Knight

15 Linkoping Rd, Rondebosch 7700
Tel: 021-686-4347 Fax: 021-689-5686
Email: guesthouse@knightsbury.co.za Web: www.knightsbury.co.za
Cell: 082-552-6872

From the immaculately-swept drive to the Marks and Sparks tea and coffee tins in the bedrooms, this 65-year-old home scores highly in every category, a good ol' traditional B&B with heaps of extras. Fresh flowers and family treasures are found throughout the house, papers are delivered early, airport pick-ups arranged, rooms are pretty, bathrooms indulgent and two have free-standing Victorian tubs. You could be forgiven for confusing it all for a suburb of Sussex, England, except of course for the sunshine... and the flavour of the garden isn't really David Austin with its bougainvillaea overflowing the trellis and patio. You can breakfast here in the sunshine among the Cape robins and sunbirds. One chap from the university comes regularly to savour home-made marmalade slathered on Tom's freshly-baked bread. The Knights are an impressive double act at breakfast. Tom does fruits and cereals, while Enid makes cheese puffs, muffins and scones. Bacon and eggs come every which way, even Knightsbury style with Enid's Irish potato bread. Doubtless you'll step out of the front door past the highly-polished brass number '15' and click your heels knowing you are ready for the day. The Baxter Theatre is a mere minute's walk away, so you can breakfast, stroll and be entertained without driving anywhere. Set your GPS for this one. *Children over 12.*

Rooms: 3: all queens with en-suite bathrooms; 1 has a shower.
Price: R350 pp sharing. R450 single.
Meals: Full breakfast included.
Directions: Exit 7 from the M3 heading south onto Woolsack Drive and Uni. In Rosebank turn right at traffic lights. Then 1st right into Burg St. Linkoping is 1st left.

Map Number: 1

Little Spotte

Zaria Dagnall

5 Cavendish Close, Cavendish St, Claremont 7700
Tel: 021-762-4593 Fax: c/o Mr C Dagnall 021-595-1173
Email: zaria@mweb.co.za
Cell: 082-374-3399

With all the shopping, dining, coffee-drinking and general urban whirl of Claremont excitedly clattering about it, Little Spotte is a time capsule of stillness and calm. A narrow path leads between designery shops to this delightful Victorian bungalow. There is no doubt of its Englishness once past the bird-of-paradise flowers in the front garden. The owners keep it a living space, in case they themselves want to come down from Jo'burg to use it. Thus you are blessed with antiques, yellowwood and oak furniture, and an astoundingly well-equipped kitchen. The cottage is self-catering, but Zaria is a very hands-on manager who will see you settled, make sure flowers, chocolates and a few breakfast commodities are arrayed for your arrival… and she is also a dynamic source of recommendation to lesser-known wineries, walks in Cape Town, local coffee-houses and restaurants. The cottage itself is far bigger than you might expect at the front door, with a central courtyard with table and green parasol, completely secure from the noise of the city and opened onto from the main bedroom and the dining area. Mod cons include TV/video with MNET and a fully-equipped laundry and your local food shop is no less than Woolworths (M&S equivalent if you're a Brit and getting confused). A lovely pied-à-terre bang in the middle of one of Cape Town's most lively restaurant districts. *Very central for all city sightseeing spots.*

Rooms: 1 cottage with 2 bedrooms: 1 twin with en-suite shower; 1 double with en-suite shower.
Price: Minimum 2 nights: R500 in low season for the cottage. In high season R600 for 2 people, R700 for 3 and R800 for 4. Discounts for longer stays.
Meals: Fully self-catering, although Zaria will put a few things in for your first night.
Directions: Faxed or emailed when booking.

Cape Town, Western Cape

The Studio

Eulalie Spamer
No.10 Seymour St, Wynberg 7800
Tel: 021-761-9554 Fax: 021-797-8183
Email: eulalie@eulaliespamer.com Web: www.eulaliespamer.com
Cell: 072-446-8152

'The Studio' was for 30 years the design office of an architect of international repute. Recently adapted to create a duplex apartment with garden, it is now available for let. There are plenty of intriguing design quirks. Take the main bedroom for example: the only solid wall doubles as the bed-head, while the rest of the room is contained by glass with a wrap-around balcony (with potted roof-garden), allowing sweeping views of the flat peak of Table Mountain and the Constantiaberg. These views can be enjoyed without even getting out of bed. Eulalie, with her customary good taste, has kept interiors simple: antique European and Asian pieces, white sofas and masses of earth-tone scatter cushions on day beds. The large living room gives directly onto the pool terrace and its outdoor candlelit dining area, fringed with potted palms and topiary. And the small eat-in kitchen is well-equipped. Long lets are typical, but if you are lucky enough to find a slot you are equally welcome for a short stay.

Rooms: 1 duplex garden studio with 1 queen and 1 single in main room; 1 on internal gallery share bathroom.
Price: Self-catering only: R750 per day, minimum 3 nights. Sleeps maximum of 4.
Meals: First morning's breakfast provisions left for you. Restaurants nearby.
Directions: Off M3 Trovato Link pass Herschel Walk turn-off. After Herschel Walk it's the 4th road to your left.

Map Number: 1

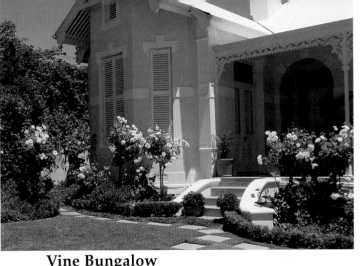

Vine Bungalow

Eulalie Spamer
7 Ellerslie Rd, Wynberg 7800
Tel: 021-761-9554 Fax: 021-797-8183
Email: eulalie@eulaliespamer.com Web: www.eulaliespamer.com

The Vine Bungalow (and that's 'bungalow' in the colonial, wrought-iron-verandah sort of sense) is an opportunity (if you can get in) to live far more stylishly than I can see myself managing ever! Everywhere you look the finest of the fine gazes evenly back: shiny wood floors, Jim Thompson fabrics, embroidered white cotton sheets, restful cream marble-tiled bathrooms. And all the kitchen and washing appliances are aristocrats and top of their range. All these basics are a pleasure in themselves. But Eulalie has created a home, and guests are treated to the full force of her great taste for interiors and a wonderful collection of art and artefacts to boot. You take the whole house and self-cater so it will suit longer stayers or families best. Guests are provided with a light meal on arrival (fruits, cheeses, rôtisserie chicken and a bottle of wine for example) but thereafter you will need to get down to a supermarket – it's 500 metres to Wynberg Village. Eulalie lives next door so is on hand to help you settle in. A family had just arrived from the UK and were out on the breakfasting stoep by the swimming pool when I visited. They looked… delighted.

Rooms: 1 house with 3 bedrooms, 2 with en-suite bathrooms (1 shower and 1 'five-star mandi'), living room and eat-in kitchen.
Price: R1,200 – R1,800 a day for the house.
Meals: Light meal on arrival. Otherwise self-catering.
Directions: Off M3 Trovato Link pass Herschel Walk turn-off. After Herschel Walk it's the 4th road to your left.

Klein Bosheuwel

Nicki and Tim Scarborough

51a Klaassens Rd, Constantia 7800
Tel: 021-762-2323 Fax: 021-762-2323
Email: kleinbosheuwel@iafrica.com Web: www.kleinbosheuwel.co.za

Who needs Kirstenbosch? Nicki has manipulated the paths and lawns of her own garden (which is pretty well an extension of the Botanical Gardens anyway – less than a minute's walk away) so that the views are not dished out in one vulgar dollop! Instead you are subtly led into them, with glimpses through mature trees (flowering gums, yellowwoods and camellias) and lush flower beds. And finally your stroll leads you down to umbrellas on a ridge with Table Mountain and the Constantiaberg laid out magnificently before you and the sea distantly below. "Keep it plain" is Nicki's motto, so the upstairs bedrooms are simply white and all naturally endowed with garden views. The salt-water swimming pool is hidden deep in the garden and Klein Bosheuwel is the sort of place where you could just hang out for a few days. I was introduced to one English guest who had clearly no intention of going anywhere that day – the cat that got the cream you might have thought! *Ask when booking about children. Tim and Nicki also own Southdown next door.*

Rooms: 4: 1 twin en/s bath; 2 queens with en/s bath and shower; 1 queen en/s large bath.
Price: R350 – R410 pp sharing. Singles R580.
Meals: Full breakfast included. Can organise other meals on request.
Directions: Fax or web site.

Map Number: 1

Southdown

Nicki and Tim Scarborough
51a Klaassens Rd, Constantia 7800
Tel: 021-762-2323 Fax: 021-762-2323
Email: kleinbosheuwel@iafrica.com Web: www.kleinbosheuwel.co.za

This is the second of Nicki and Tim's brilliantissimo B&Bs. They should give lectures on the art of hosting. Southdown was bought in March in a state of near-dereliction and has already been whipped into heavenly shape. With a small-scale Lost Gardens of Heligan on her hands, Nicki peeled back the jungle to find pathways, walls and, best of all, enormous stone-paved circles just in the right spot between the house and pool. Table Mountain towers behind. It is well known that people with fine gardens have fine houses and this is a leader amongst them. The house is a colonial Georgian pile orientated towards the exquisite view. Breakfast is taken in a spectacular dining room with a glass wall looking to sea in the distance. The eggs may be poached, but the mounted animal heads definitely aren't – one of Nicki's sons works in nature conservation. The house is filled with beastly surprises: zebra skins, porcupine-quill lamps, onyx lamp stands, a whole stuffed eagle, a wildebeest's head, a piano, deep carpets and couches, marble bathrooms and terraces off most rooms. Tim and Nicki do not live in-situ, but magically appear (like the shopkeeper) when needed. They are nonetheless full-on hosts, oozing vigour and enthusiasm and have a habit of adopting their guests as friends. I for one am going there for Christmas! A fabulous place. *Kirstenbosch gardens and restaurant 2 minutes' walk.*

Rooms: 3: 1 queen, 1 twin and 1 king, all with en-suite bath and shower.
Price: Double occ. from R395 – R450 pp. Singles R630.
Meals: Full breakfast included.
Directions: Emailed or faxed on booking. Also on web site.

Dendron

Shaun and Jill McMahon

21 Ou Wingerd Pad, Upper Constantia 7806
Tel: 021-794-6010 Fax: 021-794-2532
Email: stay@dendron.co.za Web: www.dendron.co.za
Cell: 082-4911-647 or 082-296-0691

(Quite) A few years ago, Shaun bought a Land Rover in Taunton (UK) and drove it here. Hardly odd when you see the place, now replete with relaxed family atmosphere, collie dogs and cricket pegs (or whatever they're called) on the front lawn. You get all the benefits of living the South African good life by default here. Green-fingered Jill genuinely loves having guests and her enthusiasm for life is evident in everything. The cottages are private in leafy, jasmine-scented gardens and have a kitchenette stocked with basics, a braai and views to the mountains on the right and False Bay in the distance. Two cottages have terracotta-tiled or wooden floors and beds with Indian cotton throws – perfect for families. The other two are newly-renovated cottages with kilims, safari prints and plump sofas. All are fully serviced. Evening pool-side views at sunset and moonrise, helped along by wine from over-the-hedge Groot Constantia vineyard, will make you want to throw away the car keys and stay (which is exactly what Shaun did when he first clapped eyes on the place). When you are hungry, Jill will send you off there through the back gate and across the vineyards to the Jonkershuys restaurant for dinner. Return by torch- and moon-light. Dendron (GK = tree) is a small slice of heaven. Don't stay too long, jealousy will take root!

Rooms: 4 in total: 2 cottages with 1 double and 1 twin both with bath and shower; 2 cottages with twin, 1 with bath & shower, 1 with shower only.
Price: Four in one cottage R250 pp. Two sharing R325 pp. Single on request.
Meals: Essentially self-catering, but breakfast for first morning provided and afterwards if requested at R30 pp.
Directions: Fax on request.

Map Number: 1

Hunter's Moon Lodge

Heather Nicholson
57 Southern Cross Drive, Constantia Upper 7806
Tel: 021-794-5001 Fax: 021-794-0184
Email: heathernicholson@telkomsa.net Web: www.hunters-moon.info
Cell: 084-722-4469

Hunter's Moon is truly a splendid Tuscan Villa, even compared to the other glitterati temples and ambassadorial homes of Southern Cross Drive, one of Cape Town's most desirable addresses. Even compared to real Tuscan villas! This impressive mansion is surrounded by terraced Italian gardens with lavender walks, rose-clad arches, citrus and olive trees, all planted around fountains and pools. Outside and inside it's a place that will open the eye a little wider. Sturdy oak doors open onto a beautiful two-story atrium complete with koi pond and courtyard. There are three dining rooms; one seats twelve and you'll find another, more intimate, by the pool for just four. The pale marble staircase sweeps like the train of a dress up to a colonnaded balcony walk that overlooks the lower courtyard directly below… where there are antiques, and modern art, and day beds deep in cushions, and light which pours in from the glazed roof. The bedrooms owe much to Versace, one decorated in yellow and black, and all have hand-painted trompe-l'oeils on the walls. The villa is set on a terraced hillside with long long views over the vineyards of Constantia, to the Muizenberg mountains and as far as Gordon's Bay and the Cape of Good Hope. Heather was in Europe when we visited, but lives next door and will do B&B or you can rent the whole house per day. Very classy and a new addition to the Cape Town scene. *Children over 12 welcome.*

Rooms: 6: 1 large single, 2 double/twins & 3 suites, all with en-suite bath and shower.
Price: Room rates only. From R990 (low single) – R2,175 (high suite).
Meals: Full breakfast included. Catering can be arranged.
Directions: Take M3 from Cape Town towards Constantia. Follow Kirstenbosch signs. Take Rhodes Drive on the right towards Hout Bay and follow for 3km. Southern Cross Drive is on left and No.57 is half way down on the right.

Map Number: 1

Kaapse Draai

Annelie Posthumus

19 Glen Avenue, Constantia 7806
Tel: 021-794-6291 Fax: 021-794-6291
Email: kaapsedraai@hotmail.com Web: www.kaapsedraaibb.co.za
Cell: 082-923-9869

Annelie has been charming Greenwood Guide travellers since the very first edition and should be in the running for some sort of award for B&B brilliance. Relaxed, simple and beautiful seems to be the rule here. Her daughter is an interior designer and their talents combine to make the house a peaceful temple to uncluttered Cape Cod-style living. Neutral furnishings and white cottons are frisked up with pretty floral bolsters and country checks. Sunny window-seats are perfect for reading guide-books on the area and there are posies of fresh flowers in each room. I was lucky enough to stay with Annelie and once installed in my room, she invited me down for a soup later. She is a prolific gardener and you can walk (perhaps with Annelie's dogs) from the tropical greenery of Kaapse Draai with its mountain stream, huge ferns and palms into lovely Bel-Ombre meadow and the forest next door. From there it is a three-hour walk to the Table Mountain cable station. Porcupines come into the garden at night from the mountain (they love arum lilies apparently) and there are many birds too, including the noisy (and palindromic) hadedah. A grand old willow tree is what you'll park your car under. Delicious breakfasts are taken outside in the sunshine whenever possible. All I can say is – do. *Wine estates and Constantia shopping village nearby.*

Rooms: 3: 1 double and 2 twins with en-suite shower.
Price: R295 pp sharing. Singles R350.
Meals: Full breakfast included. Annelie sometimes cooks if the mood is upon her. But do not expect this....
Directions: Ask for fax or email when booking.

Map Number: 1

At Villa Fig

Bruno and Lindsay Rolando
6 Glendyrr Walk, Constantia 7806
Tel: 021-794-7049 Fax: 021-794-1378
Email: villafig@mweb.co.za

Airbrush together your ideal of a top-notch hotel and a relaxed home for a notion of how Bruno and Lindsay host at Villa Fig. Both artists, they took four years to salvage the Burmese teak for the frame of the structure, two years to restore the timber and that was before they started building! It's made for hot summers with tall ceilings and wide doors to let in both breeze and view. Acres of grey marble soften the reflection of sunlight pouring through the skylight above the Escher-esque staircase and metre-high cymbidium orchids, which flower joyously out of giant oriental pots. There are no interior walls downstairs, just four black, cast-iron columns, which accentuate the sense of space. And what about the art! Lindsay's (Roy) Lichtenstein-inspired canvases, bronze sculptures, Persian rugs…. One bedroom has a balustraded balcony shaded by an ancient pecan tree and through elephantine doors the main bedroom reveals 50 square metres of pure shimmering luxury. Tired after swimming or tennis? Then the upper deck, complete with pergola, has been positioned with precision for you to watch the sunset behind Table Mountain whilst you loll like Cleopatra on deep cushions and a mosaicked-by-Bruno chaise-longue.

Rooms: 5: 2 suites of 1 queen and 1 twin with en-suite bath and shower; 2 kings with en/s bath and shower; 1 king with en-suite shower.
Price: R300 – R450 pp sharing. Singles on request.
Meals: Full breakfast included.
Directions: Emailed or faxed on booking.

Lusthof

Judy Badenhorst
Rose Way, Constantia 7848
Tel: 021-794-6598 Fax: 021-794-8602
Email: lusthof@mweb.co.za Web: www.lusthof.co.za
Cell: 083-412-3455

Everyone in the world seems to know Judy, whether through the Old Cape Farm Stall, from Buitenverwachting wine estate, from the Spaanschemat River Café… or in our case through obscure family links in Britain. You probably know her yourself. All her projects seem to be touched by magic and become social temples for the Constantia faithful. We spent our first two weeks in South Africa staying in her guest cottage in the garden and it was a terrible moment when we finally had to leave the nest and look after ourselves. The cottage, with cable TV, heaters for winter and kitchenette, has doors onto its own patio, where you can lie on sunloungers and admire the flower garden or wallow in the newly-installed swimming pool. Judy is truly a maestro in the kitchen and literally anything that is made by her will be worth camping overnight for. If she doesn't have time to make breakfast herself, then it will be equally good at the River Café. You shouldn't choose Lusthof if you are after a fully-catered guest house with 24-hour service. But if you like to feel part of the furniture, and among friends, then this is the place for you. Mention must finally be made of Chebe, Judy's huge, shaggy, good-natured, lemon-loving bouvier – an integral part of the set-up. Chebe is a dog by the way. *Airport pick-up and car rental can be organised.*

Rooms: 1 twin cottage with shower and kitchenette.
Price: R250 – R350 pp sharing.
Meals: The cottage is self-catering and has a fully stocked kitchenette. Or Judy will provide dinner, breakfast and picnics on request.
Directions: Ask when booking for a full map.

The Sutherlands

Liz and Derek Sutherlands

14 Riesling Rd, Constantia 7808
Tel: 021-794-5485 Fax: 021-794-5485
Email: jdgsutherland@hotmail.com

Liz welcomed me into her home with a broad smile and icing dust on her hands – she had just finished baking for afternoon tea. Guiltlessly guzzling warm muffins and drop-scones loaded up with jam and whipped cream, we chatted about Scotland where she was brought up. Looking after people is second nature to Liz and evidently her guest fan-club adores it, since most of her bookings are in months, not days. No fripperous airs and graces here, just good people, comfortable living… an air of staying-with-friends-in-the-country. You can B&B in a guest room in the house, classically co-ordinated, big, fresh, white, with 'posturepedic' beds and a private patio. Or families can take one of two self-catering options in the building adjacent to the main house. These are kitted out with kitchens, braai area, gingham-covered sofas, terracotta-tiled bathrooms, lilac or white bedspreads… and many thoughtful extras such as toys and a paddling pool. If you actually *like* playing golf, Derek is a keen player and arranges tee-off times on the six courses found within ten minutes' drive. Pianists will gravitate towards the baby grand in the house sitting room. Guests/friends often take up residency here to recover from ill health. If you haven't already guessed, Liz is an ex-nursing sister. The sort of ideal nursing sister you hope against hope to get if you unfortunately end up needing one.

Rooms: 3: B&B in house: 1 king with bath and shower. Self-catering: 1 with 2 singles en/s bath & sh; 1 with double and 1 single and sofa bed, with b & s.
Price: B&B R250 pp. Self-catering R200 pp. Kids under 12 R50.
Meals: Full breakfast included and served out on the patio in good weather. Many restaurants at hand in Constantia for dinner.
Directions: Take the M3 south toward Muizenberg and come off at the Kendal Rd off-ramp. 3rd left into Old Kendal Rd. 2nd left into Riesling Rd. No.14.

Shambhala Guest House

Janine Bloomberg

Unit 12 Vierlanden Estate, Durbanville 7550
Tel: 021-975-2426 Fax: 021-975-2426
Email: shambhalaguesthouse@hotmail.com
Web: www.beststay.co.za/shambhalaguesthouse Cell: 083-444-5750

In a nutshell, Shambhala is a super-friendly B&B, run by a super-friendly Janine, in a secure and purpose-built village, in a safe and quiet suburb of Cape Town. The sun floods in through wide windows or there's a strip of funky halogen lights for when it doesn't, and you eat on benches at a big whitewashed table. There are quirky chicken-wire cupboard doors, farmyard animal artefacts, curvy violet couches and masses of magazines and books too. The bedrooms are neat and pretty. The upstairs one has a telescope so that you can study the distant and spectacular mountains of the Franschhoek valley. If I was staying here I'd make my own breakfast, then eat at Janine's espresso bar (yes, I can vouch for that too) for lunch. Bird fundis (fundi is SA for enthusiast) can watch the red bishops, weaver birds and bitterns who nest through the fence next door in the bird sanctuary. If you've got kids then this is a good 'un for security. There are hip-high walls around the house and you can lock all the gates. And Janine has attended strongly to the detail at Shambhala, from toys to bells on doors. There's also a pool on the 'village garden' just outside the front gate. The ducks don't mind that either thanks. A group of friendly walkers meet every Sunday morning at the café, by the way. It's free (and you're free) to join in. *Janine can organise good baby-sitters.*

Rooms: 3 queens with en-suite bath and shower.
Price: R300 pp summer, R250 pp winter. Min R600 for whole house.
Meals: 1 full meal included per person at café in Durbanville. R40 – R50 in café. Can be delivered.
Directions: In Durbanville, pass Tygervalley Centre. At Wellington Rd turn right. 2km down turn left into Boland. At T-junc right into Vierlanden Estate. Turn right again, follow road to Unit 12.

Vygeboom Manor

Callie and Luli Hamman

14 Valmar Rd, Valmary Park, Cape Town – Durbanville 7550
Tel: 021-975-6020 Fax: 021-976-5029
Email: vygeboom@gtrade.co.za Web: www.vygeboom.co.za
Cell: 083-270-4021

Vygeboom is a destination in itself. Callie is a prosthodontist and microlight pilot, Luli an artist and these disparate talents merge seamlessly to create a fantastic guest house experience in Cape Town's northern suburbs. Durbanville is an ideal location for visitors, with easy access to the bright lights and beaches of Cape Town, but also on established wine routes (including the ruling triumvirate of Paarl, Stellenbosch and Franschhoek). Prisoners of the game of golf will also find themselves embarrassed for choice. But this assumes, of course, that you feel like going anywhere. Luli has based the themes of each amazing room on her own gigantic and wonderful murals, doffing the cap to Rubens, Matisse, Manet etc. Comfort, however, does not play second fiddle to artistic whimsy – beds are huge, bathrooms luxurious. Add to this charming hosts (Callie does his dentistry next door), spectacular views to the distant wall of the Hottentots Holland Mountains, a vast sitting room with a three-quarter size snooker table and a large pool in the garden. At the same price as last year Vygeboom remains outstanding value. *Callie can organize microlight trips for guests – an exciting way to go whale-spotting in season. Free access to health club/gym.*

Rooms: 5: 1 double, 4 twins (3 with en-suite bath, 2 with en-suite shower).
Price: R300 – R400 pp sharing. Ask about specials for families and groups.
Meals: Full breakfast included and barbeque dinners by arrangement.
Directions: Junction 23 N1, R302 north for 5km. Turn right into Valmar Rd.

Langebaan Beach House

Claire Green
44 Beach Road, Entrance in Jacoba St, Langebaan 7357
Tel: 022-772-2625 Fax: 022-772-1432
Email: lbh@intekom.co.za Web: www.langebaanbeachhouse.com

This very popular, friendly B&B was once Claire's family's seaside retreat in the days when Langebaan was a small fishing village. It has grown since then, but still has a nice holiday feel. The house is Claire's home, complete with two typically upbeat labradors (and two cats), and set right on the lagoon. The garden goes directly down to sand and water. The original part is over 100 years old, while the rest has gradually been added as the family expanded – most of it is now for guests. Two of the bright bedrooms are 'suites', with their own sitting rooms and views to the water. There is a big communal sitting area where Claire's collection of model boats lives and the garden has a plunge pool and sun-loungers. Breakfast is served in the glass-enclosed verandah looking down to the beach. The sea is safe and swimmable by the way, if a little chilly. All water sports are allowed – swimming, motor- and wind-powered vessels, fishing and water-skiing – and the Cape Sports Centre (where you can hire most water sports gear) is just up the beach. 250,000 migrating birds, including flamingos, live at the wilderness end of the lagoon. P.S. Next door there are two excellent restaurants where you can get bowls of calamari for R36! Claire herself is relaxed, warm-spirited and extremely knowledgeable about what's going on in her neck of the woods. Which is a lot.

Rooms: 4: 2 suites, each with sitting room; 1 double and 1 twin. All rooms have en-suite shower.
Price: Suites from R300 – R450 pp sharing. Other rooms from R200 – R300 pp. Singles on request.
Meals: Full breakfast included. For other meals there are lots of great restaurants in Langebaan – 5 within walking distance.
Directions: Directions will be faxed or emailed when you book.

Map Number: 2

The Oystercatcher's Haven at Paternoster

Sandy Attrill

48 Sonkwasweg, Paternoster 7381
Tel: 022-752-2193 Fax: 022-752-2192
Email: honihiki@global.co.za Web: www.oystercatchershaven.com
Cell: 082-414-6705 or 083-267-7051

Sandy and Wayne, ex film and advertising people, do things in style and their guest house is a knock-out! The Cape Dutch house sits on the fringes of the Cape Columbine Nature Reserve, a spectacular, fynbos-covered, hand-shaped headland, bearing its lighthouse aloft like a nine-million-watt jewel. All along the coast and a mere 40 metres in front of the house knobbly fingers of grey and black granite merge into the sea and around the rocks there are secret white sandy coves where the dolphins come throughout the year. It is quite simply beautiful and I can assure you that the Oystercatcher is a haven by anyone's standards. Heave yourself out of that plunge-pool, off the rocks and away from the view (available from your bed) and head inside the house. The interior, with its white walls, untreated timbers and reed-and-pole ceilings, is intentionally blank-yet-rustic to showcase some exquisite pieces, such as a four-foot-high Angolan drum, some Malinese sinaba paintings (you'll have to come and see them if you don't know what they are), Persian rugs, art-deco couches, courtyards…. Just about everything is a hook for an eager eye. Bedrooms are bliss, trust me….Want hurricane-lamp-lit suppers on the beach? Walk this way.

Rooms: 3: 1 queen with en-suite bath and shower; 1 queen and 1 twin, both with en-suite showers. All rooms have private entrances.
Price: From R320 – R410 pp sharing. Singles from R450.
Meals: Full breakfast included. Meals by arrangement and you can eat on the beach if the weather permits. Picnics from R60.
Directions: From Cape Town take the N1 and then the R27 north following signs to Vredenburg. Follow signs straight through Vredenburg to Paternoster (15km). At crossroads turn left and travel a full 1km towards the Columbine Reserve. Turn right into Sonkwas Rd, it is No. 48.

Map Number: 2

Blue Dolphin

George Koning

12 Warrelklip St, Paternoster 7381
Tel: 022-752-2001 Fax: 022-752-2001. Need to call and ask for the line.
Email: bluedolphin@mweb.co.za Web: www.bluedolphin.co.za

The Blue Dolphin concept is simple, natural and refreshing. Four very comfortable rooms, with views of the sea, a verandah with a day-bed for lying on and listening to the surf, a sandy beach that stretches from the house... and two great restaurants up the road for lunch and dinner. The house is open, wooden, breezy, with whites and blues dominating in tune with the beach and sea. All you have to do is lazily watch out for dolphins (and whales in season), kick sand along the strand, eat your breakfast, chat with George, read a book... chill those nerves, untie those muscles. Book early for the flower season (end of August/beginning of September). The dune fynbos blooms impressively and a rash of tiny brightly-coloured flowers emerge like magic from the very sand itself. George has kept the number of rooms down to just four so that he always has plenty of time for everyone. The bedrooms are well kitted-out with heated towel rails, satellite TV, mohair blankets, great beds and linen. Next door is the new Baby Dolphin, a self-catering option, but you can have breakfast at the Blue Dolphin. It has a giant fireplace, a wide, sea-facing verandah and a track straight out to the beach. *Columbine Nature Reserve and the Fossil Museum are nearby.*

Rooms: 4: all doubles with en-suite shower.
Price: R250 pp sharing. Singles R350.
Meals: Full breakfast included. Excellent meals at Voorstrand and Ahoy Galley restaurants in Paternoster.
Directions: Directions faxed on booking.

Map Number: 2

Hoekie

Volker and Ingrid Wessolowski

Paternoster 7381
Tel: 022-752-2077 Fax: 021-423-3055
Email: info@amakhanda.co.za Web: www.amakhanda.co.za
Cell: 082-660-6660

Volker was a boat designer and engineer before he created Hoekie. It means 'little corner' in Afrikaans and there are indeed many nooks and crannies about the place where to relax in the sun; a wooden chaise-longue built from beach-flotsam by the pool, an upstairs courtyard between two gabled bedrooms, a chunky wooden picnic table on the verandah which enjoys the view. And what a view! You can see over the quiet lane and out to a wide golden beach and the ocean beyond. Back inside, the creative hand has not been stayed and those of us who don't mind a lick of luxury won't feel out of place either. The sitting room is decorated in earthy tones, a high, open-plan space that connects to a swish kitchen and a glass-roofed dining room; there's a boat prow over the wall and Volker's exquisite miniature schooner and a hand-made staircase. A huge kudu-leather couch dominates one corner under the sleeping platform and (although not quite finished when I visited) distressed wooden furniture and white percale linens were ready to go into the bedrooms. Ingrid is a down-to-earth and very attentive soul. She runs her own tour company and has another two guest houses in Cape Town. She learnt to cook at the Four Seasons in Hamburg, so food is excellent with freshly-baked bread at breakfast. The exquisite beaches of Cape Columbine nearby can be explored in the Hoekie 4WD. Take a picnic. *Ask about self-catering.*

Rooms: 3 bedrooms, all en-suite with bath/shower.
Price: R150 – R250 pp sharing. House can be privately hired for a minimum of R2,000 per night.
Meals: By arrangement only. Self-catering optional when whole house taken. Restaurants are nearby.
Directions: Faxed or emailed upon booking.

Villa Dauphine

David and Ann Dixon
166 Sandpiper Close, Golden Mile Bvd, Britannia Bay 7382
Tel: 022-742-1926 Fax: 022-742-1926
Email: dadixon@mweb.co.za Web: www.villadauphine.com
Cell: 083-409-3195

Cosseted within its own walls, Villa Dauphine shuns the harsh sandveld of the interior and focuses instead on the bay whose broad arc passes not twenty yards from the stoep. Here you sit and peacefully beat out the rhythm of the waves. Two finned backs breached some 30 metres from shore, my first ever sighting of wild dolphins. David and Anne were unimpressed. The day before great schools of them had been leaping, frolicking, doing crosswords and playing chess right in front of the house. You can take boat rides out to cement the friendship and navigate the Berg River for bird-watching. The house is country cottage pretty, thatched and beamed with solid furniture, pots of fresh flowers, terracotta tiles, lots of whites and woods. Two atticky bedrooms are found up wooden steps, which lead from a flowery, sun-trapping, wind-breaking courtyard. The other is in the house itself. David used to be a vet and he and Anne are real bird enthusiasts. If you are too, they'll point you off to the Berg River (above 190 bird species) but everyone must visit the beautiful West Coast National Park nearby (250,000 migratory birds and a stunning turquoise lagoon). Golf courses and excellent restaurants nearby. Come here in spring and the countryside is carpeted in flowers. They appear out of nowhere and grow right down to the water line.

Rooms: 2 'units': 1 suite with 2 double bedrooms with a shared bathroom (bath & shower); 1 twin with en-suite bath and shower.
Price: From R200 – R275 pp sharing. Singles on request.
Meals: Full breakfast included. Dinner by arrangement.
Directions: From Cape Town take R27 to Vredenburg turn-off. Turn left to Vredenburg. At first lights, turn right to St Helena Bay. 10km to Stompneusbaai sign. Turn left. 17km turn left to Britannia Bay. 2km. Turn right at White Entrance to Golden Mile. Turn right and after 2nd speed bump turn left.

Map Number: 2

Kersefontein

Julian Melck
between Hopefield and Velddrif, Hopefield 7355
Tel: 022-783-0850 or 022-783-9900   Fax: 022-783-0850 or 022-783-9900
Email: info@kersefontein.co.za Web: www.kersefontein.co.za
Cell: 083-454-1025

Nothing has changed at Kersefontein since the last edition. Julian's convivial dinner parties are still a reason to book in on their own. And Julian himself remains a Renaissance man, described on his business card as 'Farmer, Pig-killer, Aviator and Advocate of the High Court of S.A.' He farms cows, sheep and horses on the surrounding fields, and wild boar appear deliciously at dinner. He also hires and pilots a six-seater plane and a flight round the Cape or along the coast is a must. He modestly leaves out his virtuosity as a pianist and organist and some of us trooped off one Sunday morning, braving a 40-minute sermon in Afrikaans, to hear toccatas by Bach, Giguot and Widor at the local church. When not eating, riding or flying, guests lounge on the pontoon, swim in the river or read books from Kersefontein's many libraries. Or they use the house as a base to visit the coast or the Swartland wineries, which are really taking off. The homestead is seventh generation and the rooms either Victorian or African in temperament, with antiques handed down by previous Melcks. You are fed like a king, but treated as a friend and I am always recommending people to go there.

Rooms: 6: 3 doubles and 3 twins; 1 with shower, 2 with bath and 3 with bath and shower.
Price: R350 – R450 pp sharing. No singles supp. Aircraft hire prices depend on the trip. Julian will also do fly/picnic trips out to various destinations.
Meals: Full breakfast is included. Dinners by arrangement: R120 – R150 excluding wine.
Directions: From Cape Town take N7 off N1. Bypass Malmesbury, 5km later turn left towards Hopefield. After 50km bypass Hopefield, turn right signed Velddrif. After 16km farm signed on right just before grain silos. Cross bridge and gates on the left.

Boschkloof Cottage

Mariet and Doempie Smit
Boschkloof, Citrusdal 7340
Tel: 022-921-3533 Fax: 022-921-3533
Email: boschkloof@kingsley.co.za Web: www.citrusdal.info/boschkloof
Cell: 082-734-9467

We bumped along six or so sandy kilometres, past orchards of citrus trees and stumbled upon some sort of prelapsarian idyll! A private valley, cocooned in the Sneeuberg Conservancy, in the foothills of the Cederberg, flanked by sandstone mountains, its orange groves watered by a natural stream, the rocks and plants etched in hyper-real clarity by a setting sun. There are Bushman rock art sites, natural pools in the river to cool off in and hiking on mountain trails to be done from the house in the early morning and evening. We parked under an oak tree and were met by Mariet, her two small daughters and two large dogs. On return from a dip in the river we met Doempie and a glass of wine and were soon being treated to crayfish kebabs from the braai, seated under the oak with views up the kloof and a sensational tone to the air. It just made us well to be there, but they say it was entirely the worst time of year (February)! The Smits live in one of the old farmhouses, their guests next door in the other. Although it is a self-catering arrangement, you are in such close proximity that you might as well be at a B&B, except with far more space and privacy. And the cottage? No time for detail – just trust me, it's lovely!

Rooms: 1 cottage with 2 bedrooms; 1 double (with extra single) with bath and shower and 1 twin with a small bathroom with a shower. Can sleep 6.
Price: R400 for 2 people. R80 for each extra person.
Meals: Fully-equipped kitchen – this is a self-catering cottage. Mariet can provide breakfast materials for you by prior arrangement.
Directions: N7 to Citrusdal – turn into village, go left into Voortrekker Rd and right into Muller St. Carry straight on, it becomes a dirt road, follow it for 7km.

Petersfield Farm Cottages

Hedley Peter and Johann Human
Petersfield Guest Farm, Citrusdal 7340
Tel: 022-921-3316 Fax: 022-921-3316
Email: info@petersfieldfarm.co.za Web: www.petersfieldfarm.co.za
Cell: 083-626-5145

Hedley and Johann are instantly likable and funny hosts and Petersfield is Hedley's family farm (citrus and rooibos tea), the property ranging over the back of the mountain behind the main house, forming a huge private wilderness reserve. De Kom, an idyllic, simple-but-stylish stone cottage perched high in sandstone mountains will appeal to your inner romantic. This charming electricity-free cottage is lit by hurricane lamps and flares with gas for the stove, fridge and hot water. A private plunge pool with river stones at the bottom overlooks this secret valley with the Olifants River and purpling Cederberg peaks as a backdrop. And what a setting, guarded to the front by a citrus orchard, to the rear by craggy sandstone and looking deep and far from the stoep down the mountain. There is a secluded farm dam nearby (300 metres) to swim in or picnic by while watching nesting eagles. Or, 2km away, there is (electrified) Dassieklip cottage, a sweet wooden mountain cabin secreted in its own kloof and reached down an avenue of oaks. It too has a plunge pool to cool off in and other mod cons such as fridge, air-conditioning, TV and CD player. Bring your own food for both cottages, although breakfast materials for you to cook can be provided. *Wood is provided at no extra charge and pets are also welcome.*

Rooms: 2 cottages with 2 bedrooms each.
Price: Week-nights: R350 for 2 people, R430 for 3, R500 for 4, R550 for 5/6. Weekends, public holidays, flower season (15 Aug-15 Sept): R400 for 2, R500 for 3, R600 for 4, R700 for 5/6. Prices are per night and for whole cottage.
Meals: Self-catering, but breakfast materials provided in the fridge by prior arrangement.
Directions: From Cape Town 4km after Citrusdal on your left on the N7 travelling towards Clanwilliam.

Rockwood Cottage

Pam and Noel Mills

Rockwood Farm, PO Box 131, Citrusdal 7340
Tel: 022-921-3517 Fax: 022-921-2653
Email: amills@new.co.za Web: www.citrusdal.info/rockwood
Cell: 072-222-3344

Rockwood is an extremely beautiful protea farm in the Cederberg highlands 800 metres above sea level. Both the main house where Pam and Noel live and their large and lovely guest cottage (self-catering) have front stoeps that overlook a succession of dams, the hinterland channelled away for miles and miles by rugged sandstone mountains. The highest peaks of the Sneeuberg Conservancy are often covered with snow in winter. The guest cottage is cradled among giant rocks with the eponymous rockwood trees growing from beneath. And to the front a story-book stream burbles past the stoep and oak trees there. A wide expanse of lawn leads to more treasure. Noel has created a natural rock swimming pool that is filled all year round by a river with fresh, drinkable water that cascades gently over the rocks. A sundowner either in the pool or in the jacuzzi just above allows you time to digest the magnificent view and feel properly smug. Behind this there is a deep gorge and waterfall, an idyllic world of water and rock, full of wild flowers in season with two bush trails cut through natural gardens. Pam and Noel will happily show their guests all there is to do on the property and in the region, still so unspoiled by tourism. *Children over twelve permitted.*

Rooms: 1 cottage with 2 bedrooms; 1 double and 1 twin sharing 1 bath with shower above. Plus an outside bedroom with twin beds and en-suite shower.
Price: R500 per night for two people, R100 for each additional person. Also R100 per day for use of the jacuzzi (electricity doesn't come cheap in the hills!).
Meals: The cottage is self-catering. Noel and Pam will point you towards local restaurants which are 5 minutes away.
Directions: From N7 into Citrusdal. At four-way intersection in centre of village straight over and up mountain for 7km. 2nd white gates on your left.

Map Number: 2 & 3

Mount Ceder

André and Jaen Marais

Grootrivier Farm, Cederberg,
Koue Bokkeveld 6836
Tel: 023-317-0113
Fax: 023-317-0543
Email:
mountceder@lando.co.za
Web: www.mountceder.co.za

Do not lose confidence as you rumble along the dirt roads that lead through the Koue Bokkeveld nature conservancy to this secluded valley – it's always a couple more turns. Finally you will arrive in the very heart of the Cederberg, dry sandstone mountains rising all around you in impressive dimensions. You will be given the key to your new home and drive off along half a kilometre of sand track to one of three fantastic rustic stone cottages. The river flows past the reeds and rock right by the cottages, clear, deep and wide all year round. You can swim and lie around drying on flat rocks. Birds love it here too. I imagine sitting out on that stoep, on those wooden chairs, looking at that view, beer or wine in hand… a piece of heaven as they say. You can either self-cater or you can eat at André and Jaen's restaurant back at the lodge. There are a few other cottages nearer the lodge, which are fine, but you must ask for the stone cottages, which are in a league of their own. A pristine slice of unspoiled nature, cherished by a very knowledgeable Marais family who will help with Bushman rock art, horse-riding and fauna and flora. Do not reach for your red pen by the way… that *is* how you spell ceder (in Afrikaans) and that is how you spell Jaen!

Rooms: 3 river cottages with 3 bedrooms each.
Price: R720 – R1,200 per cottage per night self-catering (cottages sleep 6); or R360 – R670 pp for dinner, B&B.
Meals: You can either self-cater or eat in the restaurant at Mount Ceder.
Directions: From Ceres follow signs to Prince Alfred Hamlet/Op-die-Berg up Gydo Pass past Op-die-Berg. First right signed Cederberge – follow tar for 17km then straight on on dirt road for another 34km into a green valley.

Tulbagh Country House

Ginny Clark
24 Church St, Tulbagh 6820
Tel: 023-230-1171 Fax: 023-230-0721
Email: tulbaghguesthse@mweb.co.za Web: www.tulbaghguesthouse.co.za
Cell: 082-416-6576

This 200-year-old B&B in the heart of the historic village of Tulbagh looked too inviting to drive past without taking a peek. Built in 1809 and still retaining many of its original features, the house is the epitome of classic Cape Dutch living and has been beautifully restored to its former glory by Ginny. Antiques and original artwork catch the eye at every glance and guests are free to roam and admire. Seated on her twin gargantuan couches, or around her dining table, Ginny will happily impart her extensive knowledge of Church Street's history, thereby completing the picture of the historic charm of the Witzenberg Valley. She treats her guests as friends and they naturally treat her likewise. In her guest book, Ginny has appraisals galore, markedly for her breakfasts, a table spread with antique crockery, silver cutlery and the feast itself: 'For those who follow, beware Ginny's breakfasts – they are wonderful' and such like. We crossed the road, escorted by a peacock, to find the self-catering cottage. Simple and charming, this cottage, which was formerly a wagon shed, is kitted out with board games, reference books and a large French-cricket-sized garden that stretches to the river. The authenticity of Ginny's hospitality makes a stay here a real treat. *Ask about children. A few minutes' walk to very good restaurants.*

Rooms: 3: 1 king en/s bath with shower above, 1 suite with 1 double + 1 twin, en/s bath. Self-catering cottage for 6 with 1 dbl, 2 twin, 1 bath with shower + sep toilet.
Price: R230 – R250 pp sharing. Single R280 – R300. Self-catering cottage: R150 pp for a couple, R100 pp for 4-6 people.
Meals: Full breakfast included for the rooms. Breakfast an optional extra for self-catering cottage.
Directions: From Cape Town take N1 to exit 47 Wellington/Franschhoek/Klapmuts turn-off, left onto R44 via Wellington. Follow R44 to Tulbagh. In village centre take a left to be parallel to main road.

Hunters Retreat Guest Farm & Manley Private Cellar

Esther and David Jordan
PO Box 318, Tulbagh 6820
Tel: 023-230-0582 Fax: 023-230-0057
Email: esther@lando.co.za Web: www.lando.co.za/huntersretreat

I leaned happily against my car while Esther dished out tea for the churchgoers who use Hunters church twice a month. What a setting. Pure bands of green and blue as rolling vineland meets berg meets sky. The high-thatched cottages down by the wetlands of the dam have their own patios of perfect peace, disturbed only by flashes of brilliant colour as the red bishops weave their nests in the reeds. There are birds everywhere (egrets and kingfishers among them), including a family of solemn blue cranes that check you out like dogs at the gate. Since the last visit, David has turned his erstwhile sheep farm into a wine farm (the sheep caused havoc in the vines and so needed to be relocated), has his first wine in barrels and has won three medals in the young wine show. I loved the aroma of thatch in the cottage too, which has two roomy family suites. There is plenty of space here, an outdoorsy sort of place, great for animals and kids. Grown-ups can go for walks round the dam and commune with the birds. *Historic Tulbagh has a handful of museums and good restaurants. There are other rooms available at Hunters, all fine, but the thatched cottages are our special recommendation.*

Rooms: 2 family suites each with 1 double bed, 2 single beds, a bath and shower.
Price: From R225 – R245 pp sharing.
Meals: Full breakfast included and served until 10 am.
Directions: From Cape Town take N1 to exit 47 Wellington/Franschhoek/Klapmuts turn-off, left onto R44 via Wellington. Follow R44 for an hour to Tulbagh. Straight thro' town, 1.4km on left.

Map Number: 3

Bartholomeus Klip Farmhouse

Lesley Gillett
Elandsberg Farm, Hermon 7308
Tel: 022-448-1820 Fax: 022-448-1829
Email: bartholomeus@icon.co.za Web: www.parksgroup.co.za
Cell: 082-829-4131

Heavenly scenery cossets this Victorian homestead in its lush gardens and stands of oak and olive. The wall of the Elandsberg Mountains rises up from the game reserve, reflected in the dammed lake by the house. Here guests can have breakfast on the balcony of the boathouse before heading out for an excursion onto the wheat and sheep farm. You are also taken on late-afternoon game drives to see the zebra, a variety of Cape antelope, buffalo, quaggas (a fascinating experiment to reintroduce an extinct variety of zebra), eagles, flocks of blue crane... and the largest world population of the tiny, endangered geometric tortoises. But just to be out in such nature! The spring flowers are spectacular and there are more than 850 species of plant recorded on the property. Back at the homestead you can cool down in the curious, round, raised reservoir pool, sit in chairs on the stoep; or, if you have more energy, bike off into the reserve or go on guided walks in the mountains. Staff are very friendly, food is exceptional and a reason to stay on its own (and all included in the price). I recommend splashing out on at least two nights. A great place indeed and very popular so book ahead of yourself if possible. *Closed June*.

Rooms: 5: 2 doubles and 3 twins; 5 with bath and shower.
Price: R2,380 – R2,600 pp sharing. Singles rates on application. Includes meals and game drives.
Meals: Coffee and rusks, brunch, high tea, snacks and sundowners and 4-course dinner included in price.
Directions: From CT take N1 towards Paarl. Exit 47, left at Stop. Follow Agter-Paarl Rd over 4-ways. L signed Ceres. Follow 30km, past Malmesbury sign to L. Go next R signed Bo-Hermon. Gravel road for 2km. Bartholomeus Klip signed to L – 5km.

Map Number: 2 & 3

Tigertrap Cottages

Jackie Solomon
PO Box 566, Riebeek West 7306
Tel: 022-461-2289 Fax: 022-461-2335
Email: tigertrap@iafrica.com Web: www.tigertrap.co.za

We called Tigertrap home for four months and by the end had to be crow-barred out of the place, so happily ensconced were we. We could not have landed up anywhere more perfect... hundred-year-old cottages with reed and pole ceilings, stone bathrooms, bedrooms with double doors out to private stoeps and gardens, fridges stocked with all the necessaries, DSTV, fantastico linen and sofas and showers and free-standing baths. Happily intermingled with all this, Jackie and Mike provide a never-ending supply of different goods: good conversation, good humour and overwhelmingly good cheer – the best you'll find. The cottages have steps up to a seventeen-metre, salt-water swimming pool and I did thousands of lengths (well hundreds... well, maybe one thousand) before the old earache set in. You probably don't want to hear about that. Lying on a lounger by the pool on a Saturday afternoon, staring up at the Kasteelberg that looms behind the main house, the line of its craggy summit etched against a reliably blue sky, a wind chime softly blowing in the breeze, the odd squawk from a chicken, a stamp of hungry impatience from the horses in the paddock... such was the scenario for the contentedest hours I have spent in South Africa. So thanks Mike and Jackie for four months of ideal living. We can only pity those whose stay will be measured in mere days.

Rooms: 2 cottages: 1 with 3 bedrooms, all en-suite, (2 with bath, 1 with shower); 1 with 2 bedrooms, both en-suite (1 bath and 1 shower).
Price: R480 – R520. No single supplement.
Meals: Full breakfast included. Cottage freezers stocked with home-made dinners.
Directions: Riebeek West is 1 hour north of Cape Town. Ask for directions when booking.

Belair

Janet Plumbly
Suid Agter-Paarl Rd, Paarl 7624
Tel: 021-863-1504
Fax: 021-863-1602
Email: info@belair.co.za
Web: www.belair.co.za
Cell: 082-572-7062

A straight 300-metre drive up two narrow strips of weathered red brick, past roaming gangs of guinea-fowl and rows of vines, takes you up to Belair, a beautiful guest house on its own farm beneath the round dome of Paarl Mountain. The view from the doorstep (and the garden and pool) across the valley towards Franschhoek and the Groot Drakenstein is spectacular… and it is rather lovely inside too. Steps lead up from a large threshing-circle style driveway into the hallway and open sitting room, which mixes antique furniture with comfy sofas and bookshelves bursting with swashbucklers. Behind is the bright breakfast conservatory, which looks onto a rose-filled garden. There are definitely green fingers at work here. Janet's light but stylish touch is in evidence everywhere at Belair, from the terraced gardens to the bedrooms themselves, each with its own distinct character. My favourite was the 'red' toile room at the end. From the house, it's a short walk up to the dam where bird life abounds among the reeds (look out for buzzards when it all goes quiet), a great spot for a sundowner. For the more energetic, Paarl Mountain Nature Reserve is further up the hill, and there are lots of golf courses nearby. *Cape Town Waterfront is also only 35 minutes away and there are great restaurants in and about Paarl.*

Rooms: 4 doubles with en-suite bathrooms. 2 are twins joined together.
Price: R200 – R400 pp sharing. Single supplements not specified.
Meals: Full breakfast included.
Directions: On R101 (Suid Agter-Paarl road) next to Fairview Wine Estate.

Map Number: 2 & 3

Kleinfontein

Tim and Caroline Holdcroft
PO Box 578, Wellington 7654
Tel: 021-864-1202 Fax: 021-864-1202
Email: kleinfon@iafrica.com Web: www.kleinfontein.com
Cell: 072-108-5895

After a long day I was delighted to find myself, first with a G&T in hand and then with one of Caroline's sumptuous meals before me. We discussed the name Tim should call his new wine. The farm is named after the small spring that feeds their guava and young olive trees, organic vegetable garden and vines. I suggested 'Tuinfontein' (garden spring) in honour of Caroline's indigenous, bird-friendly garden, which was opening that weekend for the Wellington garden festival. Caroline's other passion is her horses which graze in the paddocks in the valley, encased by the Hawakwe and Limietberg mountains – fantastic walking ground and a spectacular outlook from the verandah where all meals are taken, weather permitting. Guests stay in one wing of the thatched Cape Dutch farmhouse which Caroline and Tim have recently restored. It has retained its original character with poplar beams and ceilings made from reeds harvested on the farm. Both suites have roomy living areas with fresh flowers, TV and an array of spirits and wine that you can help yourself to. A nice surprise when slipping between the white linen sheets at night was the hot-water bottle that had warmed my bed for me! And in the morning I breakfasted on butter, cream and milk fresh from the Jersey cows, newly-laid eggs and honey straight from the beehive. Tim and Caroline specialise in 'home hosting'. *Closed June and July.*

Rooms: 2 suites, both with sitting room. 1 with en-suite bath and shower, 1 with en-suite bath with shower overhead.
Price: R1,150 pp sharing. Single supplement + 20%. Includes all meals, drinks and laundry.
Meals: Breakfast, tea/coffee tray, picnic lunch and 4-course dinner included in the price.
Directions: Directions are down dirt roads so map can be emailed or faxed.

Oude Wellington Estate

Rolf and Vanessa Schumacher
Bainskloof Pass Rd, Wellington 7654
Tel: 021-873-2262 Fax: 021-873-4639
Email: info@kapwein.com Web: www.kapwein.com

There seems to be so much to catch the eye even as you rumble along the 800-metre gravel road to Oude Wellington: vineyards on both sides, ostentatious peacocks, geese and hadedas, pet ostriches peering over a fence. And that afternoon four pregnant alpacas that had just arrived all the way from Australia were to be added to the menagerie. Rolf and Vanessa are clearly the hospitable types (how else could ostriches find a home on a winery?). It took them two years to restore the whole estate to its former glory as a wine-grape farm. Four rustic double rooms are in the original farmhouse (built in 1790) with high, thatched ceilings, low pole beams, whitewashed walls and yet underfloor heating and air con; the other two are in the more modern main building (well, 1836!), along with the beautiful farm kitchen with old-fashioned pots, pans and irons, billiard room and bar, and a terrace overlooking the vineyards, where breakfast is served in the summer. There is a partly-shaded pool off to the side of the main house, a brandy still in the barn, and handily on the premises is a restaurant popular with the locals (always a good sign). Guests are also invited to watch wine-making taking place at the right time of year. "We farm and dine and love company," say Rolf and Vanessa in their brochure!

Rooms: 6: all doubles with en-suite Victorian baths.
Price: R250 pp sharing. R350 single.
Meals: Full breakfast included. Restaurant on premises.
Directions: Turn into Church Street (Kerkstraat) in Wellington which becomes the Bainskloof Rd (R301/3). 2.5km out of Wellington on right-hand side follow brown signs to Oude Wellington.

Map Number: 2 & 3

Roggeland Country House

Gordon Minkley
Roggeland Rd, Dal Josaphat Valley, Paarl 7623
Tel: 021-868-2501 Fax: 021-868-2113
Email: rog@iafrica.com Web: www.roggeland.co.za

The highlight of a stay at Roggeland must be the food! All reports glow with praise: 8-12 different wines to taste pre-dinner, an opportunity to chat to other guests and Gordon himself; then four mouth-watering courses each with a different wine specially chosen to accompany it. Vegetarians will be particularly happy and meals and wines are never repeated during your stay. The house is an 18th-century Cape Dutch homestead with large, thick-walled rooms – sometimes huge – with a variety of original features: beam and reed ceilings, thatch, antique furniture. The dining room, for example, is in an old kitchen with its original grate and cooking implements. Some bedrooms are in the main house and some are separate from it, but none let the side down. Character abounds; floors slope, beams curve and attractive bright-coloured walls are often uneven with age; and there are always fresh flowers and home-made soaps in the rooms. Roggeland is family-run and the atmosphere is friendly and caring as a result. Farmland and mountains surround the property and the Minkleys will organise evening rides on horseback into the foothills. Great hospitality and very good value too. *Children by arrangement. Mountain biking and fishing.*

Rooms: 11: 6 twins, 4 doubles, 1 single. All with en/s bathrooms, 7 with baths and showers, 4 with baths and showers overhead.
Price: Seasonal R520 – R970 pp sharing. Single supplement in high season + 50%.
Meals: The highlight is a 4-course dinner with a different wine at each course and wine-tasting, all included in price. Full breakfast too. Lunches on request.
Directions: Approximately 60km from Cape Town, take exit 59 onto R301 towards Wellington. After 8km on R301 turn right at Roggeland sign. Follow sign onto gravel road for 1km.

Map Number: 2

Auberge Rozendal

Tanya Louw-Ammann
Jonkershoek Valley, Omega Road, Stellenbosch 7599
Tel: 021-809-2600 Fax: 021-809-2640
Email: rozendal@mweb.co.za Web: www.rozendal.co.za

Kurt, Tanya's father, swears by his home-made vinegar apéritif. This concoction of ten-year-old matured vinegar infused with lavender, coco, carrob, wild olives, seaweed and chillies is said to aid digestion and blood circulation. Apparently some guests love it, although I confess that I winced when swallowing. But then Tanya started to laugh when my stomach rumbled afterwards – the digestive catalyst obviously does the trick! Here on the organic bio-dynamic wine farm their philosophy is health and well-being and the proof is in the eating. With a focus on organic food, delicacies such as abalone, crayfish and free-range duck breast are not to be missed. Meals are served either on the verandah under the vines or in the dining room with its gallery of canvasses by world-famous local artists such as Paul Emsley (Tate exhibitor), Cecil Skotnes and Larry Scully. From their 26 hectares, the Ammann family harvest fruits and vegetables, collect eggs from the chickens and milk from their Jersey cows and guests can even participate in the trampling of the grapes in February/March. Separated from the main house, the purpose-built rooms fronted with olive trees and rose bushes have terraces with magnificent views that stretch over vineyards to either Table Mountain or the Botmaskop mountains. If the fresh air and natural environment do not provide you with enough feel-good endorphins, there is a massage therapist who visits on request.

Rooms: 16: 9 queens, 7 twins, all with en-suite bath with shower overhead.
Price: R410 pp sharing. Singles R550.
Meals: R50 for breakfast. 4-course evening menu R150, 3 courses for R130. Lunch also available.
Directions: From Cape Town take N2, then take exit 33 to Stellenbosch on R310. Turn R at T-jct. After station turn left onto Adam Tas Rd. At second traffic light turn R onto Merriman Rd. At roundabout look out for L'Auberge Rozendal sign. After 2km turn left into Omega St. A.Rozendal signposted at top of Omega St.

Babylons Toren

Margie and David Louw

Klapmuts – Simondium Rd, Simondium 7670
Tel: 021-863-3494 Fax: 021-863-1804
Email: babylon@mweb.co.za Web: www.babylonstoren.co.za
Cell: 082-334-3340

Babylons Toren (the Tower of Babylon) is named after the koppie or rocky hill by the house, thought to resemble a ziggurat by earlier (much earlier – the house was built in about 1700) romantics with a bit of imagination. The property is all that you would hope for from a working Cape Dutch farm. There are the old gabled house, the surrounding outbuildings and vineyards, the backdrop of mountains, the sporadic sound of tractors, many dogs… and Margie has opened up one of the courtyard outbuildings – these were once dairy, butchery, bakery – and created a rustic, but very stylish cottage for guests. The ceiling is of pole beams and cut reeds (the width of the house was apparently dependent on the length of the wagon that carried these beams), walls are thick and whitewashed, and the main bedroom itself is of grand dimensions with high ceilings and a decorative mosquito net over twin beds. You can self-cater or indulge in Margie's healthy breakfasts, which are served under a tree with the Simonsberg Mountain not inconsequential in the corner of your eye as you pour yourself another cup of tea. The large pool in the garden is as much yours as your hosts'. In fact a major reason why Margie has guests at all is to share what Babylons Toren has to offer with new people. *27-hole golf course nearby. Horse-riding easily arranged.*

Rooms: 1 cottage with 2 double rooms sharing 1 bathroom with bath. Self-catering or B&B. One-group booking only.
Price: R200 pp sharing. Singles supplement. Self-catering for two people R360, for four people R480.
Meals: Full breakfast included. For other meals self-catering or restaurants aplenty in the area.
Directions: From Cape Town take the N1 exit 47 onto R44 towards Stellenbosch. Turn left signed Simondium/Franschhoek. Follow road for 6km. Babylons Toren is on your right in vineyards.

Glenconner

Emma Finnemore

Jonkershoek Valley, Stellenbosch 7612
Tel: 021-886-5120 Fax: 021-886-5120
Email: glenconner@icon.co.za Web: www.winelands.co.za/glenconner
Cell: 082-354-3510

Looking up at the imposing mountains, which rise on both sides of the property, and surrounded by lush vegetation – including all that wild strelitzia and agapanthus – it's almost impossible to believe that you're just four kilometres from Stellenbosch. Such a spectacular location. Sit with a glass of wine on whichever stoep belongs to you for the night and watch the lowering sun paint the mountains a deep pink. You don't need to do any more than this to leaven the spirits by many notches. There are three private-terraced, light-filled, fruit-coloured, country-furnished sleeping locations to choose from: the homestead room with its four-poster bed and English country feel; The Studio, open-plan with quaint stripy sitting areas; Rose Cottage, which is a Victorian-style cottage set in secluded surroundings, ideal for its alfresco shower. A round, spring-water-fed swimming pool sits directly in front of the homestead and a tan-coloured river is a little further away for paddling, picnics and otter-sighting. If all this is not enough for you, the Jonkershoek Nature Reserve is just down the road with some of the best hiking in SA, from two-hour to two-day trails. If you'd prefer to ride through the reserve, experienced riders can borrow one of Emma's five horses who, otherwise, graze on the luminous green grass in the paddock. Why haven't we discovered this one before?

Rooms: 3: 2 self-catering B&B cottages (The Studio, double, twin & bathroom; Rose Cottage, twin, bathroom & alfresco shower); 1 double room in The Homestead.

Price: R295 – R350 pp sharing B&B, R250 pp sharing self-catering. Discounts for extended stays.

Meals: Continental breakfast included in B&B or R45 for self-caterers. 5 minutes drive into Stellenbosch with restaurants aplenty.

Directions: From CT, N2 to Stellenbosch, follow signs to Jonkershoek Nature Reserve. 4km from Stellenbosch turn right and cross over bridge opposite Neil Ellis vineyard.

Map Number: 2

Graceland

Sue McNaughton
Stellenrust Rd, Stellenbosch 7599
Tel: 021-881-3121 Fax: 021-881-3341
Email: graceland@iafrica.com Web: www.gracelandvineyards.com
Cell: 082-441-2680

Sue and Paul live in a huge thatched house at the end of a long driveway, which opens up at the back onto a large lawn, large garden, large swimming pool, correct-sized tennis court and a small putting green. Beyond this is the cottage, which houses one of the bedrooms, while the other is a secluded gem in the loft with antique furniture, thatched roof and pole beams. The free-standing bath, the loo and World War I officer's washstand are screened off from the sleeping area. The lawn gradually gives way to the vines and cellars beyond. Wine tastings are a must... usually at 6 in the evening. Guests are free to roam the property with walks up through the vines to the awesome Helderberg (the distinctively craggy mountain you can see from Cape Town). Every morning Sue's whim and her guests' preferences determine what you eat and even what you eat off. In fact Sue is so generous with both her energy and the space she gives you that you may experience a moment of distress when the time comes to leave. Suddenly it will dawn on you that all this is in fact someone else's! But you can at least take something away with you – I recommend the shiraz. The name Graceland derives from the three Graces who feature on every bottle of wine the vineyard produces (shiraz and cab sav).

Rooms: 2: 1 twin cottage with shower; 1 double with bath.
Price: R300 – R400 pp sharing. Cheaper rates for longer stays.
Meals: Full breakfast included.
Directions: Take R44 south out of Stellenbosch for 5km and it is on the left-hand side. 400m along dirt track on right. There is no right-hand turn on R44 from south.

Map Number: 2

65

Langverwagt

Janette Le Roux
Langverwagt Rd, Kuilsrivier
7579
Tel: 021-903-1203
Fax: 021-903-1207
Email: rleroux@iafrica.com
Web: www.langverwagt.co.za
Cell: 082-783-9987

Barely four kilometres from the endless 'drive-thrus' of downtown Kuilsrivier is the wonderful and improbable working farm and guest house of Langverwagt. But this is more than just a blessed relief from Cape Town's urban sprawl. The final 500m of the drive up the hill from the main road are along a dirt track, through young shiraz vines and a final flourish of hydrangeas. The old farm (1800) has been restored over the past three years, emerging from a tangle of vegetation to become a place of quirky beauty, with a large sunken garden and a myriad of trees providing plenty of shade. The dozens of enormous antique Spanish pots scattered around the buildings are one of the farm's many idiosyncrasies; the accommodation itself is another. You stay in a converted 18th-century slave-house (there are pictures of the last two Langverwagt slaves on the walls), whose thick walls and high, thatched ceilings keep the large rooms cool. The stable-like doors add to the unfussy charm of the place, as do the glass frames on the walls indoors, which highlight sections of the original brickwork. Breakfast is served on a stone patio, which has great views across the suburbs to Table Mountain. Walks around the property are highly recommended and fishing is possible on the two dams. You will thank me for finding so near Cape Town such a friendly family farm.

Rooms: 4: 2 doubles with en-suite bath; 2 doubles with en-suite shower.
Price: R275 pp sharing. Singles R330.
Meals: Breakfast included and served till 10.
Directions: From Cape Town take N2 past the airport. Next left onto R300 over M12. Then leave R300 signed Bellville. Right into Kuilsrivier. After 6 or 7 lights turn left and follow signs to Zevenwacht for 2.5km. House signed up drive to right.

Malans Guest House

Laetitia Malan

4 Keerom St, Stellenbosch
7600
Tel: 021-887-8859 Fax: 021-887-9909
Email: malansgh@hotmail.com
Web: www.malansgh.de
Cell: 083-664-1517

Cape Winelands, Western Cape

Laetitia has uniquely and beautifully decorated each of her guest rooms with antique furniture, kilims on beds, fresh flowers and even proper home-found shower caps in the bathrooms! (Ladies with long hair will know what I'm talking about.) She also collects Voortrekker wedding dresses that date back to the 1860s, while her other lace collections are displayed under glass-covered breakfast tables. And what a breakfast room!: antique Chinese vases and vessels, exotic orchids, furniture inlaid with mother-of-pearl, 'grandparent' clocks, newly-painted frescoes and a flower-imprinted Chinese screen. Laetitia admitted that she may have lived in China in a previous life. She also collects porridges (!) after a fashion: try Matabela porridge (a traditional black-corn variety), maize or oatmeal at breakfast. And if you're not a porridge fan (no reason why you should be), there are plenty of mueslis, fresh fruits, bacon, eggs and all. Laetitia and her daughter treated me to their home-made chocolate cake and my first-ever rooibos tea, and sitting on the verandah in the sunshine I felt serene. A rare quote from one of our other hosts in this book: "I have stayed there myself and I often send guests on to her. Incredible value for money and an experience in its own right. A very interesting owner, with staff who know the art of hospitality and the most beautiful antiques." This all turns out to be pretty exact. *Nearby: cycling, horse-riding, golfing, fly-fishing and wine-tasting.*

Rooms: 5: 1 queen and 1 double with en-suite showers; 3 twins with en/s bath and shower.
Price: R275 pp sharing. R350 single.
Meals: Full breakfast included. Restaurants aplenty nearby.
Directions: From Cape Town take N2, then R310 to Stellenbosch. Drive into town, at railway turn right into Dorp St. After right-hand bend turn left up The Avenue, first left to Neethling St and first left again into Keerom St.

Map Number: 2

Natte Valleij

Charlene and Charles Milner
R44 betw' Stellenbosch and Paarl, Klapmuts 7625
Tel: 021-875-5171 Fax: 021-875-5475
Email: milner@intekom.co.za Web: www.nattevalleij.co.za

Come and lose yourself in the depths of this wild and fecund garden – or do I mean jungle? Ancient trees such as the rare gingco (the oldest in South Africa, once thought extinct), several 200-year-old oaks and a wealth of growth besides keep the pool, 'moon gate' and old brandy stills secreted in their midst. Guests stay in the simple B&B room next to the main house, its verandah festooned with grandiflora, and eat a breakfast in this most lovely of Cape Dutch homesteads (pictured above), built in 1775. If the weather's fine then you eat out on the patio under its cooling roof of vine. Or you can take one of the cottages lost down garden paths. Vineyard Cottage (pictured below), with direct access to the swimming pool, is the oldest building on the property, its original 1714 reed ceilings still intact. While Cellar Cottage is the most recent addition at 'Nutty Valley', small, cute, rustic, perfect for couples. Come for great charm, rather than luxury, from house and hosts alike. Walks are in all directions up mountains and into surrounding vineyards. *Local bird-watching tours with Charles are a speciality. Well positioned on the Stellenbosch and Paarl wine routes. Self-catering available in the cottages. Horse-riding from the farm.*

Rooms: 3: 1 B&B room, double with en/s bath; 2 cottages (self-catering or B&B): Cellar Cottage sleeps 2 (plus 2 kids' beds); Vineyard Cottage sleeps 6.
Price: B&B R210 – R240. Rates for the whole cottage per night depending on how many people and length of stay: Vineyard R450 – R750; Cellar R390 – R450.
Meals: Full breakfast included in B&B and an optional extra in cottages.
Directions: From Cape Town take N1 exit 47. Turn right onto R44. Farm 4km on left.

River Manor Country House & Spa

Johan and Leigh Swanepoel
No.6 The Avenue, Stellenbosch 7600
Tel: 021-887-9944 Fax: 021-887-9940
Email: rivermanor@adept.co.za Web: www.rivermanor.co.za

Since the first edition of this guide, River Manor has annexed the listed building next door, and it is fair to say that Johan and Leigh have gone from strength to strength as a result. A central Stellenbosch historical house has become two, and thanks to unwavering Swanepoel enthusiasm and attention to detail, both with their guests and with the decor – the African colonial theme has been successfully carried over to the second, older house – the experience remains a rich one. The new rooms are as large as those in the original house and also furnished with antiques. Beds and bedding are fit for a king and there are many added comforts such as soft towelling bathrobes and port and sherry trays. Old maps on walls, restored leather suitcases and travellers' trunks complete the effect. With the second house also came another garden, where you will find an intimate health and beauty spa (massage, steam room and spa) overlooking a second pool, ideal for pampering the weary or the self-indulgent. Breakfast is served at the poolside or in the large conservatory, another new addition to the original building. Guests have plenty of different spaces in which to relax between exploratory walks around town. *Closed for the month of June.*

Rooms: 16: from Petit (small) to Classic (very nice indeed) to Superior (yet nicer).
Price: Seasonal from R295 – R952 pp sharing. Singles from R550 – R1,600.
Meals: Full breakfast included. Restaurants nearby.
Directions: From CT take the N2 turning to Somerset West. Follow signs to Baden Powell Drive and then to Stellenbosch. On entering Stellenbosch, turn right at 2nd set of traffic lights into Dorp St, follow the road all the way to the top, round to the right and take first left which is The Avenue.

Map Number: 2

Summerwood Guest House

Hilary and Malcolm Forbes

28 Jonkershoek Rd, Stellenbosch 7600
Tel: 021-887-4112 Fax: 021-887-4239
Email: summerwood@mweb.co.za Web: www.summerwood.co.za
Cell: 072-309-1870

You notice the huge stinkwood tree first, then the swimming pool (a proper one for swimming in). The smooth, well-tended lawns of the garden seem to beckon the guests, who convene round tables on the terrace in the evening or take a few hours out from wine and history to brave the sun by day. The house itself was built in 1904 by an Italian architect – light and airy, with pretty 'Italian' windows. All the bedrooms are furnished with a summery feel (lots of yellows) and uncluttered, allowing for much clean wall and floor space. The 'room at the top' has panoramic views of garden and mountain. Hilary and Malcolm take the greatest care that their guests are properly orientated, find the best restaurants (some of the best around are a short walk away, as is the Jonkershoek nature reserve and its mountain trails, if you feel like building up an appetite). They clearly revel in the relaxed and friendly atmosphere they have created at Summerwood. *Stellenbosch is only twenty minutes from Cape Town International Airport. Closed in June.*

Rooms: 9: 5 king-size doubles, 4 twins. All have en-suite bathrooms with baths and showers.
Price: R440 – R725 pp sharing. Singles R650 – R1,000.
Meals: Full breakfast included and served until 9.30 am. Restaurants nearby.
Directions: Exit 33 from N2, L to Stellenbosch R310. At T-jct turn R for 2.5km. 2nd lights turn R up Dorp St to pancake roundabout. L into Meul St, next roundabout R into Plein St, becomes v. Riebeeck St. Keep L at fork, house on R.

Map Number: 2

Cathbert Country Inn

Ann and Robert Morley
Franschhoek Rd, Simondium, Franschhoek 7620
Tel: 021-874-1366 Fax: 021-874-3918
Email: info@cathbert.co.za Web: www.cathbert.co.za
Cell: 082-414-0604

Ann and Robert have a complete set of correct attitudes, as far as we are concerned: they have purposefully kept Cathbert's small (only eight rooms), "so we get to know our guests"; it's smart without going over the top and yet totally relaxed; and the food is a major focus. Bedrooms have views over a reservoir, farmland, vineyards, and the Simonsberg Mountains loom behind the house. Guests can walk up Kanonskop from Cathbert, a hill from which they used to signal to ships out at sea. You sleep in chalets with open-plan bed/sitting rooms and are refreshingly simple in style (and well-equipped with towelling bathrobes and other welcome luxuries). Each chalet has its little front garden where you might be honoured with a haughty visit from one of the resident peacocks, whose home this really is. Ann spends her day between reception and the kitchen where she is *maestro* – (set) menus are based on what she finds freshest around her. Her food is truly delicious, beautifully presented (only to residents) – 'modern' without being outré – and a real pull for Cathbert's burgeoning fan club. Robert, meanwhile, acts as (and *is*!) the charming and knowledgeable sommelier and host.

Rooms: 8 suites: 2 standard, 4 luxury, 2 executive. All with en-suite bath and shower. All king-size/twin beds. All air-conditioned.
Price: R450 – R600 pp sharing. Single supplement + 50%.
Meals: Full breakfast included. Set menu, 4-course dinner (except on Sundays).
Directions: From CT take N1, take exit 47, turn right at end of ramp, over 4-way stop, left at next road towards Franschhoek. Pass Backsberg Wine Estate. At the stop just before railway crossing turn right onto private tar road. Follow for 2.5km.

Map Number: 3

Lekkerwijn

Wendy Pickstone

Groot Drakenstein, Franschhoek Road, near Boschendal 7680
Tel: 021-874-1122 Fax: 021-874-1465
Email: lekkerwijn@new.co.za Web: www.lekkerwijn.com

Lekkerwijn (pronounced Lekkervain) is a 1790s Cape Dutch homestead with a grand Edwardian extension designed by Sir Herbert Baker. You would probably have to pay to look round if Wendy didn't live there. It positively creaks with family history. You can tell when one family have lived in a grand house for generations – all the furniture, fittings and decoration look so at home. This is not some country house hotel nor some converted annexe. You share the house fully with Wendy, whose family have lived here since the late 19th century – unless of course you would prefer the privacy of the wagon house cottage and ballroom cottages. My strongest impressions are of the central courtyard with its gallery and cloister, the yellowwood floors and beams and the towering palms planted by Wendy's grandfather, the informal taste of the nursery bedroom, a wonderful breakfast... and Wendy herself, who is full of character and so caring of her guests.

Rooms: 5: 3 doubles in the house, 1 with en-suite bathroom, 2 private bath + shower; 2 cottages provide self-catering option for couples, either alone or with children.
Price: R250 (winter rates) – R500 (summer rates) pp sharing. Singles on request.
Meals: Full breakfast included for B&B. You can self-cater in the cottages and breakfast in the courtyard of the homestead is an optional extra.
Directions: On R45 at intersection with R310 from Stellenbosch (after passing Boschendal), alongside the new Meerrust entrance walls.

Map Number: 2 & 3

Résidence Klein Oliphants Hoek

Ingrid and Camil Haas

14 Akademie St, Franschhoek 7690
Tel: 021-876-2566 Fax: 021-876-2566
Email: info@kleinoliphantshoek.com Web: www.kleinoliphantshoek.com

Sometimes it all comes together so satisfyingly! Ingrid and Camil opened their first restaurant in a Dutch windmill, at the venerable age of 23, then worked their way across Europe – Turkey, France, Belgium – before moving out to South Africa in 2000 and falling in love (at first sight) with Klein Oliphants Hoek. The building has been reincarnated many times in its hundred and some years, built by an English missionary as a chapel in 1888 and at other times a school and a theatre. I'd only been at the guest house a very brief while before I knew instinctively that no single aspect of the place was going to let the side down. The centrepiece inside is the chapel hall itself, with its high-vaulted ceiling, fireplace and original beams, now the guest sitting room; but there are the bedrooms, the scented garden, the verandah and salt-water pool, the views. The highlight, for me, are Camil's evening meals which mix I'm-at-home-and-these-are-my-friends informality, guests drifting in and out of the kitchen (try doing that in London), with the hautest of haute cuisine, created on (and in) a restored wood-burning stove. Ingrid selects wines for each course to complement the dishes and explains why she has chosen them too – like a wine lesson. All in all, a real treat. *Closed in June.*

Rooms: 7: 3 twins and 4 doubles; all with en-suite showers and baths. The top luxury room has a private sundeck on roof with a built-in jacuzzi with mountain views.
Price: R450 – R1,000 pp sharing. Single supplement.
Meals: Full breakfast included. 6-course dinner extravaganza R225, excluding drinks. No evening meals on Wednesday and Sunday.
Directions: Akademie St is parallel to the main road in Franschhoek (Huguenot St), two streets up the hill.

The Garden House

Barry and Annette Phillips
29 De Wet St, Franschhoek 7690
Tel: 021-876-3155 Fax: 021-876-4271
Email: info@thegardenhouse.co.za Web: www.thegardenhouse.co.za
Cell: 083-340-3439

As soon as I met Barry, who runs the local newspaper (The Franschhoek Tatler), and Annette who rescues cats, a small inner voice instinctively told me, "Ah, this is somewhere I feel at home." Annette and Barry have fully immersed themselves in village life since their impulsive on-holiday decision in '01 to leave London and buy their Cape Victorian house. They haven't looked back since and their enthusiasm is palpable. And why wouldn't it be, quite frankly. Franschhoek, with mountains on three sides, is recognised as the food and wine capital of the Cape. From the restaurants and wineries we sampled when we went out in Barry's 'Maigret'-style 1951 Citroën it certainly seemed to be! Guests stay in an air-conditioned, stylishly-decorated cottage with wood-beamed bedroom and bathroom. If the cottage is already taken, Annette and Barry invite you to share their home in their comfortable, yet compact, guest room. Come morning, Barry took me on a rigorous mountain-bike ride – he has two of them to lend – while Annette prepared a smoked trout breakfast for our return. Village folk talk and I had already heard on the other side of the valley about Annette's local trout treat. Lovely, down-to-earth people who may well ply you with a sundowner before you head out to dinner. *Nearby fishing and horse-riding.*

Rooms: 2: 1 queen with en-suite bath and shower; 1 standard double with en-suite bath and shower overhead.
Price: Courtyard Room: R450 pp sharing, 2 or more nights R400. Main House room: R325 pp sharing.
Meals: Breakfast included.
Directions: N1, then R45, then, as you come into Franschhoek, turn left into de Wet St just before the canon and go up the hill. The Garden House is on your right.

Map Number: 3

Akademie Street Guesthouses

Katherine and Arthur McWilliam Smith

5 Akademie Street, Franschhoek 7690
Tel: 021-876-3027 Fax: 021-876-3293
Email: katherine@aka.co.za Web: www.aka.co.za
Cell: 082-655-5308

The parade of flowers and stepping-stones through citrus trees, fig trees, rose bushes and bougainvillaea made an otherwise rather thundersome day (ooh and the gale that was blowing!) much brighter. The airy cottages, which sit detached within the flower arrangements, open out onto private stoeps, gardens and even swimming pools. Vreugde, meaning 'joy', is a garden suite for two that has a neat kitchenette in an alcove and a sofa on the terrace. Oortuiging is a restored 1860s cottage for four that retains the old Cape style with antiques throughout. And Gelatenheid is a luxurious villa with, again, a private swimming pool and a wide wrap-around balcony. At the end of the balcony, suitably screened by tree-tops, is an outdoor, repro Victorian bathtub in which you can soak while gazing out at the mountain views… then wrap up in a towel from the heated bath rail. Inside, an expansive open-plan studio is home for just two people (though there's space enough for a four-bed house), with high wooden ceilings, Venetian blinds and French doors… a decadent holiday home. As full as a full breakfast can be (including boerewors – a type of SA sausage if you really didn't know) is served under the vines at the homestead. Katherine and Arthur – he was formerly Mayor of Franschhoek and they are both sooo nice – are easy smilers and happy to help with any day-tripping tips.

Rooms: 3 cottages: Vreugde: twin beds, en/s bath + shower; Oortuiging: 1 twin + 1 double, both en/s bathrooms; Gelatenheid: 1 king + en/s bath + sh'r.
Price: R275 – R650 pp.
Meals: Full breakfast included.
Directions: From Cape Town take N1 then R45. Akademie St is parallel to main road in Franschhoek, two streets up the hill.

Map Number: 3

Auberge La Dauphine

Liz and John Atkins
PO Box 151, Excelsior Rd, Franschhoek 7690
Tel: 021-876-2606 Fax: 021-876-2398
Email: guests@ladauphine.co.za Web: www.ladauphine.co.za

The location is perfect, a sanctum of blooming plum blossom, vineyards and oak trees throwing dappled shadows on the freshly-mowed lawn, magnificent mountains rising steeply from the Franschhoek valley. Here I found serenity intact, with indigenous flowers and carved-out benches where to sit and soak it all in. Liz is passionate about her garden and encourages guests to make full use of it and to enjoy sundowners with a glass of wine by the dam. An extra element she is hoping for is the inauguration of a Zimbabwean sculpture exhibition amidst her greenery. The fruit-coloured bedrooms are refreshingly air-conditioned and some have a split-level sitting-sitting area, making them feel like mini-cottages. Having run a B&B in the UK for fifteen years, Liz and John know what people like and are, as you might expect, experts at the English breakfast. This is served on the stoep of the homestead with that most wondrous view of the mountains beyond the stud farm next door. While at breakfast guests can ask for wine tours, tastings, trout fishing or horse-riding to be arranged for them, borrow a book from the extensive library or take a peek at John's motoring collection. He is the proud owner of the one and only original AC Cobra in SA, and also has a prolific display of signed photos of racing-car drivers and other motor memorabilia. *A self-catering cottage to sleep four is also available.*

Rooms: 6: 1 family room, 2 split-level suites, 2 doubles, all with en-suite bathrooms. 1 self-catering cottage that sleeps four.
Price: Seasonal. From R250 – R450 pp sharing.
Meals: For B&B full breakfast is included.
Directions: Drive through Franschhoek and turn right at the monument. After 1.3km Auberge la Dauphine is on the left.

Longfield

Pieter and Nini Bairnsfather Cloete

Eikendal Rd, off R44,
Somerset West 7130
Tel: 021-855-4224
Fax: 021-855-4224
Email: ninicloete@iafrica.com
Web: www.longfield.co.za

Longfield occupies a sensational vantage, gazing out like an Inca from the dramatic Helderberg across the panorama of the Winelands and all the way to Cape Point. The luxurious new cottage, adjoined to the homestead, is decorated in a relaxed country-house style: tables and chairs, as in the cottage up the hill, are rare early Cape family heirlooms; the bedroom, through folding double doors, has French antique beds; the fabrics are Colefax & Fowler and pictures are an eclectic mix of style and artist. Glass doors and arched windows with inside shutters frame the sweep of vineyards below to Table Mountain. Both cottages are light and airy, with fresh flowers, up-to-date mags, coffee table books on SA wine, flora and fauna etc, pretty china and touches of Africa in the *objets d'art*. Comfy beds are made up with finest quality hand-embroidered linen and there are spoiling lotions in the pretty bathrooms. Sit out on the terrace of one or in the private garden of the other, with a glass of chilled white wine from the surrounding vineyards, to savour the sun setting behind Table Mountain. At night the lights of Cape Town make a spectacular display. The cottage up the hill has a fully-equipped kitchen, the new cottage a well-equipped kitchenette; fridges and cupboards are restocked each day with breakfast materials for you to help yourself to. *Restaurants, wineries, golf courses all within easy striking distance.*

Rooms: 2 cottages: both twin beds with bath and separate shower.
Price: R250 – R400 pp sharing. Single supplement by arrangement.
Meals: Breakfast included.
Directions: From CT take N2 past the airport, take exit 43 Broadway Bvd. Left at lights. From the next lights 6.3km exactly, then right into Eikendal Rd. Follow up gravel road, jink left onto tarmac and follow to top and Longfield House.

Zandberg Farm Country Guest House

Hilary and Lance Beal
96 Winery Rd, Somerset West 7135
Tel: 021-842-2945 Fax: 021-842-2945
Email: info@zandberg.co.za Web: www.zandberg.co.za

Hilary and Lance's model village is a lush oasis. The grapes on the surrounding vineyards ripen in blazing sunshine, but dive into Zandberg, where huge oak trees, stands of bamboo, grassy lawns and a large swimming pool mean cool, green light, water, birds… altogether another world. Guests emerge from their cottages to the communal sitting room (with a blazing fire in the winter) for early evening drinks – they're on the house – and as often as not will go on to dine at the restaurant, 96 Winery Rd, a buzzy and popular restaurant by the entrance to the farm. A pleasure to dine in style and then only have to stagger a few yards to your bed. They also do a braai for guests on Sunday evenings – R60 a head. Yoga is on the menu in the mornings in the old Cape Dutch barn for those in need of a stretch and for those in need of reflexology, acupuncture, massages or iridology there is a therapist on hand in the treatment rooms. The old coach house has become the bar and the next building is the breakfast room where champagne is a daily ritual. Further exploration uncovers a chapel with stunning stained glass made by Hilary, a tortoise sanctuary with 20 tortoises, a small village for the staff, a lake, even a patch of jungly bushland. The further I walked the more I liked it. *6 golf courses within 10 minutes' drive.*

Rooms: 13: 11 cottages; 7 with bedroom and sitting room; 5 with open-plan bedroom. 2 suites; 2 separate double rooms share 1 bathroom.
Price: Seasonal. R275 – R680 pp sharing.
Meals: Full champagne breakfast included. Braais on Sunday evening. Every other evening of the week bar drinks are free from 6 – 7 pm.
Directions: From CT take N2 to exit 43. Left onto R44. 6km then left onto Winery Rd (M6). Number 96 on the right. 30 minutes from Cape Town.

Map Number: 2

Manor on the Bay

Hanél and Schalk van Reenen
117 Beach Rd, Gordon's Bay 7140
Tel: 021-856-3260 Fax: 021-856-3261
Email: manorotb@mweb.co.za Web: www.manoronthebay.co.za
Cell: 082-896-5790

Hanél and Schalk van Reenen are a young couple, and their enthusiasm for the job is palpable. They have poured great vats of time and energy into restoring their property, moving an impressive tonnage of earth to create a raised garden at the front, below a long terrace. This is a great place for watching sunsets over False Bay or even whales in spring, and the view is conveniently framed by two large palms. A brace of Old English sheepdogs, Yuka and Kayla, complete the very friendly reception committee. Beach Road, you won't need telling, is just next to the sea, and a hop, skip and a dive takes you across the road and into the water. If you don't fancy the walk, however, there's also a pool out the back. Of the six rooms, four are sea-facing and open onto the terrace, but the other three are just as enticing and luxurious, and look out over a large garden that climbs up the Gordon's Bay hillside. Breakfast is either healthy (in Hanél's case eaten after an early run on the beach – you don't have to join her, so don't worry) or hearty, and is served in the bright dining room or on the terrace outside.

Rooms: 6: 3 doubles, 3 twins; all with en-suite bathrooms, 4 with sea view, 2 looking on to the garden court.
Price: R380 – R600 pp sharing. Singles + R200.
Meals: Full breakfast included.
Directions: From Strand on the R44, take Beach Rd turning just before BP garage. From N2 take Sir Lowry's Pass to Gordon's Bay and cross over on to van der Bijl St, down to Beach Rd and L.

Map Number: 2

Wildekrans Country House

Alison Green and Barry Gould
Houw Hoek Valley, Elgin 7180
Tel: 028-284-9827 Fax: 028-284-9624
Email: wildekrans@kingsley.co.za Web: www.wildekrans.co.za

From the tufts of moss poking out between the old flagstones of the front path I knew that this was my sort of place. The 1811 homestead is raised above its garden and looks down on lawns, abundant roses, pear orchards, the large swimming pool and old oak trees. The scene is magnificent with the 'wild cliffs' ('wildekrans') of the berg setting the property's limits, rising from a meadow at the back of the garden. Take a stroll beside landscaped watercourses and lily ponds that neighbour the orchards, and you will encounter wonderful, some might think surreal, sculptures that have been positioned with much thought, and I think argument, where they now stand. They add a touch of the unexpected to this magical garden. Finally a rickety bridge – that inspires little in the way of confidence, but is quite safe – crosses a stream and you find yourself at the foot of the steep, forested mountain. A path leads straight up or you can cross a neighbour's land in search of gentler gradients. The bedrooms are charming, each with a four-poster bed, originally parental gifts to Alison and her many sisters, and views out to the garden. There is a large pool, a contemporary art collection and the Wildekrans winery nearby.

Rooms: 4: 3 four-poster doubles in the homestead with en-suite bath (one has a shower too); and 1 self-catering cottage.
Price: B&B R270 – R310 pp sharing. Singles R350. Self-catering R185 – R275 pp sharing.
Meals: Full breakfast included. Dinners from one-course simple country supper (R55 – R65) to three-course (R85 – R95). All meals are self-served.
Directions: On N2 from Cape Town for 1 hour approx., past Grabouw and 12km further turn left signed Houw Hoek Inn. Through Houw Hoek gate posts (no gate), follow road round to left. Farm on your right.

Map Number: 3

Paul Cluver Guest House

The Cluver Family
Grabouw 7160
Tel: 021-844-0605
Fax: 021-844-0150
Email: info@cluver.co.za
Web: www.cluver.com

I trundled through vineyards and more vineyards, fruit trees (apples, pears and plums), past grazing springbok, eland, tame ostriches, horses, cows, blue crane (twelve of them), past the Reebok river, a large oak tree and finally I arrived at the Cluver family's early eighteenth-century house, mule stable and school. What an estate! All 2,000 hectares of it! And the Cluvers set their substantial – and one assumes very time-consuming – wine and fruit production to one side in order to accommodate, welcome and feed their guests. Inge, one of Dr Cluver's daughters, introduced me to part of their family history: a Grégoire on the wall depicts the house and its outbuildings from before Inge's grandmother's time and antiques passed down through generations of Cluvers are plentiful. The buildings have been totally renovated with clay-tiled floors and now there are such things as electric blankets, heating and a lounge with satellite TV and videos. There are three rooms in the homestead and the other two are the converted cottages (the mule stable with its fireplace is especially popular in winter). You can have breakfast in bed; or a breakfast picnic basket is a tempting option to take on a riverside amble among the rich array of proteas and disas. *The Paul Cluver Amphitheatre season runs from January to March.*

Rooms: 5: 4 twin rooms and 1 double. All en-suite showers.
Price: R240 – R400 pp sharing.
Meals: Full breakfast included. Lunch and supper on request.
Directions: From Cape Town take N2, past Somerset West, over Sir Lowry's Pass. You will see the Orchard farm store on the left and the Paul Cluver Wine Estate sign follows shortly on the left (about 20km from Somerset West).

Map Number: 3

Foresthall Luxury Tented Camp

Kate and David Hall

Grabouw 7160
Tel: 021-844-0441 Fax: 021-844-0441
Email: foresthall@iafrica.com Web: www.foresthalltents.co.za
Cell: 082-550-9054

Camping? This isn't the camping I remember! Where are the sleepless nights, the trips through the rain to the facilities block by torchlight, the lukewarm baked beans? Hoorah instead for a novel, luxurious, comfortable and exciting form of outdoor sleeping. Foresthall is quite a find in both senses. The 'tents' are semi-canvas, semi-fixed with a concrete floor, wooden beds, proper mattresses, upholstered armchairs, water-releasing sinks, taps, toilets and a shower en-suite. Yet the springbok horns toilet-roll holder, kudu horns towel hook and lack of electricity remind you that you are truly 'out there'. When night falls, lanterns galore light the way to your 'bedrooms' and down to the communal 'tent' with its corrugated roof, wood-burning fireplace, curl-up-your-legs sofa bench and proper kitchen with all utensils. For those in need of outside-tasting food there is a large South African barby (braai). You can sit and eat on the sun-deck overlooking the two crystal-clear, spring-water lakes. The surrounding landscape is tailor-made for chest-beating activities such as swimming in the dams, quad-biking and motor-biking in the mountains or white-water rafting; or less heart-stoppingly playing golf; or just (and it sounds plain after all that) walking through the forests and vineyards. David and Kate will clue you up with local rentals and routes and off you go….

Rooms: 4 doubles with en-suite showers.
Price: R180 – R280 pp sharing. Single supplement. Group bookings welcome.
Meals: Hot water, tea, coffee, muffins and rusks are delivered to your tent in the morning. Otherwise self-catering.
Directions: Will be emailed or faxed.

Wild Olive Guest House

Gloria and Peter Langer
227 Hangklip and Bell Rds, Pringle Bay 7196
Tel: 028-273-8750 Fax: 028-273-8752
Email: g-langer@mweb.co.za Web: www.wild-olive.de
Cell: 082-442-5544

After restauranteering for 27 years, Peter decided to dedicate his love of cooking to his B&B guests in the white sandy-mouthed bay of Pringle. Food is certainly the *spécialité de la maison*. I couldn't believe my luck when I noticed the certificate in the kitchen declaring him a top-ten SA chef of 1999. While preparing the freshly-caught yellow-tail he informed me that in the summer, when the bay is calm, he takes guests out in his engine-powered dinghy (rubber duck to South Africans). The guests catch the crayfish and Peter cooks it for supper. The breakfasts eaten on the sundeck (with ocean view... and whale view too between July and November) boast fresh, home-baked breads, pancakes, croissants, fruit, muesli, yoghurt and the full 'English' breakfast. I almost popped. The bedrooms have private terraces and baboon-proof window locks. I scanned the mountainside for primate life in my (private and enclosed) open-air washroom. I can imagine that when it is sunny it must be so lovely to have your skin sun-kissed while showering. I had blustery weather, but still wanted to test it out (hot water – phew). There is an inside option too, of course. Two of the bedrooms have this novelty and the other has an up-a-ladder bed for couples with children (12+). Gloria and Peter are very attentive and professional hosts. *They have also recently installed a natural rock swimming pool surrounded by trees.*

Rooms: 3: 2 queens, I with en-s bath with shower overhead & 'al-fresco' shower, I with en-s shower & 'al-fresco' shr & separate loo; I twin/king with loft & en-s shr.
Price: R225 – R300. Singles on request.
Meals: Full breakfast included. Dinner available on request.
Directions: From Cape Town on N2, turn towards Gordon's Bay, follow coast road for 30 km to Pringle Bay turn – follow signs.

Barnacle B&B

Jenny Berrisford
573 Anne Rd, Pringle Bay 7196
Tel: 028-273-8343 Fax: 028-273-8343
Email: barnacle@maxitec.co.za Web: www.deadduck.co.za/ads/barnacle
Cell: 082-925-7500

Come and explore Jenny's seaside idyll. Several different natural environments collide right outside her cottage. From the deck at the back – with views all the way to Cape Point – you walk down rickety (but safe!) steps to her lawny enclaves in the marsh reeds where narrow paths lead you to the river and beach. The sea is a hundred yards of the whitest, finest sand to your left; beyond the river fynbos and milkwood 'forest' climb the mountain, a nature reserve. You don't have to be a kid to love this. There are otters in the river, baboons on the mountain, estuarine and fynbos birds aplenty... and Jenny is a horticultural expert in one of the world's most amazing natural gardens. Rooms are simple, rustic and country cosy, one with a Victorian slipper bath (recently expanded by knocking two rooms together to allow far more space and light), another with a solid brass bed and the whole place is super relaxed... a hidden gem. *Jenny has canoes and paddle skis to take out on the river. This area has been proclaimed a world biosphere reserve. Kichenette in the reconfigured double room.*

Rooms: 2: 1 outside annexe double with en-suite shower and small sunroom; 1 double with en-suite 'slipper' bath and kitchenette. Annexe can be self-catering.
Price: R170 – R250 pp sharing. Singles R240 – R300.
Meals: Full breakfast included. Restaurants in Pringle Bay.
Directions: From Cape Town along N2 turn towards Gordon's Bay before Sir Lowry's Pass – follow coast road for 30km to Pringle Bay turn – follow signs down dirt roads.

Buçaco Sud

Jean Da Cruz
2609 Clarens Drive, Betty's Bay 7141
Tel: 028-272-9750 or 028-272-9628 Fax: 028-272-9750
Email: bucaco@hermanus.co.za Web: www.bucacosud.co.za
Cell: 083-514-1015

Everything in this beautiful place has been designed and built by Jean, including the house itself, which sits halfway up a mountain in South Africa's first Biosphere Reserve, a nature lover's paradise with tranquil lakes, stunning beaches, the Harold Porter Botanic Gardens and a penguin colony. Buçaco Sud was once Jean's castle in Spain (or Portugal I should say), now a flight of personal fancy come true. The upstairs sitting room has windows on both sides, and light streams through to mountain views in one direction and sea views in the other. Guest bedrooms are eye-catching, full of startling colours, flowers and eclectic 'stuff' collected by Jean or donated by friends. They all look down over the sea, except 'Shangri-La' at the back – perhaps my favourite – where you can walk straight out through French windows onto the Kogelberg mountain. Local artists' work (for sale) adds even more colour to the vibrant decor. It's not a place for TVs and mobile phones. Genuine care, a sense of humour and enthusiastic hospitality in a house where every detail is home-spun. *Dinners and lunches available at Casitas, Jean's restaurant in Kleinmond. Arabella Gold Estate is about 18km away.*

Rooms: 5: 4 doubles and 1 twin; 4 with en-suite shower, 1 with en-suite bath.
Price: R190 – R300 pp sharing. Singles on request.
Meals: Dinners and lunches at Jean's restaurant Casitas. Will cater for weddings.
Directions: Follow R44 from Gordon's Bay along the coast for 30km, house signed to left in Betty's Bay. 1 hour from Cape Town.

Map Number: 2

96 Beach Road

Annelie and Johan Posthumus
Kleinmond 7195
Tel: 021-794-6291 Fax: 021-794-6291
Email: kaapsedraai@hotmail.com Web: www.kaapsedraaibb.co.za

When the family bought "the beach house" in 1954, the milk was delivered by bike. Kleinmond still feels like a sleepy little town but it's hardly surprising that more have fled here since. The house is but a kite-tail's length from the sea, the blue Atlantic stretching forth beyond a strip of fynbos. You can choose to watch the whales passing by (from August to December) from two spots, the sea-side verandah or the upstairs bedroom. The latter runs from one side of the house to the other under a vaulted ceiling and ocean-side the walls stop and the glass starts, forming a small square sitting room jutting out towards the blue. Here there is a soft couch and a rocking chair, perfect for siestas, sunsets (and of course whale-watching). Downstairs is equally adorable. It feels a bit like a Nantucket Island house: white, light, airy and adorned with simple understated beach furnishings. Interior designers, *nota bene*! It is totally self-catering here, but walk a kilometre west and you'll find some untouristy cafés in the old harbour; a three-minute drive east will take you past a decent restaurant and miles of white sandy beaches, perfect for kids, flying kites, swimming and walking. Kleinmond is near the Arabella Golf Estate, the Kogelberg Biosphere with its myriad fynbos species, the wild horses of the Bot River Estuary and Hermanus, but avoids its touristyness.

Rooms: 2: 1 double with en-suite shower, 1 twin with bath.
Price: Max 4 persons. Minimum R600 per night or R1,000 if 4 persons. Min 2-night stay.
Meals: Self-catering.
Directions: In Kleinmond town face east. Drive through 3 stop signs and turn towards the sea on 6th Avenue. Keep going to the sea then turn left and No 96 is the penultimate house from the corner.

Otters Inn

Estelle and Pieter Spaarwater

28 Marine Drive, Vermont, Greater Hermanus 7201
Tel: 028-316-3167 Fax: 028-316-3764
Email: otters@hermanus.co.za Web: www.wheretostay.co.za/ottersinn
Cell: 082-898-7724

Estelle and Pieter are hugely enthusiastic about the charms of the Overberg and love talking about its history, environment and potential. From their house (built in 1926 by the Speaker of the South African parliament) near Hermanus you can visit most of the area's 'jewels' within 30 minutes. You can also join Estelle on a twelve-kilometre beach hike to walk off the superb breakfast, which always includes a house speciality such as crêpes filled with crayfish. Those of a less active disposition can, in season, watch whales frolicking right in front of the house. The Spaarwaters can show you a tidal swimming pool, and there is a fynbos garden too with tiny orchids, a natural playground for local birds. The guest house is arranged around a central hall and an enclosed verandah, and the four wood-floored rooms have shutters, mohair rugs, silk duvets and particularly attractive beds. They are bright and fresh in feel and the Spaarwaters have brought great taste to bear. Two have their own sea-facing sitting rooms and two have bigger bathrooms with baths and showers – you choose. They have a swimming pool too and many books (on whales) to read beside it. *Excellent golf nearby. Closed End of May – mid-July.*

Rooms: 4: all doubles/twins; 2 with en-suite bath and shower; 2 with en-suite shower and private sitting room.
Price: R325 – R390 pp sharing. Single supplement 40%.
Meals: Full breakfast included and served till 9.30 a.m.
Directions: From Cape Town take N2 for 110km until signed left to Hermanus. Follow R43 until signed right to Vermont/Onrusrivier. Follow this road straight down to the sea. Left at the bottom, house on left.

Map Number: 3

Schulphoek Seafront Guesthouse

Petro and Mannes van Zyl

44 Marine Drive, Sandbaai, Greater Hermanus 7200
Tel: 028-316-2626 Fax: 028-316-2627
Email: schulphoek@hermanus.co.za Web: www.schulphoek.co.za

Waves roll into the bay, five foot high when I visited, and crash against rocks right in front o
Schulphoek Seafront Guesthouse. The sitting room has one of the most exciting sea views yo
could hope for and, naturally, whales steal into Schulphoek Bay during the season for privat
viewings. The best room, Scallop – I don't think there is any doubt, despite the extremely hig
standard! – is upstairs, the whole seaward wall an expanse of window with a sliding glass doo
and parapet. The smells of the sea are powerful. The other rooms, although without sea views
have solid, hand-crafted oak beds and spectacular bathrooms with double sinks, double showers
huge baths… I mean, you will not find better *anywhere*. Not many places in this area feel the nee
to provide in-house dinners but your hosts are not taking chances on outside eateries. Guest
who want to guarantee themselves delicious food stay in (herbs, salad and veg picked straigh
from their vegetable garden) and eat at one long table, on chairs made from vintage wine vats
You can choose from an exhaustive cellar of the finest South African wines. Schulphoek is ar
intimate, state-of-the-art seaside lodge, but still the sort of place where guests socialise with eacl
other, drinks are on an honesty system and meals are all eaten together. *Closed in May.*

Rooms: 7: all doubles with en-suite bathrooms; I
with shower, I with double shower, 3 with bath and
shower, 2 with spa bath and shower.
Price: R495 – R700 pp sharing. Single supplement
+ 50%. Cheaper rates for longer stays. R4,500 (low
season) – R5,800 (high) for whole guest house per
night.
Meals: Professional kitchen with chef. 4000 bottles o
wine. Full breakfast included. Lunch & dinner on
request – advance booking essential.
Directions: R43 into Hermanus from the N2. Take
Sandbaai turn-off into Main St. At 3rd 'stop' sign turn
left, into 3rd street. Continue to next junction and
they are across the road (3 flags).

Windswael Seafront Whale Inn

Thea Claassen
36 Marine Drive, Vermont, Greater Hermanus 7201
Tel: 028-316-3491 Fax: 028-316-1853
Email: windbb@hermanus.co.za
Web: www.hermanus.co.za/accom/windswael Cell: 082-558-9834

A South African magazine picked the heavy sleeperwood table on rocks yards from a frothing sea as one of the top ten breakfast spots in Africa. Humpbacks and southern right whales sometimes blithely creep into your field of vision and add a touch of the sensational to this daily ritual. The food will make demands on your concentration too and in the whale season you can imagine the happy confusion as freshly-squeezed orange juice, a selection of fresh fruit, sizzling bacon and sausages and creamy eggs battle with magnificent sea-going mammals for your undivided attention. There is much to do from here apart from whale-watching. Great white sharks breed close by, there's walking in the mountains or lounging on local beaches. The brick house is not the most beautiful from the outside, but once through wide sliding doors Thea's inspirations are given free rein – she even wove many of the rugs on show herself. There are Art Deco chairs, wind chimes and mobiles, rough-hewn nude sculptures (the work of Thea's daughter), hanging abalone shells, wildlife paintings. At the back is a brick courtyard and half-thatched braai where high-spirited barbecued seafood dinners are another speciality. Windswael offers far more than just breakfast. *Excellent golf nearby. Internet access.*

Rooms: 4: 1 double, 3 twins. All with en/s bathrooms, 1 with bath and 3 with shower.
Price: R350 – R550 pp sharing. Singles R400 – R600.
Meals: Full breakfast included. Other meals on request.
Directions: Take N2 from CT and follow signs to Hermanus. About 10km before Hermanus take second Vermont turn-off, signposted to Onrus. Turn R and follow road winding down to seafront. At T-jct turn L into Marine Drive. 3rd house on L.

Map Number: 3

The Artist's House

Gail Catlin-Segal Donald Lamont and Neill Leitch
Hermanus 7200
Tel: 028-313-1533 Fax: 028-312-2520
Email: info@artistshouse.co.za Web: www.artistshouse.co.za

Gail Catlin, one of South Africa's leading contemporary artists, has opened up her family house t share its treasures with lucky visitors. She is described as 'a fairy' and the magic she has worke on every detail of her home is indeed spellbinding. Gail has designed and hand-made everythin herself, including the aromatic bath crystals, scrubs and shampoo. I marvelled at the splinters c mirror safely impressed in the floor next to one of the sunken baths and at the mother-of-pea buttons imbedded in the stepping stones to the front door, not to mention her own pictures an private art collection. Gail uses liquid crystal as the base medium for her creations and it is such privilege to stay among her gallery of paintings. On my arrival, I was given a ceramic lily pad fille with sweet rose water to wash away my weary travelling look (which I have now perfected). and then came a relaxed, friendly and delectable stay, made even more delectable by the culinar creations conjured up for me. The house, open-air jacuzzi and organic vegetable garden are se in a valley against the mountains of the Overberg and an expansive lake below. And with all th peaceful relaxation (including reflexology and aromatherapy on request), Hermanus and whale are only seven kilometres away. If I sound impressed... well I was!

Rooms: 6 in the main house, all with lake or mountain views.
Price: Seasonal R350 – R580 pp sharing. Singles on request.
Meals: Breakfast is included. Lunch, picnic basket and four-course dinner on request.
Directions: From CT take N2, then R43, then turn left onto R320 towards Caledon. The tar road turns into a dirt road. Turn left at the Karydeskraal signpost, go 4km around dam and turn right at Artist's House sign.

Beach House on Main

Brandon and Nikki Smit

325 Main Road, Hermanus 7200
Tel: 028-313-2783 Fax: 028-313-1576
Email: info@beachhouseonmain.co.za Web: www.beachhouseonmain.co.za
Cell: 082-783-8005

Welcome to whale-ville! Hermanus, the whale-watching capital of South Africa, is bursting with B&Bs catering for the expectant tourists, but this is the one which, to me, felt most like a home and a relaxing place to unwind after hearty walks along the bay. Although the house is on Hermanus's main street, it is set back from the road behind a flowered garden and the ocean front and cliff path are just a hop away (one minute, if that). Being on the edge of Hermanus, the house backs onto fynbos and then mountain. You can lounge by the sheltered swimming pool or sundeck, or make use of Brandon's talents at Arabella Golf Estate. Brandon is a golf pro with many years of experience as an instructor and he gives discounted private lessons to his guests at the eighteen-hole championship golf course, Arabella, 30km away. Breakfast gets ticks in all the GG boxes: freshly-squeezed orange juice, real coffee and the healthy option along with the fried. On request, Nikki and Brandon cook a crayfish BBQ for dinner in season, and picnic baskets are packed full for those one-day excursions. Rooms are simply and stylishly decorated, in keeping with the beach house theme (light, airy and elegant) and all have fans and heaters.

Rooms: 3 doubles: 1 with en-suite bath and shower, 1 with en-suite shower, 1 with adjacent bath and shower (exclusively for the use of guests in that room).
Price: R200 – R350 pp sharing.
Meals: Full breakfast is included. Picnic baskets and crayfish BBQ on request (summer months only and dependent on availability).
Directions: From CT take N2 and then the R43 to Hermanus. Drive through Hermanus town centre and Beach House is on your left on the main road, approx 1km from Hermanus Golf Club.

Map Number: 3

Cliff Lodge

Gill O'Sullivan and Gideon Shapiro

6 Cliff St, De Kelders 7220
Tel: 028-384-0983 Fax: 028-384-0228
Email: clifflodge@netactive.co.za Web: www.clifflodge.co.za
Cell: 082-380-1676

This is the closest land-based whale-watching you could possibly find. I could see the whites of their eyes (I was only shooting with a camera!) and the callosities on their heads. It was as though Gill and Gideon had paid them (in plankton) to put on a special show for me; blowing, breaching, spyhopping, lob-tailing. I applauded delicately from the royal box. The viewing from my room and on the breakfast conservatory-balcony was don't-turn-your-eyes-away-for-a-minute magnetic. But the fun wasn't just in the looking. As soon as I walked through the door, Gideon, formerly a dive-master, whisked me down to the ocean for a swim through the cave (bring shoes you can swim in for the rocks) and Gill kindly booked me a whale-, sea-lion- and penguin-watching boat trip for the following morning. For the 'help-danger' adrenaline rush, there is also the shark-cage diving. The guest house décor is classy and modern and there are whale-spotting terraces for those rooms on the side of the house. On the cliff edge is also a small swimming pool. Gill and Gideon are wonderfully hospitable hosts and really look after their guests. After the best breakfast you could possibly have – not only because of the food but also the panorama – indulge in an aromatherapy massage from Gill, nature reserve walks in front of the house and the nearby flower-farm. Cliff Lodge rocks.

Rooms: 3: 1 twin/king with bath and shower, 1 double with bath and shower overhead, 1 twin with bath and shower overhead
Price: R400 – R700 pp sharing. Single supplement + 50%.
Meals: Full breakfast included.
Directions: N2, then R43 through Hermanus. Past Stanford towards Gansbaai. Turn right at first De Kelders turn-off, then right into De Villiers Rd, left into Kayser Rd and right into Cliff St.

Map Number: 3

Anlo Guest House

Annelie Rheeder
Guthrie St, De Kelders, Gansbaai 7220
Tel: 028-384-1201 Fax: 028-384-1201
Email: anlo@kingsley.co.za Web: www.anloguesthouse.co.za
Cell: 082-896-0367

Ezette and her sister Annelie will give you a big ol' South African welcome, organise your excursions for you and cook you delicious meals. The supper I had was as tasty as it was large: soup, bobotie, chicken, pumpkin, a ravishing vinegar pudding and coffee that's hand-made to their own specifications. The guest house is an involving, upbeat place, many guests excited by their first whale sighting or great white shark dive. Personally I have no desire to swim in a cage while Nature's greatest killing machine salivates over my love handles, but if that's what lights your candle…. The enormous living room is the heart of the place, with sofas aplenty, rugs, music, books and a large wood-burning stove. You should try to get a room with views of the sea and doors out to the stoep where you can even whale-watch (in season) out in Walker Bay – it's only 150 metres down to the cliffs if you want to get closer. Bedrooms are comfortable with many thoughtful extras: underfloor heating, after-sun cream, proper bottles of shampoo, make-up remover etc. The new section of the house, guarded by a most convincing talking parrot, is a more ideal place to have meals, freeing up the old dining area as a games room. And now they have upgraded the top apartment with aircon, DSTV, fridge, sitting area and balcony. *French is spoken here and Mervyn, Ezette's husband, is an in-house tour guide.*

Rooms: 5: 1 double with shower & bath, 1 double with shower, 1 twin with bath, 1 twin with shower & bath, 1 family unit/honeymoon suite with en/s bath & sep' shr.
Price: R300 – R550 pp sharing. Singles + R100. Dinner B&B R400 – R650 pp sharing. Special rates for groups for DB&B or B&B.
Meals: Full breakfast included. Dinners on request. See above DB&B price.
Directions: Take R44 from Hermanus for about 45km on road to Gansbaai. Signposted at first sign towards De Kelders. House about 3km before Gansbaai. Map can be faxed.

Map Number: 3

Fair Hill Private Nature Reserve

Val and Tim Deverson
R43 between Stanford and Gansbay, Stanford 7210
Tel: 028-341-0230 Fax: 028-341-0230
Email: fairhill@yebo.co.za Web: www.fairhill.co.za
Cell: 082-788-2086

A gate in the middle of nowhere, then a sandy track which leads into the fynbos, arriving finally at Val and Tim's single-story guest house. I guarantee that you will be stunned by the quality of natural silence that envelops you as you step from your car. I think you can hear the fynbos growing! Just walk out in any direction and encounter the eland who, Jeeves-like, only materialise when you aren't looking. We stayed here for a weekend break from Cape Town (two hours max) and completely refilled our energy tanks. Walks are lovely down through Fair Hill's fynbos to the beach, which is hard to get to any other way and will most likely be deserted. Those with more momentum can walk all the way to Hermanus and, if she can, Val will pick you up there. Or you can sunbathe by the pool, protected from the wind in the lea of a natural cave. Big rooms are all blessed with verandahs whence to commune with the wilderness. To top it off, the Deversons themselves couldn't be nicer and delicious dinners are part of the (*incredibly* good value) package – with a choice at every course. Fair Hill is an authentic, uplifting and special experience. We recommend you stay for a minimum of two nights.

Rooms: 4 doubles with en-suite bath and shower attachment.
Price: B&B R310 – R350 pp sharing. Dinner B&B R420 – R460.
Meals: All dinners included with choice for each course.
Directions: From Hermanus follow R43 to Stanford. Continue past for 8.7km. Electric gates on right. From the Garden Route take R326 after Riviersonderend. At Stanford turn left, continue for 8.7km, electric gates on the right.

Map Number: 3

Blue Gum Country Lodge

Nic and Nicole Dupper

PO Box 899, Stanford 7210
Tel: 028-341-0116
Fax: 028-341-0135
Email: reservations@bluegum.co.za
Web: www.bluegum.co.za
Cell: 082-564-5663

Good food, a beautiful setting, comfort and relaxation interspersed with some conscience-easing activity – this is what the word 'holiday' means to me. And clearly to Blue Gum Country Lodge, who like to add a touch of English opulence to the formula: Pimms, complimentary afternoon tea and scones (all mmm)... oh, and anyone for tennis? Borrow a racquet for a quick game or alternatively a mountain-bike for an uphill slog and downhill breeze. If that's not your thing, dig out a bird book and sit with a check-list and a glass of wine. Beyond the ancient blue gum (the actual tree that is), weaver birds busy themselves by the dam, and grapes on the newly-planted vines dream of one day becoming bottles of sauvignon blanc, chardonnay and shiraz. The yellow buildings with sky-blue shutters are all recently built, a sophisticated lodge with beds piled high with pillows, sometimes themed rooms (zebra, monkey, elephant), swish bathrooms and numerous plush conservatories, lounges with sofas, verandahs (I lost count), bar, restaurant and breakfast room. Breakfast is more like brunch in size, content and until-late serving time, specialities a muesli bake, eggs Benedict, sweet corn fritters, crispy bacon and home-made tomato chutney. Evening cheese, biscuits and sherry are placed on each private terrace to whet the appetite before the à la carte evening supper.

Rooms: 10: 5 queens, all with en-suite bath and shower. In manor house: 4 twins, 1 king, all bath and shower except one which is double shower.
Price: Seasonal. R650 – R900. Single supplement + 50%.
Meals: Full breakfast included. Light lunches, 4-course evening dinner (R160 – R180).
Directions: From CT take N2, then R43 turn-off to Hermanus. Drive through Hermanus on R43, following signs to Stanford. At Stanford turn left onto R326 for 6.7km, then left onto dirt track for 4km.

Map Number: 3

Klein Paradijs Country House

Susanne and Michael Fuchs

Pearly Beach, Gansbaai 7220
Tel: 028-381-9760 Fax: 028-381-9803
Email: kleinparadijs@lando.co.za Web: www.kleinparadijs.co.za

Paradise would be a proud boast, so perhaps Little Paradise is a more defensible claim. But you can see why the name stuck: nature on the one hand, man-made environment on the other, and all rounded off by delicious cooking and green fingers. I'll elaborate. The property stretches up a mountain covered in indigenous fynbos vegetation and nearer the house there is a reed-edged dam with weaver birds, an old camphor tree in the courtyard and an amazing garden whose swimming pool acts as moat to a tiny island of plant life. Inside, high open spaces are punctuated with lovely things: bright paintings, vases of proteas and pincushions, a stinkwood grandfather clock for example. A-shaped rooms have soaring thatched roofs, dormer windows, beams, window-seats, balconies and the curtained-off bathrooms are truly luxurious. The Fuchs are Swiss and have brought many talents with them. Susanne was a translator and speaks English, German and French, while Michael is a chef – they open a small but excellent restaurant in the evenings. *Whale-watching possible nearby from June to November.*

Rooms: 5: 2 twins and 3 doubles all with en-suite bathrooms; 2 with bath and shower, 3 with showers.
Price: R450 – R800 pp sharing. Single supplement +50%.
Meals: Full breakfast included. Light meals and dinner by arrangement. The restaurant is fully licensed.
Directions: From Hermanus take the R43 through Stanford and Gansbaai. Go left at Pearly Beach crossing, then 1st left again. The house is on the right.

Map Number: 3

Beaumont Wine Estate

Jayne and Raoul Beaumont
Compagnes Drift Farm, PO Box 3, Bot River 7185
Tel: 028-284-9733 or 028-284-9370 (home) Fax: 028-284-9733
Email: beauwine@netactive.co.za Web: www.beaumont.co.za
Cell: 082-928-2300

Jayne's guests stay in the charming buildings of an 18th-century former mill house and wagon shed, today snug with wood-burning heaters, but left as far as comfortably possible as they were, with original fireplaces in kitchens and hand-hewn, yellowwood beamed ceilings. Outside, you can sit around an old mill stone and admire the antediluvian water wheel, while the willow-shaded jetty on the farm lake offers one of the Western Cape's prettiest settings for sundowners and wheatland views. While meandering through the flower-filled garden I realised that there is no real need to move from the farm, despite being only half an hour from Hermanus. While Jayne and her family busy themselves producing their annual 150,000-odd bottles of wine, you can swim in the informal swimming pool – being the lake – under the weeping willows where the weaver-birds make their nests or you can roam about on their land – they own half a mountain! You can even put the idea of cooking on the backburner and instead arrange to have home-cooked meals delivered to you. The Beaumonts, whose estate is in the middle of tranquil Bot River, make a pinotage for London wine merchants Berry Bros and Rudd's own label and you can wine-taste in the cellar flanked by an old wine press. To find the horses and horse-riding you only have to trot down the road. The setting is beautiful – well worth spending several nights here.

Rooms: 2 self-catering cottages. Mill House has 2 bedrooms (plus 2 extra can sleep in living room); Pepper Tree has 1 double (again 2 extras possible).
Price: R190 – R230 pp sharing. Extra people R80 pp. Call for high-season rates.
Meals: Self-catering but breakfast and home-cooked meals by arrangement. All meals self-served.
Directions: From N2 take exit 92, sign-posted to Bot River. Follow signs to Bot River and Beaumont Wine Estate is signed off to the right-hand side. Map can be faxed.

The Post House

David Donde
22 Main Rd, Greyton 7233
Tel: 028-254-9995 Fax: 028-254-9920
Email: info@posthouse.co.za Web: www.posthouse.co.za
Cell: 082-446-3884

High on the side of The Post House is an old sign cheekily proclaiming, "Food and Lodging for the Gentry". David (dad, avid 4WD'er, fisherman and renovator) is a down-to-earth owner who's got everything covered – including knowing how to host. He says he hates the sign, but their customers (including my good self) are fond of it, so majority rules for the time being. A post office in the 1860s, it was also once THE country hotel outside Cape Town. Now it thrives again with the sound of clearly delighted customers conversing about the country-chic interior design and the gurgles of David's coffee-machine, which turns out the best coffee I had in SA. The thick walls are delightfully warped and guests tend to settle either in an old English-style pub in front of fires which roar in deep inglenooks in winter, or on wide leafy verandahs for summer G&Ts. The restaurant feels more modern with wooden floorboards, pine tables and monochrome prints. Naïve oils brighten the scene and the cosmopolitan cooking is excellent. Rooms are found off to the side through a cottage garden and are named after Beatrix Potter's characters. I had pretty 'Tom Kitten' and the honeymoon suite is palatial. *The hiking round Greyton is famous in SA.*

Rooms: 12: 6 kings, 1 queen and 5 doubles. All with en-suite bath or shower.
Price: From R290 pp sharing. Honeymoon suite R800 pp sharing. Singles +50%.
Meals: Full breakfast included for house guests. Also to the public for all meals throughout the day. High tea is served at 4 pm.
Directions: From the N2 turn left signed to Greyton. Travel for 32km. The Post House is smack in the middle of the village on the left.

Map Number: 3

Roosje van de Kaap

Nick and Ilzebet Oosthuizen
5 Drostdy St, Swellendam 6740
Tel: 028-514-3001 Fax: 028-514-3001
Email: roosje@dorea.co.za Web: www.roosjevandekaap.co.za
Cell: 082-380-4086

Nick, a lawyer, chef, dad and food-magazine editor (his dog can ride a skateboard…), wants people to come here for food, space and good living. And you'll get it, at "nearly ridiculous" prices. I mean, where else can you get mussels for R25, a bottle of exceptional Springfield Sauvignon Blanc Special for R85 and listen to a live jazz band while you enjoy them! The candlelit restaurant, named by *Eat Out* magazine as one of the ten best restaurants in the Garden Route, is charming and encourages intimacy, with guests often ending up chatting to each other across the tables. It's not open for lunch though. Some rooms at the lodge face the pool, some are bonsai Cape Dutch cottages that face the mountain and next-door's sheep. The Honeymoon suite is all about the view and has a huge four-poster. They vary in feel and size, but all are adorable with bunches of wild flowers everywhere you look. Guests can bask like reptiles in the garden or pool on those hot Swellendam summer days. Nick also has a secret track to a ravine where you can swim below a waterfall. He'll pack you a picnic.

Rooms: 9: all doubles with en-suite shower, except 1 king with bath.
Price: R220 – R275 pp sharing. Singles R320 – R450.
Meals: Full breakfast included. The restaurant is open from Tuesday till Sunday evening, but not for lunch.
Directions: From Cape Town, take the 4th exit off the N2 to Swellendam. (Count the turn-off to Swellendam industrial area as the first.) After turning off, take the first street left. From the east, after turning off the N2, it's the first street on the left.

Map Number: 5

Kliphoogte

Herman and Marita Linde
Swellendam 6740
Tel: 028-514-2534 Fax: 028-514-2680
Email: kliphoogte@telkomsa.net
Cell: 084-581-4464

Three kilometres of dusty track bring you to Kliphoogte, one of South Africa's most charming farm B&Bs. Herman, absurdly cheerful for a man who gets up at 4.30 am, runs a fruit and dairy farm on the banks of the Leeurivier… while his mother Marita looks after the guest house. Herman represents the fifth generation of Lindes to work the property and will take guests on walks around the farm, or leave them in the company of the boisterous weaver-birds to swim at the lake. At meal times, Marita takes charge and cooks typical South African dinners. Bread, butter and milk are all home-made, as is the lemonade and brandy cake. After dinner, Herman will probably sing to you, and then take you in his 4x4 up a nearby hill to look at the stars. The main bedroom is a sweet, blue affair with sturdy old Afrikaner furniture, family photos and rugs made by the farm workers. The other two rooms, which also share a bathroom, are more functional (though one has a four-poster bed), but this is not a place where you will want to spend long in bed; there is too much going on outside. To sit on the Kliphoogte stoep, listening to the cicadas, and look out over the small, lush valley is to know contentment indeed.

Rooms: 3: 2 doubles and 1 twin; 1 en-suite shower, 2 with shared bathroom.
Price: R250 – R275 pp sharing. Singles on request.
Meals: Dinner by request and will be 3 – 5 courses. Marita will ask you what you want when you book. Lunches and picnics available too. Ask about prices.
Directions: Turn off N2 onto R60 (Swellendam turn-off). After 10km, Kliphoogte (blue sign) is on your left. Then 3km more on gravel road.

Jan Harmsgat Country House

Brin and Judi Rebstein

Swellendam 6740
Tel: 023-616-3407 or 023-616-3311 Fax: 023-616-3201
Email: brinreb@iafrica.com Web: www.jhghouse.com

A true country house, Jan Harmsgat is a breath of fresh air in an often-chintzy genre. Judi (a producer in the film industry) and Brin rescued it from tumbledown oblivion in 1989. They swept out the old rotted beams, mould, even pigs, and set about pouring a cellar-full of TLC into it. It is a beautiful place. The cover photo does not lie. But what it doesn't show is that the restaurant and its increasingly famous staff are starting to catch the food-media's eye… or that your hosts are so gracious. Past resident Hermanus Steyn proclaimed the Independent Republic of Swellendam in 1795 and farmed wine here originally, but I doubt he dined on butterfish bobotie stacks with coriander. Perhaps he did! His 25-metre barn-cellar (now the dining room, complete with grand piano) today looks out of a glass wall. Guests are housed in old slave quarters whose large rooms and great comfort might make you forget the history of the place. However, sympathetic renovation means that windows in the clay walls have not been enlarged, and the wonky lintels, wooden shutters and vast beams all play their part in preserving the original character here. Mine was high up in the apex of the thatch, had a free-standing Victorian bath, gilded chairs and come morning I had a colour-me-happy moment when I opened my shutters and was drenched in a sweet citron-scented breeze gusting across from the orchard. Bliss.

Rooms: 4: 1 dbl with shr & 1 twin en/s bath; 1 dbl & 1 twin, Victorian baths in room, en-suite toilet. Self-catering cottage with dbl & tw sharing bathroom.
Price: R375 (winter) – R650 (summer) pp sharing. Singles R450 – R720. Cottage R450 pp sharing.
Meals: Full breakfast included. Lunch by arrangement only. From 2004 the restaurant is open for dinner to the public (book before 10 am).
Directions: From Cape Town on N1 to Worcester turn R into R60 (Robertson) at Worcester. Carry on thro' Robertson and Ashton. Turn R after Ashton and stay on R60. House on left after 21km. From CTN on N2 to Swellendam turn onto R60. 24.5km after Swellendam towards Ashton, house on R.

Braeside B&B

Janine and Chris Taylor

13 van Oudtshoornweg, Swellendam 6740
Tel: 028-514-3325 Fax: 028-514-1899
Email: ctaylor@sdm.dorea.co.za Web: www.braeside.co.za
Cell: 082-499-0222 or 083-261-1923

Braeside is a vibrant, inspirational and pioneering place. One of the strings to Janine's bow is the 'culture share' experiences that she (a social worker) organises with the local community. They asked her to bring visitors out to the township to interact with them since they couldn't afford to travel themselves. So she did. And it worked. It remains a rare opportunity in South Africa to get an insight into a real African community. Janine always goes too and will translate, do the introductions and then you can join in and share life and whatever else is going on for a few hours. Visits differ each time. The choir and gumboot dancers may be at practice, you may have a beer at the shebeen, show photos of your country etc. It is a great opportunity for some cultural interfacing. Braeside House itself is old and lovely. The rooms are comfortable, with wide beds, crisp white linen and plenty of creature comforts. The internal courtyard in dominated by a semi-raised circular pool. Breakfast is prodigious (all the usuals plus smoked snoek pâté, curried omelettes and warm, wood-fired bread). It's served on the stately verandah and a tall frangipani tree drops its flowers onto the tables. Janine is a gifted host. Stay for at least two nights – it's an amazing place. *Interaction visits are strictly by arrangement only and a donation is encouraged.*

Rooms: 5: 1 double and 1 twin with en-suite shower and bath; 1 queen, 1 double and 1 twin with en-suite shower.
Price: R150 – R300 pp sharing May – September. R250 – R400 pp sharing October – April. Singles on request.
Meals: Full breakfast included. Other meals by arrangement only. Excellent restaurants nearby.
Directions: Come off N2 into Swellendam main street. With Spa on your LEFT head up main street towards mountains. Turn off main road left as the road heads right. This turn is signed to Caravan Park. Travel about 500m to T-junction, take left into Tilney St. Braeside is on your right.

Map Number: 5

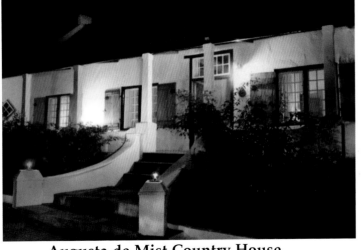

Augusta de Mist Country House

Madeleine and Rob Harrisson

3 Human St, Swellendam 6740
Tel: 028-514-2425 Fax: 028-514-2057
Email: info@augustademist.co.za Web: www.augustademist.co.za
Cell: 082-775-0834

Cool, contemporary decor meets rustic heritage architecture at Augusta de Mist, each setting the other off to great advantage. And Madeleine and Rob are grandmaster hosts at this most laid-back of guest houses. Two of the rooms are actually little cottages deep in the garden. Here under reed-and-pole ceilings you'll find a fireplace, large indigo sofas or chairs, a funky bedroom with beige and white linen and matching indigo organza curtains billowing in the breeze. The main house is an old Cape Dutch farm national monument, built 50 years after the foundation of Swellendam, i.e. at the beginning of the 19th century. Rob does up old tools and farm implements in his intriguing workshop, so all round the house you'll find wagon boxes, shutters, hinges, doors and once-cherished peasant furniture that has been tailored and restored under his furnace and bellows. The rose nursery garden is a peaceful haven with red-brick paths winding up the hill through banks of lavender towards the swimming pool with its swanky canvas brolly and loungers… and then off to the right over a stream. All the indigenous trees and shrubs mean an abundance of birds. Madeleine is a big fan of modern art; and of growing food at home; and, while we're at it, of breakfast pancakes with banana, crispy bacon and syrup! These are best in winter by the pot-belly fire and in summer at pretty tables under the grapevine. Ask about the moonlight walk through Cactus Farm.

Rooms: 6: 2 kings, 1 with shwr and 1 with bath and shwr; 1 queen, 1 double and 1 twin, all with en-suite bath & shr; 1 double with adjoining single with en/s bath & shr.
Price: R250 – R450 pp sharing. Singles plus 30%.
Meals: Full breakfast included.
Directions: Heading towards the mountains, pass the churches on your left and as the road bends to the right, turn left following signs to the caravan park. 1st road on left at top on left.

Overberg, Western Cape

Lentelus

Helena Joubert

Route 62, Barrydale
Tel: 028-572-1636 Fax: 028-572-1636
Email: helenaj@lando.co.za Web: www.lentelus.co.za
Cell: 082-579-1246

If you're passing through Barrydale from the N2, then you'll drive through the magnificent Tradouws Pass. Those-in-the-know drive from here to Montagu through the Klein Karoo, a region of semi-arid desert between two mountain ranges that snake along parallel to each other. Sound beautiful? Now imagine a valley floor that has been slowly carpeted over the centuries with fruit orchards and vineyards. One of the prettiest is the Jouberts', and you can drop in for lunch and wine-tasting at their new Joubert-Tradauw cellar. But even the longest of long lunches is never going to be enough. Helena lives up on the valley side, surrounded by orchards. Her house is on the left, yours is off to the right in the pears and is pretty near perfect. It is a flat-fronted, sandy coloured place of clean lines and honest-to-goodness simplicity. In spring the pears bloom and white blossom drifts around like warm snowflakes making it all the more blissful. Upstairs has a balcony, while downstairs at the back there is a simple courtyard garden with an outside shower. Back inside you'll find fresh linen, blankets, fleecy rugs on the beds and a sitting room with couches and fireplaces. Over at Helena's house (where you eat breakfast) we munched on "a simple Sunday night supper" of seared beef fillet, crisp salad from the garden followed by a cream cheese nut and honey tartlet. Helena hasn't missed a trick.

Rooms: 2: 1 twin with en-suite shower and bath; 1 king/twin with en-suite shower.
Price: R300 – R350 pp sharing. Single supplement R150.
Meals: Full breakfast included. Meals by arrangement.
Directions: From Barrydale take the R62 toward Montagu. 11km from Barrydale on the right.

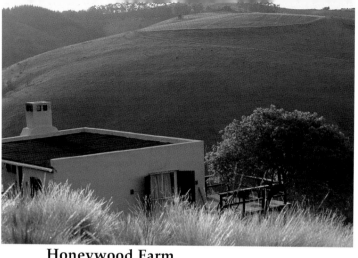

Honeywood Farm

John and Miranda Moodie

Between Swellendam and Heidelberg, Heidelberg 6665
Tel: 028-722-1823 Fax: 028-722-1839
Email: john@honeywoodfarm.co.za Web: www.honeywoodfarm.co.za
Cell: 083-270-4035

These days the Moodies (sweetly known as Mr and Mrs Honey by locals) farm bees (and, of course, honey), but the family has been here since 1807 when they moved from Orkney. Part conservancy, it's a wild, free place, right next to the bird-watching mountain paradise of the Grootvadersbosch Nature Reserve, through which you drive on the five-kilometre trip to wind-swept, wild and wistfully romantic Hunters Cottage. If the wild calls, then this little bothy tossed in a sea of green hills, lit only by hurricane lamps and warmed by an open fire is for you. Down in the valley is the Bush Camp. Incorporating parts of the original homestead site, it feels like a wooden hay-barn with a cinematic element, since a quarter of the blackwood walls slide out of sight so you can observe the scenery. It has an enormous fireplace, old couches, chunky beds and you only need to BYO sleeping-bag and sustenance. Firewood, washing-up liquid, towels and everything else are provided for you. Gold is reputedly buried on the farm somewhere, but more accessible treasures are the view of the surrounding mountains at sunset, the lake to swim in and the secret braai spots in the wooded valleys. You can sample each and every one of these, whether you've chosen a more conventional farm cottage nearer the main house or slightly bohemian Oakvale House. *Children under 12 half price.*

Rooms: 7 self-contained cottages, each with 2 or 3 bedrooms, some with en/s bathr'ms. Oakvale sleeps 6 – 8. 1 booking per cottage, except Bush Camp (sleeps 10).
Price: R150 – R200 pp sharing.
Meals: Full breakfast R40 pp. Lunch platters R55 for two sharing. Dinners R80 pp for 3 courses including wine. All meals must be pre-booked.
Directions: From Cape Town on N2 take the first road to Suurbraak (R324) after Swellendam and continue straight (you will pass the turn to Tradouws Pass) until you arrive at a dirt road. Carry on straight until you start seeing signs for Honeywood.

Map Number: 5

105

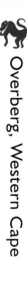

Skeiding Guest Farm

Neels and Anné-Lize Uys

Route N2, Heidelberg 6665
Tel: 028-722-1891 Fax: 028-722-2223
Email: skeiding@sdm.dorea.co.za Web: www.skeiding.co.za
Cell: 082-722-2223

Neels and Anné-Lize are fantastically energetic – you need to be to run a farm, a young family and a guest house in the same lifetime. You are welcome to become involved in the workings of the farm as far as possible. This could mean watching the 1500 ostriches being fed in the morning, but there are also indigenous beef cattle, some sheep and goats, two dogs called Asterix and Obelix… and a couple of young children too. The farm is on high, open, rolling terrain, but it's only a short drive into surprising, Garden Route-style forest and the beautiful Grootvadersbosch Nature Reserve for day hikes. The area is a birder's paradise too with 17 endemic species and they have counted at least 50 species on the farm itself. Alternatively, you can head down over South Africa's only working ferry to the De Hoop Nature Reserve or go to Witsand (35km) for the whales (June to November) and boat rides. It's an outdoorsy sort of place and bedrooms have all you need, their own patios, strong showers, ostrich-skin slippers and there are sitting rooms in the cottages too. Guests eat at the family dining table, wholesome farm fare like ostrich fillet, bobotie, pumpkin fritters etc. A friendly family farm and an education for city slickers. *Professionally run horse rides can be arranged.*

Rooms: 4: all doubles/twins; 1 with en-suite bath and shower; 2 with en-suite shower; 1 with wheelchair-friendly en-suite shower.
Price: R250 – R350 pp sharing. No single supplement.
Meals: R70 for 2 courses pp. R100 for 3 courses pp. Price excludes wine.
Directions: From Swellendam take N2 towards Mossel Bay. 45km after Swellendam (12km before Heidelberg) farm signed to left. Follow 2km then signed left again. 3 more km then signed left again. House on hill.

River Magic

Bosky and Paul Andrew
Vermaaklikheid, nr Riversdale
Reservations: Indaba, 35 Pear Lane, Constantia 7806
Tel: 021-794-6294 or 028-713-2930 Fax: 028-713-2930
Email: rivermagic@vermaaklikheid.co.za Web: www.vermaaklikheid.co.za

The village of Vermaaklikheid is straight out of *The Wind in the Willows*, with its dirt road, tiny shop and few wee cottages. I half-expected Ratty and Moley to toddle past on the river path when I visited. There are two cottages at River Magic. 'Back Track' (300 metres from the river) is surrounded by tall blonde reeds and has a clear shallow pond where birds come to drink. And down an ever-more-puddly-and-goaty track through the grassy river flats is 'Glory Be'. To get there you first have to row your boat across the tea-coloured river to the jetty. The low, thatched house peeps out from on top of the riverbank and, like 'Back Track', it is the stuff of childhood dreams (imagine Bilbo Baggins's home and you're most of the way there). The cottages are comfortable, not extravagant, with simple beds, wooden furniture, Paul's paintings on the walls, lino floors, big fireplaces (BYO wood and charcoal) and well-loved couches. You can paddle off on the canoes on bird-watching expeditions (more than 100 species live here in the reeds and fynbos-covered cliffs). Fishing, swimming and hiking are excellent too. A very special spot.

Rooms: 2 cottages: Glory Be sleeps 12 (3 dbles, tented garden hut, and a 4-bed room), shared ablution block; Back Track sleeps 6 (2 twins en/s shr, 1 tented hut).

Price: From R130 – R150 pp sharing. Minimum R350 per cottage per night. Min R500 – R800 over long weekends and R800 – R1,000 over Christmas holidays.

Meals: Self-catering, bring your own wood, towels and torches. Seafood restaurant nearby.

Directions: From Cape Town take N2. 3km before Heidelberg turn R at signs marked "Port Beauford; Witsand". 6km down tar road, turn L at dirt road signed Vermaaklikheid. After 14km turn L at T-jct, cross Duivenshok River over causeway. Follow signs to Vermaaklikheid & then to River Magic.

Map Number: 5

Zingela Indlela

Rienie and Deon Douglas
Farm 272, Mossel Bay
Tel: 044-694-0011 Fax: 044-694-0012
Email: drd@mweb.co.za Web: www.greatbrakriver.co.za/zingela
Cell: 082-380-0567

These 695 wild and open acres were originally an adventure and eco-tourism game farm. Now they are also home to 3000 ostriches. It's a busy place, perfect for big or small kids, especially if you're no stranger to adrenaline. Day visitors also come to quad-bike, to watch the crocs at feeding time, or you can bring your own 4WD and try the challenging boundary track. Hiking and swimming in the (croc-less!) river is also popular. Wherever possible overnighting guests are invited to join in farm life, but this is more common in winter since it can get busy in summer. The lodge is built on an escarpment overlooking the broad sweep of the land. The main atrium is huge, airy, full of Africana, including a stuffed lynx and giraffe head, leather couches… and this is where you eat too. Breakfast specialty? Scrambled fresh ostrich egg with green peppers, herbs and bacon. Brick-built in the '90s, two wings run off either side. The rooms all face the view and are decorated in an African theme. Downstairs is a bar, snooker table and just outside in the wild space that so characterises this place, a massive deck sweeps about the pool. Rienie is lovely and runs the farm, house and staff with a jolly smile and knowing eye.

Rooms: 8: 5 doubles (1 with en-suite bath/shower, 4 with shower only); 3 family suites all with doubles and extra bath & sh (1 with 1 single, 1 with two extra singles).

Price: R250 pp sharing B&B. Self-catering R210 pp sharing.

Meals: Full breakfast included. Lunch from R45 – R85 pp. Dinners by arrangement From R65 – R120 pp (excluding wine).

Directions: From N2 follow signs to R328 and Oudtshoorn. 9km from Hartenbos turn left to Brandwag. Keep left where the road forks. Pass Nyaru Game Farm (on left) and after 8km on dirt turn left into farm.

Map Number: 5

Susan Pardew Guest House

Marthie Oberholster
Susan Pardew Rd, Hersham,
Great Brak River 6526
Tel: 044-620-2349
Fax: 044-620-2349
Email:
susanpardew@intekom.co.za
Web:
www.guesthousesusanpardew.
co.za
Cell: 082-782-8975

Garden Route, Western Cape

If you're after a beachy time then you might as well do it properly. At the Susan Pardew Guest House the surf crashes continually below you and the views and salty breezes of the beach permeate every corner of the place. Obviously the big deck is a major draw and I found myself wrestling the catch off the door to get out there before I'd even said hello to Marthie! The big deck, which leads directly onto the dunes and fynbos and down to the beach, is also the venue for breakfast and there is a plunge pool encased within it too. You are treated to both sunrise and sunset from here and Mossel Bay glimmers most appealingly at night. Dolphins are a common sight, as are whales in season. The bedrooms are all very large, with unusual modern furniture, the two rooms upstairs more like apartments with sitting areas, microwave and fridge, DSTV, hob and sink. The upstairs verandah and its fantastic views of the ocean are shared by all the rooms. Marthie does dinners for guests or there's an indoor braai installed. The Susan Pardew by the way was a ship that was wrecked here in 1872 in case you were expecting her to bring the tea in the morning.

Rooms: 5: 4 doubles with en-suite bath and shower; 1 twin with en/s shower.
Price: Self-catering R400 – R500 per person per night (breakfast at R45 pp). B&B is R300 – R500 pp sharing. Singles R350 – R550.
Meals: Full breakfast included. Dinners by arrangement from R80 (excluding wine).
Directions: From Cape Town take N2 past Mossel Bay. 20km further turn off onto Great Brak River ramp. 1st right, under road, left at T-junction. Over bridge, turn right signed Glentana. 1km turn right into Hersham Drive. Keep straight to the end.

Map Number: 5

Riversyde

Dora Hattingh

2 Long St, Great Brak River 6525
Tel: 044-620-3387 Fax: 044-620-3387
Email: riversyd@mweb.co.za Web: www.riversyde.co.za
Cell: 082-784-5885

Dora asked me to fill in a questionnaire about her guest house and I realised then that she had every angle covered – impeccable food, personality, award-winning service, comfort, beds, linen garden. All got top marks, and not because I was sucking up! There are only four rooms in the house, all large with deep carpets and egg-shell blue or salmon pink walls. One has a little balcony two overlook the river and two have free-standing iron baths behind screens in the bedroom with you. For some reason I loved this – perhaps because I could watch TV from the bath. You must make sure you book with Dora early enough to give her time to include you in her delicious dinners. But perhaps the most remarkable aspect of Riversyde is the river side. The tidal Great Brak River runs beside the lawns of the garden, just 5 metres from the house, and there is an island rich in bird life just yards from the jetty. Dora can make you a picnic and you can paddle off down the river on a canoe or take the motorised raft to some secluded sandy beaches; or otherwise stay at home and sample the very reasonably priced traditional South African lunches, delicacies and sweet treats from the café menu. Few hostesses take such deserved pride in what they do. *Good base for golf, beaches and day-trips to Oudtshoorn, Mossel Bay and George.*

Rooms: 4: all doubles with en-suite bath, or bath and shower.
Price: R330 – R600 pp sharing. Single supplement 50%.
Meals: Full breakfast included (included if you are self-catering too).
Directions: From Mossel Bay take N2 towards George, exit 409 signed left into Great Brak River. Follow past 2 stop signs. House on right before bridge.

Fairview Historic Homestead

Philda Benkenstein
36 Stander St, George 6530
Tel: 044-874-7781 Fax: 044-874-7999
Email: benkenstein@mweb.co.za Web: www.wheretostay.co.za/fairview
Cell: 082-226-9466

This picturesque, listed Victorian house on the eastern edge of George is an intriguing place to stay. With its high ceilings and abundant Victoriana, Fairview has the feel of an old English rectory, although the vivid colours owe more to African than Anglican themes. All the bedrooms are a treat: the two in the main house still have their original 1880s floorboards, beams and fireplaces; the Orange Room, complete with dashing white trim, bathes in afternoon sunlight, while the Yellow Room soaks up the morning. The sitting room has the same high ceilings and wooden floors, with shuttered sash windows and enormous linen press. There is a self-catering cottage apartment with its own orange tree and garden around one side, and Philda will have another room for guests upstairs by May 2004. The whole place has a happy family atmosphere, enhanced by the original home features, which have been retained wherever possible. Philda loves to host and have people in her beautiful home. She will cook too and if you do eat here, as the GG guests visiting were, then you'll enjoy mainly South African fare. Husband Desmond is a green-fingered doctor and the creative force in the glorious garden. There are tropical fruit trees, an immaculate veggie patch, swathes of clivia... and plans for much more.

Rooms: 4: all doubles with an extra bed. All have en-suite shower, 1 has en-suite bath. One self-catering apartment.
Price: R200 – R320 pp sharing. Singles plus 50%. Self-catering rates on request.
Meals: Full breakfast included. Dinners by arrangement.
Directions: From CT on N2 take York St turn-off to George. Turn right at T-jct into Courtenay St. Over railway bridge and turn left into Second Street and turn left at stop sign into Stander St, house on right.

Hoogekraal Country House

Colin Bryan
Glentana Rd, Glentana, George 6530
Tel: 044-879-1277 Fax: 044-879-1300
Email: guest@hoogekraal.co.za Web: www.hoogekraal.co.za

To say Hoogekraal is unique is an understatement. Where else would you find larger-than-life Colin, ex-bodyguard and chef Johann, sublime views of sea and mountain, a surfeit of antiques, hoards of Ming and Imari porcelain, 25 kilometres of deserted beach… and a seven-foot-high Christ? Once lord of over 120,000 Cape morgen (a measurement of land… x 2.2 for an acre equivalent) the house has a rich and varied history which reads like a South African equivalent of *Gone with the Wind* (minus the nanny, and with a more enticing set). Today the land may have gone but the sense of affluence remains. Accommodation is in Cape Dutch farmhouses where the rooms are a salad of styles with 18th- and 19th-century antiques, comfy beds (the rooms with the brass ones are best) and a suspicion of the '70s, mainly in the bathrooms. Hoogekraal is one of the original pioneer estates and has been in Tonie's family for generations. However, since he is often involved in South African current affairs, it is Colin who is more likely to entertain you with stories if you get involved in the five-course banquet. Starting with drinks in the 70-square-metre sitting room, the gastronomic endurance test continues in the red dining room with porcelain, silver, candles, two soups, two mains, eight veggie dishes and tipsy tart. Politics, history and the well-known names signed into the visitors' book are what you should discuss. Culture vultures will find reception under the flagpole…. *Children over 12.*

Rooms: 6: 3 suites, 3 rooms. Suites: 1 double, 1 twin, 1 'family unit', all have 2 bedrooms, extra bed & sitting room. Rooms: 2 doubles, 1 twin, all en/s bath and/or shower.
Price: R300 – R500 pp sharing for B&B. Singles + 50% from October to April.
Meals: Full breakfast included. 5-course dinner R200pp. 4 courses R175 pp (including wines, sherries, port or brandy).
Directions: Take the Glentana off-ramp from the N2. Drive 1km toward the sea and it is signed left. Up dirt road and reception is under the flagpole.

Map Number: 5

The Waves

Liza and Iain Campbell

7 Beach Rd, Victoria Bay, George 6530
Tel: 044-889-0166 Fax: 044-889-0166
Email: thewaves@intekom.co.za
Web: www.gardenroute.co.za/vbay/waves/index.htm

Iain and Liza have an amazing photo from 1906 when The Waves was the only house on the beach, used as a holiday home by an Oudtshoorn farmer. It is not surprising a few others have since joined the club. The hamlet is closed to vehicles – only residents hold the key to the gate, so you can park your car securely at night. I'm no surfer, but the waves here are enticing, rolling up the perfect arc of the small bay at a height that is challenging, but not scary. Iain will get you a wetsuit and surfboard or fins and a snorkel. Or if you like your activity less damp, there is horse-riding nearby, dolphin- and whale-watching in season and walks along the bay front. The house is right on the sea (see above) and all three bedroom suites (each with its own lounge) look out, although you may spend more time on the verandah watching the waves roll in. They are hypnotic. Breakfast is served here in the sunshine and often goes for hours. The Outeniqua Choo-Tjoe (yes, it's a steam train) runs through Victoria Bay twice a day. Both Iain and Liza are consummate hosts, love what they do and share a great sense of fun. Bay life could be addictive. *Fully no smoking anywhere. Children over 12 only.*

Rooms: 3: all doubles with extra beds, 1 with en-suite shower, 2 with en-suite bath and shower.
Price: R375 – R650 pp sharing. Singles R495 – R850.
Meals: Full breakfast included. Meals can be ordered in and a table will be set for you.
Directions: From Mossel Bay on N2 go past George exits where highways merge. 1km further on signed Victoria Bay to right – follow down hill 3km. Park and walk along beach road to collect the key for the gate.

Map Number: 5

Strawberry Hill Country Lodge

Di and Bill Turner

Old George-Knysna (Seven Passes) Road, Wilderness, PO Box 4822, George East 6539
Tel: 044-877-0055 Fax: 044-877-0055
Email: getaway@strawberryhill.co.za Web: www.strawberryhill.co.za

Bill and Di wouldn't swap this for all the tea in China. Their hill-marooned farm looks across to the mountains and the view here has previously had guests applauding and trying to order prints! The garden plunges straight from the pool and lawns to two deep gorges and nothing spoils the unfettered view. The area is home to ferny afro-montane forests and Bill will happily tell you the way along numerous hiking tracks to the best pools; having been resident here since 1970 he is more than well qualified to do so. Every evening Di and Bill invite their guests to join them for wine and snacks on the verandah or beside the log fire. Di had just got back from a mammoth hike collecting fynbos plants for the Cape Nature Conservation when I visited. The lodge is very luxurious, homey and no details (like chocolates on your pillow) have been overlooked. The cottage is now available to rent as well, tailored to children with a playground and tree house in the fenced garden, pretty country furnishings and animal murals in an upstairs bedroom. Last edition Simon did the walk down to the 'frothy confluence' of the rivers and says it is absolutely not to be missed. *Great hiking and well-situated for exploration of the Garden Route.*

Rooms: 4: 3 doubles in house; 1 suite (sleeps 2 extra on divan) with en/s shower; 2 doubles with en/s bath & sh; 1 self-c house with 3 doubles sharing bath & sh.
Price: For B&B: R250 – R500 pp sharing. For self-catering: R500 – R1,200 for house (sleeps 6).
Meals: Full breakfast included. Light self-service supper provided (request in advance). Cottage less R30 if self-catering for breakfast.
Directions: From George towards Wilderness on Knysna Rd. L onto old George-Knysna rd signed Saasveld Technikon. Strawberry Hill after 7.5km on R. From Wilderness: up Heights Rd behind hotel. At T-Junc (3.5km) L towards George. SH is 3km on L.

Map Number: 5

Eden B&B

Bev Campbell

Erica Rd, PO Box 623, Wilderness 6560
Tel: 044-877-0149
Email: bcampbell@telkomsa.net

At GGHQ, we consider it a good sign if we make notes *before* we visit a place. One phone call to Bev and I'd taken down first-class directions, remembered old acquaintances, talked elephants and admirals and assured her that I was half the man my predecessor was (Guy is 6'10, whereas I was designed to be fired from a circus canon). Bev used to live on a citrus farm in Addo, but has now relocated to this hilltop wilderness. Amongst the homes of golf stars and polo players, Eden is something out of the ordinary. But then so is Bev. Not many people can lay claim to having built (and sold) a village. Now she's perched between forest and sea, in a house hand-made by a 'wood expert', with individually painted walls, where you join her for breakfast. You sleep in the uncluttered woodcutter's cottage next door, which has a quaint little kitchen, old wood-burning stove, beds that embrace you and a shower that steams with hot water. Her two dogs – one a pedigree Jack Russell, the other a jolly good effort – will accompany you round the garden. The legacy of the previous owner, it teems with irises, watsonia, strelitzia, clivia and an incredible selection of succulents. Further afield, toward the mountains, you can gambol through lush meadows and pine forests, wildlife in full song. "I make no apologies for the noises off," says Bev. "This is Africa!"

Rooms: 3: all twins, 1 with en-suite shower, 2 sharing bath and shower.
Price: R175 – R200 pp.
Meals: Full breakfast included. Plenty of restaurants 5 mins away in Wilderness.
Directions: From George turn off N2 into Wilderness Village. Left past Wilderness Hotel to T-junction. Stay left on Heights Road, up hill, past Bundu Café and map of Africa settlement. Erica Rd on left, right fork to Eden on right.

Moontide Guest House

Maureen Mansfield
Southside Rd, Wilderness
6560
Tel: 044-877-0361
Fax: 044-877-0124
Email:
moontide@intekom.co.za
Web: www. moontide.co.za

It's a rare pleasure for us to stay somewhere on *holiday* and to experience it over a period of days. And Moontide was a palpable hit with all five of us. Its position is hard to beat, right on the banks of the lagoon, its wooden decks shaded by a 400-year-old milkwood tree. Here you can sit out for bountiful breakfasts or with an evening drink from your bar fridge, and watch giant kingfishers diving for fish – well, we saw one anyway. Bird life is profuse on the lagoon. The long, white-sanded Wilderness beach is only a one-minute walk from the house, but you can also take a canoe straight from Moontide up the lagoon into the Touw River and then walk along forest trails to waterfalls to swim in fresh-water rock pools. Whatever we did it was a pleasure to return, play cards in a relaxed sitting room, or read in the cool of our bedrooms. I was delighted with 'Milkwood' because I'm a sucker for dozing on a futon, in a loft, under thatched eaves, with river views by my head. But I would like to return and try them all. Since we descended *en masse*, Maureen has built herself a tree-top sanctuary. The deck, day-bed, even the free-standing bath, look out across thatched roofs to the river. Sportingly, she's decided it's too nice to keep for herself!

Rooms: 5: Luxury Suite (king & 2 twins); Treetop, (double, bath & outside shr); in house (double & 2 singles); Stone Cottage (twins & shr); The Boathouse (twins & shr).
Price: R260 – R460 pp sharing. Single rates on request.
Meals: Full breakfast included.
Directions: From George on N2 ignore Wilderness turn-off. Cross Touw River bridge, first left signed Southside Rd. Moontide at the end of cul-de-sac.

Map Number: 5

Wilderness Manor

Johan and Marianne Nicol
397 Waterside Rd, Wilderness 6560
Tel: 044-877-0264 Fax: 044-877-0163
Email: wildman@mweb.co.za Web: www.manor.co.za

Marianne has a flair for interiors. You won't need one of the hundreds of books (African art and history, its wildlife and architecture, war memoirs, children's classics and psychology texts) that rub sleeves throughout the house to find this out. Overlooking the lagoon, the glass-encased sitting room is coir-carpeted with Afghan kilims, a low-slung ivory sofa and a pair of Morris chairs, given to the Governor of Gauteng. There's an old billiard table, too, somewhere under a pile of maps. African artefacts have been begged, borrowed or bought: Ndebele pipes and beads, bartered-for carvings and stones from the Cradle of Mankind. The bedrooms have similar horn-and-hide hues, all the luxurious trappings you could wish for, and room for Indonesian chairs and chests, chocolate leather sofas, slipper baths and dark canopied beds with reading lights. In the morning, linen tables were dressed with bone-handle cutlery and lilies in a square metal vase placed on an old country bench next to fruit and muesli. Your hosts are discreet and attentive, and after serving up a faultless (and greaseless) breakfast, will give you a map and bountiful beach-bag and set you off to explore your surrounds. Bird life is rampant in the area and walks in the surrounding forests are a must. It is only a five-minute stroll along lagoon-side boardwalks to the beach, town and some good restaurants.

Rooms: 4: 2 kings with en-suite bath and shower; 2 twins, one with en/s bath and shower, one with shower only.
Price: R400 – R700 pp sharing. Single supplement plus 50% (100% in summer). Winter rates available.
Meals: Full breakfast included.
Directions: From George, follow N2 to Wilderness (beware of speed cameras on descent). Turn left into Wilderness Village and follow road to T-junction. Turn right along lagoon to Wilderness Manor on left.

Forget-me-not B&B

Mary and Derek Woolmington

21 Boekenhout St, Upper Old Place, Knysna 6570
Tel: 044-382-2916 Fax: 044-382-2913
Email: mary@forget-me-not.co.za Web: www.forget-me-not.co.za
Cell: 083-505-4225

Derek and Mary, a warm and down-to-earth English-Irish couple, embody all that we look for in hosts. Having built businesses and raised family, they're starting out on their own again. Hence Forget-me-not (Self-catering and B&B, to give it its full title), with its sloping slate roof, dormer windows and gravel drive set behind a picket fence. The house is edged with wisteria, primroses and forget-me-nots and other flowers Mary can't quite put a name on (and nor can I obviously) – she puts it down to "Outeniqua Rust", a lethargic malaise blamed on easy living. Inside the sweep of a maranti staircase leads to two bedrooms. Iris has pine floorboards, leaning walls, blanket box and hanging space. There's a cushioned window-box from which to sit and stare. The Rose room, more feminine in shades of pink with floral motifs, has Oregon pine furniture. An elongated bathroom harbours a bath tucked under the eaves. Everyone eats at the house (usually outside above the lawn, orchard and pool), even those in the self-contained flat, whose wooden deck faces the lagoon, Knysna Heads and the hills. All guests get use of the pool and the braai area and the house is within walking distance of the Waterfront and a short drive to the beaches. The long list of activities, both on water and inland, can be booked on your behalf by Derek and Mary.

Rooms: 3: 1 king and 1 queen both with en/s bath and shower; 1 self-contained apartment.
Price: R150 – R250 pp sharing.
Meals: Full cooked or Continental breakfast and variety of fruit and fruit/veg juice boosts. Plenty of local restaurants.
Directions: Head east out of Knysna and turn left onto Old Toll Rd, Upper Old Place. At T-junction turn right and take first left into Boekenhout St. Forget-me-not on right.

Map Number: 6

Glenshee

David and Fiona Ramsay

Eastford Downs, Eastford Nature Reserve, Welbedacht Lane, Knysna 6570
Tel: 044-382-3202 Fax: 044-382-3202
Email: glenshee@mweb.co.za Web: www.gosouth.co.za/glenshee/
Cell: 082-789-5062

David and Fiona were the first to build up here on the mountain, their pink-washed home blessed (not by chance) with majestic valley views down the steep sides of the Eastford Nature Reserve to the curve of the Knysna River far below. Views they couldn't resist sharing with others… which is where you come in. They built the house themselves, the hundred-year-old windows and doors salvaged from Karoo farms, and the wide wooden deck has become the irresistible focal point of the house. And now they have built a grey fibre-glass plunge pool too, further inducement to spend at least one lazy day at Glenshee. The three bedrooms are fresh, light, airy and countrified with wicker bedsteads, excellent linen, your own private deck and viewpoint. David and Fiona really enjoy their guests and operate in traditional B&B fashion, offering much expert advice, over sundowners or tea, on secret spots they have found all along the Garden Route. Or they will point out the best walks from the house through the forests and fynbos. Fiona spends at least an hour each morning preparing the breakfast (Health, Continental or English) and these are taken on the deck with the invigorating view as backdrop. A real home and delightful hosts. *Despite Glenshee's imperious mountainside position it is just 8 minutes from Knysna town centre.*

Rooms: 3: 1 double with en/s bath; 1 twin with en/s shower; 1 double/twin with en/s bath and shower.
Price: R250 – R400 pp sharing. Singles on request.
Meals: Health, Continental or English breakfast included. 3-course dinner by arrangement: R80 – R120 pp. Local restaurants in Knysna.
Directions: From George, before Knysna, turn left into Welbedacht Lane, go straight for 2km to crossroads. Go right signed Eastford Downs follow for 250 metres, then straight through the gateposts into Eastford Downs. Glenshee is 800 metres down on the left.

Map Number: 6

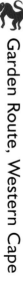

Lindsay Castle

André and Laura van Blerk

Noetzie, Knysna 6570
Tel: 044-375-0100 Fax: 044-382-0877
Email: reservations@knysnacastles.co.za Web: www.knysnacastles.com
Cell: 082-560-5710

There is something peculiarly invigorating (and perhaps just peculiar) about trudging through sand and over glistening rocks, in salty sea air, crashing surf on one side, lush hillside vegetation on the other, to your own beach-marooned, stone-turreted castle. King Arthur meets Robinson Crusoe. Since our last edition Laura has taken up the reins, a delightful host, well-travelled, knowledgeable. Joining other guests, I settled on the sofa as she lit candles. We sipped tingling tonic, watched the fire dancing in its hearth and inhaled some very encouraging smells emanating from the kitchen. Dinner is eaten together around a medieval-looking table made of railway sleepers – fresh mussels fetched from below that very night. Later, I ascended the wooden ladder to my turret and lounged in bed, surf washing comfortingly on the shore below, stars twinkling through misty windows. If you come in winter, you'll watch waves of phosphorescence wash in and, in the darkness, ghostly footprints glow in the sand. Lindsay Castle, with its airy, stone interior, terracotta tiles and blue and white fabrics, is somehow very in tune with the surrounding, pounding sea. Whales (in season) and dolphins cavort in the bay and there are otters, bushbuck and the rare oyster-catcher too. You can hike, fish and swim in the estuary or sea. Romantics only need apply.

Rooms: 4: all doubles, all with en/s bathrooms (two are in the turrets, one is a honeymoon suite).
Price: R650 – R900 pp sharing.
Meals: Full breakfast included. Lunches and dinners by arrangment (approx R150 for dinner with wine).
Directions: From Knysna, go through the town towards Plettenberg Bay and turn right after approx. 4km at sign for Noetzie. Follow the road for 5km until you arrive at the castle.

Map Number: 6

Narnia Farm Guest House

Richard and Stella Sohn

off Welbedacht Lane, Knysna 6570
Tel: 044-382-1334 Fax: 044-382-2881
Email: narnia@pixie.co.za Web: www.narnia.co.za
Cell: 083-325-2581

Narnia combines just about every element we search for in a place to stay. It's defiantly itself – the style (luxuriously ethnic, but never overdone) is so unusual and so genuine that you know it is the extension of real people, not some pretentious interior design job. Stella (graphic design graduate, protea farmer, mother of two) is one of those people and Richard (lawyer, 'architect' and father of four) the other. Narnia is entirely their creation, a dream slotted round one or two key requirements: the house should have a deck with a clear view to the Knysna Heads; and there should be a big, open, friendly entrance hall. Otherwise the house has grown organically into some mad ship with wooden decks, gangways and staircases, swing chairs, heavenly colours of tropical brilliance ("In a previous life I must have been a Mexican," says Stella), a prize-winning garden, long views in all directions, and smaller surprises everywhere. They are great ones for inventively recycling stuff that you or I might throw away. Stella and Richard amaze me with their great energy and skill with people, despite holding down so many jobs. *Bushbuck are often spotted by the dam on the farm and visitors to the garden include porcupine, monkeys, bushpigs, lynx and 85 species of bird*

Rooms: 4: 2 doubles with en-suite bathrooms; 1 cottage with 1 twin and 1 double and shared bathroom (self-catering or B&B).
Price: R295 – R425 pp sharing. Singles on request. Children under 12 half-price.
Meals: Full breakfast included and served from 8.00 – 9.30 am.
Directions: On N2 from George turn into Welbedacht Lane just before Knysna. Then follow signs to Narnia Farm Guest House.

Map Number: 6

Sandgate

Karen and March Turnbull

11 De Smidt Drive, Leisure Island, Knysna 6570
Tel: 021-674-4257 Fax: 021-683-9560
Email: march@turnbull.co.za Web: www.sandgate.co.za
Cell: 082-579-0090

When I first spoke to March he was on the beach, looking for a stick to write my number in the sand with and sounding ridiculously laid-back. I was intrigued to see where he lived. Sandgate is a pleasingly modernised Cape farmhouse, which you can have to yourself. In a quiet corner of leafy Leisure Isle, where hedges are neatly trimmed and lawns run into one another, this bright summery house sits back from a tidal beach, with views to the Knysna Lagoon. The tin-roofed verandah extends along the house, populated with cushioned cane chairs, to a deck and solar-heated pool, surrounded by arum lilies and bougainvillaea. Behind the white walls and marant sash windows, there are acres of space for family and friends. Bedrooms are large, with white timber ceilings and panelled cupboards and decorated in beachy blues and whites. Downstairs the large farm-style kitchen opens onto a dining room and a terracotta-tiled sun-room beyond The beach buggy in the garage, by the way, is for guests to use. GG statisticians have detected a trend amongst our readers to arrive as strangers, depart as friends and return as neighbours. I you suspect you are one of them, test the waters here first and experience Garden Route living at its best. You'll be as relaxed as the Turnbulls in no time. *Don't forget your golf clubs; there's a separate self-contained cottage too.*

Rooms: 5: 1 king with en/s bath, 1 queen and 1 twin with en/s shower and 2 twins sharing bath and shower; additional double with shower in cottage.
Price: R1,400 – R3,500 per day (sleeps 12). Includes weekly linen change and service. 5-day minimum stay.
Meals: Self-catering only.
Directions: From Knysna, turn down George Rex Drive, Leisure Isle signed on right. At end of causeway onto island, turn left at stop into Cearn Drive. Follow road around island and turn right into De Smidt Drive. Sandgate is the second house on the right. Parking at rear.

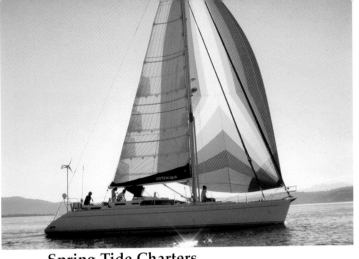

Spring Tide Charters

Stephan and Evelyn Pepler

34 South Jetty, Knysna Quays, Waterfront Drive,, Knysna 6600
Tel: 044-533-4006 Fax: 044-382-5852
Email: info@springtide.co.za Web: www.springtide.co.za
Cell: 082-829-2740

As I took the helm on board the Outeniqua, 50 feet of shimmering beauty somehow suddenly under my command, and sailed her across Knysna lagoon at a leisurely six knots, I felt very special indeed. The Outeniqua is sailed daily (in the lagoon or out in the Indian Ocean, weather permitting) by Stephan and his young friendly crew who clearly love what they do and it's not hard to see why. The coastline around Knysna is spectacular, with regular sightings of marine life and pelagic birds. The vessel itself is also exceptional, and I'm not just saying that because Stephan spent four and a half years building and fitting her out! Every immaculate thing on board, excluding the hull, is his own work. Anyone who has climbed aboard will agree, from President Mbeki to their new-born son (and future crew) Alix. The day starts with a call to the harbourmaster to raise the bridge by the moorings, as you head off across the lagoon to the Heads, two majestic sandstone cliffs that lead out to the open sea and a whole world of excitement. Various day trips include a 4-hour day sail with lunch, a 2.5-hour sail and the 3-hour sunset cruise where you can indulge in Knysna's famous oysters and wash them down with a fine South African bubbly. Evenings are spent anchored in the calm lagoon where a private chef conjures up a gourmet dinner from the galley. A wonderful experience. Advance bookings essential.

Rooms: 2 cabins – ideal for a family or two couples. Day sails and champagne sunset cruises available.
Price: Overnight charters R1,950 pp. Day sail and cruises start at R290 pp.
Meals: Full breakfast and dinner included.
Directions: Knysna Quay Marina is on the Waterfront Drive. Park on the waterfront, next to the station. Yacht moored next to 34° South restaurant.

Map Number: 6

The Gallery Guest House

Lolly Hahn-Page
10 Hill St West, Knysna 6570
Tel: 044-382-2510 Fax: 044-382-5212
Email: gallery.guesthouse@pixie.co.za Web: www.galleryguesthouse.co.za
Cell: 083-309-3920

Lolly manages the happy trick of combining her work as an artist with running a friendly, laid-back guest house in a peaceful part of Knysna. She is a strong force for the promotion of arts and crafts in the town, itself a honeypot for those that can hold a pencil steady. Thus "The Gallery". Her own and local artists' paintings and sculptures dot the walls and cover the carpets in the guest house, one of the longest-running in Knysna. When she can, Lolly steals away to her private studio, handing the reins to the charismatic Miriam, grand-daughter of the King of Lesotho (!). The main room where breakfast etc happens is upstairs and the adjoining wooden deck has tremendous views out over the Knysna Heads, Leisure Isle and Pledge Park nature reserve. There is lots to do in town, what with sunset boat rides, the Outeniqua Choo-Tjoe, sea swimming, canoeing etc and Lolly is very knowledgeable. Best of all she has special private places – sunset spots, music venues, beaches, walks and restaurants – you will only find with her help. The bedrooms themselves are simple, showcasing more local artwork, but cater for all your needs. Choose The Gallery for the irrepressible personality of both house and hostess. *Nine good restaurants within 2 mins.*

Rooms: 4: 2 twins and 2 doubles; 1 with private bath, 3 with en-suite bath or shower.
Price: From R200 pp sharing. Single rates on request.
Meals: Full breakfast included and served from 8 to 10 am.
Directions: From George take N2 to Knysna. At 2nd lights turn left into Grey St, then 2nd left into Hill St West, to end of cul-de-sac. Map on web site.

Beacon Lodge

Al and Clo Scheffer

57 Beacon Way, PO Box
1694, Plettenberg Bay 6600
Tel: 044-533-2614
Fax: 044-533-2614
Email:
beaconlodge@worldonline.co.
za Web:
www.beaconlodge.co.za

This is a small (just two rooms), personal, friendly and involving B&B – and I mean B&B in the proper sense where you share the house with your hosts. (Both rooms have their own separate entrances, mind you, if you want to slip about more furtively.) The patio (for breakfasts, garden bird-watching or reading) has long views out to sea and it's only a short walk to the beach and the lagoon, presumably where you will want to spend at least some of your time. To this end Al and Clo have all beach necessities at the ready – umbrellas, towels and the like. The larger of the two rooms was my favourite (and also the more expensive – my wife will tell you this is typical) with sea views through a huge window and anti-glare solar blinds. There is seagrass on floors, plenty of immaculate seaside white in walls and towels and colour is added in the form of fresh flowers. The Scheffers take the greatest care of their guests. *Fridge facilities provided. Great restaurants within walking distance. Whales and dolphins in season. Closed mid-Dec – mid-Jan and either June or July. Enquire first!*

Rooms: 2: 1 twin and 1 double, both with en-suite bathrooms with showers.
Price: R165 – R330 pp sharing. Single rates on request.
Meals: Full breakfast included. There are good restaurants in town for other meals.
Directions: From Knysna take the N2. Take the second turn into Plett at the Engen 1-stop garage – the house is 600 metres on your left.

Bosavern

Vivienne and Gerald Dreyer
38 Cutty Sark Ave, Plettenberg Bay 6600
Tel: 044-533-1312 Fax: 044-533-0758
Email: info@bosavern.co.za Web: www.bosavern.co.za
Cell: 082-922-4721

The striking S-shaped waves of Bosavern's timbered ceiling mimic the sea and combine with minimalist white interiors and mirrors to strike a harmonious note with the blue ocean far below. Glass doors lead off the open-plan sitting room and onto the balcony where you can treat yourself on wicker chairs to a regal cliff-top view of the Robberg Peninsula and the white beaches of Plettenberg Bay. Powerful binoculars will pick out whales and schools of dolphins which are (can be!) plentiful in the clear water. The bedrooms downstairs have the same sliding doors that disappear smoothly into the wall and the sea breeze wafts in through a square gap of sky as if from a bright blue painting. The view from your room and private balcony is no less spectacular. Comfort is a priority, with goose-down duvets on enormous beds, fine cotton sheets, a welcoming bottle of Nederberg, gowns and slippers. Vivienne and Gerald are natural hosts, who provide great breakfasts and also picnic hampers for the beach or Robberg hikes, and mountain bikes and canoes for the madly active (a pool caters for loungers). They will also point you in the right direction for golf, and recommend a number of restaurants within easy walking distance.

Rooms: 5: 4 twins/doubles & 1 double; 3 with en-suite shower, 2 with en/s bath and hand showers.
Price: R350 – R620 pp sharing. Single supplement 50% out of season, 80% in season.
Meals: Full breakfast included and served from 8 – 9 am.
Directions: From Knysna take N2. Right at Shell garage into Plettenberg Bay. Turn 1st right into Cutty Sark Ave. Follow road round, then turn right again into cul-de-sac. House on left.

Map Number: 6

Cornerway House

Dee and Robin Pelham-Reid

61 Longships Drive, Plettenberg Bay 6600
Tel: 044-533-3190 Fax: 044-533-3195
Email: cornerwayhouse@mweb.co.za Web: www.cornerwayhouse.co.za

Robin and Dee recently moved from my Wiltshire school-town (as it happens) to start Cornerway House, and fantastic hosts they make too. Although new to Plett, they've wasted no time in unearthing its treasure – Robin is active on the tourism board – and will ably point you off to the beach with sundowners or to the Robberg Peninsula walk, an exhilarating experience. After drinks in their English drawing room, we repaired for dinner, where wine flowed and conversation roamed. Dee uses what she can from the garden, herbs of course, but artichokes and strawberries too on the day I visited. When a professional cycling team came to stay they were so well fed they failed to win a single race (… not that professional then!). I retired to my room – wooden antiques, comfy bed and sash windows looking onto the garden – and at dawn joined Ocean Blue to spot whales, dolphins and sharks, returning to a proper breakfast, courtesy of Robin. Dee teaches art in the township and throughout the house there are colourful quirks, to wit the yellow-washed and lilac shutters of the house, the petunias bathing in a bath, a purple TV sitting room with bright blue cushions and the pink and yellow mohair in the garden suite. I left Robin and Dee among the frangipani, gardenia and orange trees as I wrenched myself away.

Rooms: 5: 4 twins and 1 double; 2 with en-suite shower, 3 with en-suite shower and bath.
Price: R250 – R450 pp sharing. Single supplement plus 50%.
Meals: Full breakfast included. Lunch (salads & sandwiches) from R60; 3-course dinner from R120, includes pre-dinner drinks & bottle of wine per couple.
Directions: From N2 heading east, turn right into Plett. Continue to circle and go straight over. Road descends to river and crosses it. Over circle, turn right onto Longships Dr. Continue down 0.9km to Cornerway House on right.

Map Number: 6

Gulls View

Noel and Pam Mills

32 San Gonzales St, Plettenberg Bay 6600
Tel: 072-343-7217 Fax: 044-533-3498
Email: info@gullsview.co.za Web: www.gullsview.co.za

Gulls View is named for the feathered athletes who riot and curl in the thermals that funnel up the cliff at the sea-facing end of the garden. From the verandah, upstairs main bedroom and front rooms there are views in bands of searingly simple colour; a spread of blue sea, white beaches on the peninsula, then the green of a lawny (and wholly indigenous) garden filled with birds including the Knysna Loerie. Noel and Pam (who also have a (GG) guesthouse (Rockwood) in the Cederberg) have coaxed the second oldest house in town into the 21st century and built a whole new one too. This way you can live in the new house if there are only two of you, or use both if you are more numerous. The new house has an open feel with polished timbers, nice curvy wicker chairs, soft white, cream and turquoisey-green tones and billowy ivory-coloured curtains framing the view. All of which are right and proper for the sea. The little things haven't been forgotten either; TV and VCR, stereo set, CD player and, of course, a top-notch kitchen. The house is equidistant to several beaches (down a fairly steep hill) and a five-minute walk to the vibrant and trendy town where there are excellent restaurants. Louann lives next door and will meet and greet you and look after you as much or as little as you wish. *Children over 12 are welcome.*

Rooms: Self-catering house let as a whole, with 6 bedrooms.
Price: Low season: R500 per night for 2 sharing, plus R100 for each additional person; Middle season: R600 per night as above; High season (1st Dec – 20th Jan): R2,500 per night. Rates include servicing of house on week days.
Meals: Breakfast ingredients can be supplied on request at a cost of R30 pp.
Directions: Turn off N2 into Plett' at Shell Garage. Turn right at the roundabout, then left into San Gonzales St. Gulls View is 2nd last house on the right before Signal Hill.

Lairds Lodge Country Estate

Alison and Murray Brebner
Off N2 Highway, PO Box 657, Plettenberg Bay 6600
Tel: 044-532-7721 Fax: 044-532-7671
Email: info@lairdslodge.co.za Web: www.lairdslodge.co.za

Alison and Murray are by nature black belts in the hosting arts and have created an intimate, country-house experience for gourmets, in a great location and with sumptuous bedrooms. They take their hospitality (and cooking) seriously here and every guest is treated as special. It's an involving place too, guests coming together in the evening for drinks in the drawing room to mingle amongst sofas and ottomans, books, flowers, and family photo albums. Properly acquainted, guests are then invited to eat together at one table (not obligatory, but recommended). These dinners, based round speciality seafood and venison dishes, are the highlight at Lairds Lodge. For more intimate soirées, the Brebners have added an autumnal, exposed-brick wine room where you can also dine. The concrete floor tolerates spilled wine (though you may not). A honeymoon suite has been added too, its wet-sand walls in keeping with other rooms, but with its own lounge, patio and his-and-hers sinks. Elongated sash windows and flowing curtains stretch to high ceilings, and all rooms are plump with earthy-coloured rugs, cushions and throws. The Brebners' Cape Dutch homestead sits in 24 acres of grounds – plenty of space for appetite-building walks. You can sit by the fountain in the whitewashed courtyard, or in the pool, and simply admire the view across to the mountains. Plettenberg Bay's beaches and Knysna's lagoon are only a short drive away.

Rooms: 11: 2 standard queens with en/s shower; 7 deluxe rooms (3 king and 4 twin) en/s bath + shower; 2 garden suites (1 king and 1 twin) en/s bath + shower.
Price: R450 – R660 pp sharing. Single supplement 50%. Winter rates available from May to September.
Meals: Full breakfast included. 3-course dinner, including coffee and port: R160.
Directions: You'll see the sign directing you just off the N2 highway, 8km from Plettenberg Bay, 23km from Knysna.

Lily Pond Country Lodge

Niels and Margret Hendriks
The Crags 6602
Tel: 044 534 8767 Fax: 044 534 8686
Email: lilypond@global.co.za Web: www.lilypond.co.za
Cell: 082 746 8782

Lily Pond Country Lodge borders on Nature's Valley, with its beautiful, unspoiled beaches, and the Tsitsikamma National Park. The ponds of the title are carpeted with blue, white, yellow and magenta lilies and the island in the middle is a haven on which to sit marooned, watching frogs hop from one pad to another. I had always thought they only did that in Beatrix Potter. All the rooms have private sun decks, which lead out to the largest lily pond, beyond which you can stroll off along trails, which meander mazily past more ponds and into indigenous forest. You will spot many birds on the way. The building itself is modern with mustard-yellow and terracotta-coloured walls. Inside, the modernity continues, spiced up with an African theme. The carpeted bedrooms are neat and comfortable with semi-open-plan bathrooms. One of the lounge areas has a Pygmy bed, now used as a coffee-table, and framed tribal masks on the walls; while the nautical motif in the other reflects Niels and Margret's sailing days. They are a Dutch couple who fell in love with South Africa on holiday and decided they could not leave. They are new to the hospitality business and their attention to their guests is a breath of fresh air. Margret cooks with flair and presents her dishes delicately. And Niels delivers them with equal delicatesse! *Hiking, golfing, horse-riding, whale-watching, bungy-jumping, mountain-biking, boating and fishing all available in the area.*

Rooms: 6: 4 doubles, 1 twin, 1 king/twin; 4 with en-suite bath/shower, 2 with en-suite bath and separate shower.
Price: R375 – R575 pp sharing.
Meals: Full breakfast included. Picnic lunch and four course dinner on request.
Directions: Off the N2. From CT take first exit to Nature's Valley, from Port Elizabeth take second exit after the toll. Then follow R102 for 3km and turn right at the sign.

Bitou River Lodge

Sue and Paul Scheepers

Wittedrift Rd, Plettenberg Bay
6600
Tel: 044-535-9577
Fax: 044-535-9577
Email: info@bitou.co.za
Web: www.bitou.co.za
Cell: 082-978-6164

For well-heeled South Africans "Plett" is the place to summer and its sophisticated buzz can border on the frenetic. Which is why Bitou River Lodge is such a find. Situated to the east of town, it's close to Plett's glass-plated beach houses, bijou shops and restaurants, yet feels a million miles away. Paul and Sue wanted to make the most of the natural environment and have created a peaceful haven for nature lovers. The drive sweeps past a citrus orchard and horse paddock to the whitewashed lodge, which sits on five hectares of neat flower-filled gardens, with pool, chipping-green and river frontage. Behind pepper trees and honeysuckle, stable-style bedrooms have river-facing patios, where dazzling sunbirds congregate. The lime-washed, painted-pine rooms have slate-floored kitchenettes and bathrooms, and sliding doors keep them light-filled. Farmhouse feasts are served in the breakfast room, which adjoins a warm lounge where you can settle into birding books and watch the liquid-smooth lawn gather all before it – boulders, benches and flowerbeds – as it slips silently toward the lily-leafed river. While away some time out here, watching busy birds build coconut nests and lazy ones sway in the reeds, while the ripple of canoe paddles, the splash of a kingfisher and whiz of a fly-reel provide a soothing summer soundtrack. At night, guests carry picnics down to the candlelit riverbank. *In season the bay hosts whales, dolphins and seals.*

Rooms: 5: 3 kings and 2 twins, all with en-suite bath and shower.
Price: R255 – R455 pp sharing. Singles on request.
Meals: Full farmhouse breakfast included. Plenty of restaurants in nearby Plett.
Directions: Head east from Plettenberg Bay on N2. Immediately after bridge, turn left onto the R340. Bitou River Lodge is signed on left.

Map Number: 6

Southern Cross Beach House

Sue and Neill Ovenstone

1 Capricorn Lane, Solar Beach, Plettenberg Bay 6600
Tel: 044-533-3868 Fax: 044-533-3866
Email: info@southerncrossbeach.co.za
Web: www.southerncrossbeach.co.za Cell: 082-490-0876

…and relax. With this dreamy, whitewashed, wooden house at the quiet end of Robberg Beach's long arc, it is impossible not to. Plettenberg Bay is a lively town, with lots of restaurants and bars, but people really come here for the sea, and you would seriously struggle to get closer to it than at Southern Cross. During the Christmas holidays the beach is packed, but for the rest of the year there are more signs of life in the sea. Dolphins race by all year round, revelling in their position at the head of the food chain, with southern right whales often wallowing just in front of the house from June to November. The house itself is just up a wooden gangway from the beach. Wood predominates, with blues and white echoing the ocean. The brochure says 'plantation style', but I would plump for classic Massachussetts beach house. Wooden decking looks across the bay to the Tsitsikamma Mountains to the left and the Robberg Peninsula opposite, which is geologically identical to the Falklands, bizarrely… and a fantastic place to walk. Inside is the breakfast room and living room, and set around the garden on the ground floor (Sue and Neill live upstairs) are the five lovely rooms. Barefoot, laid-back luxury.

Rooms: 5: 1 double, 1 queen, 2 twins, 1 king; all with en-suite shower, 2 with baths as well.
Price: R375 – R595 pp sharing. Single supplement R150.
Meals: Full breakfast included. Kitchenette available for putting together salads and light meals.
Directions: From roundabout in Main St, go down hill past Central Beach, over Piesang River bridge. Over the circle, past shops (Kwikspar), right into Longships Ave. Straight over 3 speed bumps (2km). Left into Gris Nez Dr. Over stop street, left into Gemini, 3rd street on L. Turn right and then left into Capricorn Lane.

Map Number: 6

The Armagh Guest House

Johan and Marion Brink

24 Fynbos Ave, Storms River, Tsitsikamma 6308
Tel: 042-281-1512 or 042-281-1587 Fax: 042-281-1510
Email: armagh@mweb.co.za Web: www.thearmagh.com

Johan and Marion are not ones to sit on their laurels, and this year their Armagh enclave includes a swimming pool at the foot of the Tsitsikamma mountains. It's the perfect place from which to stargaze in a night unpolluted by the glow of conurbation. And to think it was only in the last edition that the zesty Rafters restaurant was added to the Armagh's zesty repertoire, feeding guests with home-cooked Cape-Malay food. This remains a fiercely unpretentious guest house, where the milk of human kindness prevails. The exterior of the building is face-brick, while the rest is made almost entirely of pine with a towering roof adding to the feeling of space – the whole place is soundly eco-friendly. The main part of the building combines the restaurant, connected to the bar, and a little loft sitting area up wooden steps, which looks down over the scene, perfect for relaxing and observing life in the guest house. Outside, a conical mountain, Storms River Peak in the Tsitsikamma range, looms over the indigenous garden, patched with small flower-bordered lawns. All the bedrooms open out onto this view and have vine-covered patios whence to enjoy it. Painted walls, snoring peacefully in low-key colours, are rudely awoken by dandy-bright cushions, counterpanes and abstract pictures. The beach is minutes away, as is the world-famous Tsitsikamma National Park.

Rooms: 5: 3 doubles & 2 twins, 3 with en-suite baths, 2 with en-suite showers.
Price: R225 – R450 pp sharing. Single supplement 50%. We advise you to book in advance.
Meals: Full breakfast included. Meals available all day in Rafters Restaurant and traditional dinner every evening.
Directions: 165km from Port Elizabeth and 65km from Plettenberg Bay. Turn off the N2 Highway into Storms River Village and you'll see The Armagh on the right.

Map Number: 6

133

Red Stone Hills

Petro and Hermanus Potgieter

Oudtshoorn 6620
Tel: 044-213-3783 Fax: 044-213-3291
Email: redstone@pixie.co.za Web: www.redstone.co.za

The humbling sense of the passage of time pervades this 3,000-hectare veld, whose desert colours swirl with Van Gogh vibrancy. For a start, the current Potgieters are the fifth generation to farm this land (ostrich, vineyards, cattle and fruit), but that lineage is put into perspective by the red stone hills. They date to the enon-conglomerate period, formed 65 million years ago when the earth twisted and a torrent of sanguine mud-stone settled and solidified; a few million years later, bushmen hid in the hills' stone pockets and painted wildlife; and in the 1790s Karoo cottages completed the picture. It's all been authenticated by erudite visitors: botanists, geologists and a chap from Roberts who identified 181 birds here, including eagles, black stork and five varieties of kingfisher. But you'll find Hermanus and Petro plenty knowledgeable themselves. We drove out along dusty tracks leading past the schoolhouse his father donated to the mixed community (which still congregates there), through babbling brooks to Chinese lanterns and blankets of fynbos and medicinal succulents. Hermanus will name them all. Petro says he lives in the past whereas she's an artist facing the future. She's currently planning open-air opera for their natural stone auditorium. There are many ways to enjoy the scenery, cycling, hiking, riding, fishing… and ostrich-rich Oudtshoorn is minutes away. When you're tired out, your sleepy cottage, with original Oregon pine doors and floors and farm-made furniture, awaits.

Rooms: 6 cottages: all fully self-contained with one, two or three bedrooms and shared bathrooms.
Price: R190 – R320 pp self-catering.
Meals: Full breakfast R50, Continental R40. 4-course dinner R140 pp, excluding wine. Light meals also available.
Directions: Red Stone is half way between Calitzdorp and Oudtshoorn on the R62. Head west from Oudtshoorn for 28km, then take the Kruisrivier turn-off. Red Stone is 6km down this road. There is another well-signposted entrance between the foot of the Swartberg mountain and the Cango caves via Matjiesrivier.

Map Number:

Williamsburg Farm

Renée and Nigel Williams
PO Box 10074, George 6530
Tel: 044-745-1013 Fax: 044-745-1013
Email: wbrgfarm@lantic.net Web: www.williamsburgfarm.net
Cell: 082-896-9862

Somehow ignoring the directions below, I forged my own route along a corrugated dirt road that descended through forest to a pastoral idyll at the foot of the Prince Alfred Pass, Thomas Bain's audacious route over the Outeniqua Mountains. Well and truly in cattle country, the road to Williamsburg becomes a sequence of grids and gates. It's a good route, if you're in no particular hurry. Bordering the semi-arid Klein Karoo, Williamsburg Farm is an uncut jewel. On its 2,000 hectares are two charming farmhouse cottages: one of sandstone with porch, stable-doors, painted stone floor, original timber and gas lamps; the other whitewashed, with green pitched roof, just one room deep. Azalias at the door, a green bench on a stoep covered by leaf canopy and purple fygies smeared across the lawn draw you outside to a naturalist's haven. The local flora fascinated botanist John Burchell, and fauna in these parts is pretty lively too with baboon, duiker and leopard and a long list of birds to tick off. For those with good shoes and the drive to use them, walking trails follow streams to rock art sites and lofty lookouts. This is also the place to hone your 4x4 skills under Nigel's tutelage, on some of SA's best trails. Suitably trained, you'll attack the Prince Alfred Pass with confidence! Alternatively laze on river banks or, as I did, simply gaze at the mesmerising grandeur of the surrounding mountains.

Rooms: 2 self-catering cottages, both with two bedrooms sharing a bathroom.
Price: R100 – R150 pp. Children under 16 from R65; under-5s free.
Meals: Self-catering only.
Directions: From George, take N12 north, turning east onto N9 toward Uniondale. Before Uniondale turn right onto dirt road toward De Vlugt and Prince Alfred Pass. Continue for 9km to Williamsburg Farm on left.

La Plume Guest House

Bartel and Karin Du Toit
Volmoed, Oudtshoorn 6620
Tel: 044-272-7516 Fax: 044-272-7516
Email: laplume@mweb.co.za Web: www.laplume.co.za
Cell: 082-820-4373

You can sense La Plume's self-assured, country style in the curl of the gateway, the crunch of the gravel and the glint of a limpid pool under a cloudless desert sky. Lawns mount like steps to a colonial homestead, two bay wings book-ending a shaded verandah. Within its airy auspices are rooms of solid character with hefty beams, pine architraves and theatrical drapes. Breakfast and dinner are eaten here, at antique yellowwood tables dressed with linen, silver and crystal. There's no doubt that a certain large flightless bird is the farming focus. Soft leather is spread over tables, oversized eggs and fluffy feathers decorate most rooms and ostrich fillet makes a regular and delicious appearance at dinner. Thankfully they stop short of inviting you to make a selection (as from the lobster tank in a seafood restaurant), but only just. If you're interested, Bartel will take you on an informative tour of the farm. Bedrooms are in a collection of converted farm buildings, linked by pebble paths. They're all large, some especially so, with bold brass beds, chandeliers and mod cons stowed in heavy antique furniture. There's still space for armchairs and armoires. A hostess *par excellence*, Karin's skill in the garden is equally evident. Among the plumbago, ghoenas, hybenia and inkalilie, you are invited to take your anarondak seat in a secluded box and peer over parasols to the spectacle of the Swartberg.

Rooms: 9: 5 kings and 4 twins all with en-suite bath and shower.
Price: R350 – R525 pp sharing. Singles R450 – R650.
Meals: Full breakfast included. 3-course dinner (ostrich fillet a speciality): R130 excluding wine.
Directions: From Cape Town follow R62 through Calitzdorp. Before Oudtshoorn, take right 7km to Volmoed. Turn left, La Plume on right. From George, R12 to Oudtshoorn, then R62. Turn left on R328 to Mossel Bay. Volmoed signed to right. Follow for 7km, La Plume on left.

Map Number: 5

The Retreat at Groenfontein

Marie and Grant Burton

PO Box 240, Calitzdorp 6660
Tel: 044-213-3880 Fax: 044-213-3880
Email: groenfon@iafrica.com Web: http://users.iafrica.com/g/gr/groenfon/

A tiny gravel road twists along the sides of this idyllic valley, beside the river that gives the Retreat its name, while abandoned Cape Dutch farm buildings line the route, which eventually leads to the Burtons' Victorian-colonial homestead. They ran a popular wilderness lodge in Namibia before trawling southern Africa for a new Eden, and it took years to find Groenfontein. It was worth the wait. The view from the verandah, where meals are served, crosses a valley and climbs the Burtons' own mountain before joining the vast Swartberg Nature Reserve. What with hiking trails and mountain bikes, the opportunities for merry traipsing are limitless. If (when!) it gets hot, you can swim in river or pool, or collapse inside the gloriously cool house. The original marble fireplace and pine and yellowwood flooring remain, but much has been built by Grant himself. This year he designed two slate-floor, reed-and-mud roof rooms (away from the house), with French-window views to the Swartberg. Airy bedrooms benefit from simple combinations of yellow, beige and cream. It is an incredible area to explore with kloofs, mountain wilderness, half-forgotten roads, with many animals to look out for – klipspringer, mountain reedbuck, mongoose, jackal, caracal and porcupine among them. But, best of all, you come back to delicious dinners, welcoming hosts and a truly relaxed household.

Rooms: 6: 2 doubles and 2 twins (in house), I en/s bath & shower, 3 en/s shower; 2 king/twins, I en/s bath and shower, I en/s shower.
Price: R410 – R620 pp sharing. Singles an additional R80.
Meals: Full breakfast and 3-course dinner (without wine) included. Light lunches and picnics from R20.
Directions: From Oudtshoorn take R62 towards Calitzdorp for 30km. Turn R onto dirt road signed Kruisrivier. After 17km keep L at fork as road gets narrower and follow for 10.7km until see sign for Burton's to your R. From Calitzdorp L at Groenfontein sign – 19km to house. Drive slowly on these roads.

Map Number: 5

The Port-Wine Guest House

Andrea Nel

7 Queen St, Calitzdorp 6660
Tel: 044-213-3131 Fax: 044-213-3131
Email: portwine@mweb.co.za Web: www.portwine.net
Cell: 083-261-9025

The key to the Port-Wine is Andrea herself who juggles a young family and her excellent guest house with kindness, energy and a sense of humour. No fingers wag and no tongues tut-tut. You can dress up for (excellent) dinners if you want, or you can shuffle up, like I did, in whatever rags you woke up in. Evening meals are a major feature at the Port-Wine (as Andrea is such a good cook, although *she* doesn't seem to think so) and everyone eats together. A concerted effort has been made to remain faithful to the house's 1830s origins, where possible saving yellowwood from the ceilings and recycling it into dressers and beds; the new ceilings are of reed and beams. Four-poster yellowwood beds are solid and firm with lacy canopies. During the day guests can lounge round the pool, visit the hot springs, explore the spectacular mountain passes nearby; or in the evening climb the mountain and count the satellites when the sun goes down. Nearby are three nature reserves, playgrounds for birders, bikers, hikers and fishermen, and Andrea, who is a registered tour guide, can organise an architectural walk around the town. Of course, the big draw in town is the wine. This regional fruit-bowl produces the country's finest port (there's a festival here to celebrate the fact) and there are cellars and vineyards for you to explore.

Rooms: 6: 3 doubles and 3 twins; 5 with en-suite shower, 1 with shower and bath.
Price: R190 – R375 pp sharing. Single rates on request.
Meals: Full breakfast included and served from 8 – 10 am. 3-course dinner R85 – R115.
Directions: Calitzdorp is on the R62 between Ladismith and Oudtshoorn. Ask for precise directions when booking or follow the road signs.

Map Number: 5

Die Lang Huis

Andrew and Sandra Thom
No. 8 Van Riebeeck St, Barrydale 6750
Tel: 028-572-1954 Fax: 028-572-1954
Email: andrewthom@xsinet.co.za

Driving to Barrydale via the pass you may be lucky enough to see blooms of leucadendron tradouwense, as it is snappily known to botanists, one of the world's rarest proteas. The Klein Karoo has a drier heat than the coast, making it perfect for morning and evening exploratory walks in search of other botanic gems. Simon van der Stel is reputed to have passed this way in 1689 when we are told the countryside teemed with game. Now one may be lucky enough to see a leopard as they take refuge in the mountains. Baboons are more commonly seen. Andrew used to live in Malawi and Lesotho and a few years back, he and Sandra had everything packed for a move to Scotland... but they saw this place on a Wednesday and bought it on the Friday. Die Lang Huis is a traditional Cape cottage facing the dramatic Langeberg Mountains and is proper B&B at its best, the living space shared with the most genuine of hosts. The elegant home feels English with a definite African twist. South African paintings decorate the walls and there are European antiques everywhere. The two bedrooms are delightful, one with a four-poster. The fire always jollies in the grate in inclement weather and on fine days you can breakfast on the wisteria-covered patio at the rear of the house, enjoying the lovely garden and uninterrupted views of the surrounding hills.

Rooms: 2: 1 twin and 1 double, both with en-suite shower and bath.
Price: From R200 – R250 pp sharing. Singles R225 – R275.
Meals: Full breakfast included. Will do picnic lunches on request from R25 pp.
Directions: From N2 through Tradouws Pass to Barrydale. Turn right towards the town and take a right at the first garage and into Van Riebeek St. Cross over Sprigg St and it's 2nd on the left.

Mimosa Lodge

Andreas and Yvette Küng
Church St, Montagu 6720
Tel: 023-614-2351 Fax: 023-614-2418
Email: mimosa@lando.co.za Web: www.mimosa.co.za

My flabber is gasted by what Andreas and Yvette have achieved since they left Switzerland and moved into their two-storey Edwardian townhouse in the middle of beautiful mountain-marooned Montagu. It helps that I adore Art Deco as there's a lot of it about: chandeliers, wardrobes, cabinets, revolving bookcases, chairs re-upholstered in daring colours. The bedrooms do not resemble each other one bit. Some are in the house, others in the dazzling flower garden, with its herbs and vegetables, orchard and black marble swimming pool. Colours are used with imagination throughout, some bold, some demure, but all give a true sense of luxury and space. Each suite has a CD player and all the rooms have a host of little extras: a decanter of Muscadel, books, magazines, fresh fruit, chilled water for example. An old shop counter has become the bar where guests congregate (and salivate) before dinner. Andreas is a chef extraordinaire, well-known by gourmets from all over the world, and people travel miles to sample his international variations on a South African theme. Only freshest ingredients are used and many originate from Mimosa's own lovingly-tended garden where Yvette has planted more than 200 plant species herself. I recommend Mimosa for a special treat. *Children by arrangement.*

Rooms: 16: 7 twins, 9 classic rooms, all with en/s bathrooms; 7 with bath & separate shower, 5 with shower, 4 with bath/shower.
Price: R265 – R700 pp sharing. R390 – R1,020 for singles.
Meals: Full breakfast included. Dinner (table d'hôte) in the restaurant R130.
Directions: Ask when booking, but Mimosa Lodge is clearly sign-posted in Montagu!

Map Number: 3

Fraai Uitzicht 1798

Axel Spanholtz and Mario Motti

Historic Wine and Guest Farm
with Restaurant, Klaas Voogds
East (Oos), Between
Robertson and Montagu on
Route 62, 6705
Tel: 023-626-6156
Fax: 023-626-6156
Email: info@fraaiuitzicht.com
Web: www.fraaiuitzicht.com

Klein Karoo, Western Cape

'Fraai Uitzicht' means 'beautiful view' in Dutch – no idle promise as it turns out. The 17th-century wine and guest farm is four kilometres up a gravel road in a cul-de-sac valley ringed by vertiginous mountains. People come from far and wide for the well-known restaurant and the seven-course *dégustation* menu is basically irresistible. Matched with local wine, it features trout salad, springbok carpaccio, beef fillet with brandy sauce and decadent Dream of Africa chocolate cake. Shall we just say I left with more than one spare tyre in the car. You could also be entertained by a Xhosa choir who give performances every other Wednesday night. Where to sleep is not an easy decision as you are spoilt for choice. A few cottages take it easy in the garden, each comfortable and pretty with impressionistic oils and views of the mountains, while others offer you masses of character with metre-thick walls and timber interiors; my favourite was the loft bedroom in the eaves. Or opt for one of the garden suites with their own entrances and balconies. Make sure you take a peek at the wine cellar – guests have first option on the (uniquely) hand-made merlot. I can't count the number of recommendations we had pointing us to Axel and Mario's door.

Rooms: 8: 4 cottages, 2 with 2 bedrooms (1 x queen & 1 x twin), 2 with 1 bedroom (queen & extra sleeper couch); 4 suites, 2 with king, 2 with queen, all en/s shower.
Price: Cottages are R600 pp. Suites are R400 pp.
Meals: Continental breakfast included. R30 extra for English. Lunch and dinner available on premises.
Directions: On R60 between Robertson & Ashton. Approximately 5km from Ashton and 12km from Robertson, Klaas Voogds East turn-off, 4km on gravel road, turn-off to left.

Map Number: 3

Merwenstein Fruit and Wine Farm

Hugo and Heidi van der Merwe

8km from Bonnievale on Swellendam Road, PO Box 305, Bonnievale 6730
Tel: 023-616-2806 Fax: 023-616-2806
Email: merwenstein@lando.co.za Web: www.merwenstein.co.za
Cell: 082-377-6638

Hugo and Heidi are quite simply the kindest people you will ever meet. Hugo will show you around the wine farm, around the fruit farm too, carry your bags to the car and generally be the most natural gentleman to all who cross his path. Heidi is cut from the same bolt of cloth. When I arrived she was off with guests (or temporary adopted family) to join her cousins at a picnic up in the mountains… and this is what it's like at Merwenstein. Everyone is welcomed in as one of the brood. Staff are too, and Felicity (Heidi calls Felicity her right hand… and her left hand too) will cook dinner in front of you and print out the recipes that you like. They do special dishes that you will not find in a restaurant. If Heidi is not too busy she will show you the creche for Xhosa children from very poor families that has been started with her help in Bonnievale. A neighbour farmer does cruises on a riverboat and if you are lucky you will see the very shy Cape clawless otter. I saw the dung so I know they are there! For bird-watchers, it's possible to see 90 species in only a few days, among them water dikkop, hammerkop, gymnogene, hoopoe and five different types of kingfisher. Breakfast is mouthwatering, sometimes served on the banks of the Breede River, and one of the best I had in South Africa. *Hier wird Deutsch gesprochen.*

Rooms: 3: all with en-suite shower.
Price: R225 – R250 pp. Single supplement plus R50.
Meals: Full breakfast included. Dinner R95 pp.
Directions: Use the same turn-off as for the Merwespont Wine Cellar, 8km from Bonnievale on the road to Swellendam.

The Old Mill Lodge

Karen and Spencer Hill
Voortrekker St, McGregor 6708
Tel: 023-625-1841 or 023-625-1882 Fax: 023-625-1941
Email: info@oldmilllodge.co.za Web: www.oldmilllodge.co.za
Cell: 072-529-3040 or 082-401-9340

Old Mill Lodge and McGregor itself lie deep in the Robertson wine valley only two hours from the Mother City, but a whole world away in temperament. The semi-arid Klein Karoo is just beautiful and these photos still don't do it justice. The horizon beyond the lake (just behind the Lodge) is crowded with mountains. You can walk over these on the famous day-walk to Greyton and swim at Oakes Falls. But for the not-so-hikey you can walk to the falls and back in a few hours from this side. Chef Spencer runs the family lodge with wife Karen and their three children. It's a quiet, relaxed, can't-hurry-we-live-on-a-vineyard sort of place. The farmhouse is also the restaurant. I ate a cracking crispy duck salad washed down with a local white on the stoep, looking down over orderly lines of grapes stretching towards the village. For winters there is a sitting room with a huge fireplace and comfy sofas and a bar with the intimate feeling of an Irish pub. The cottages are found up nearer the lake in indigenous fynbos gardens. They are whitewashed, split into two (you can take both halves or just one) and each shares a simple verandah. The thatched vaulted ceilings, slate floors and crisp white linens make it perfect for hot summer nights. 'Relaxed' doesn't even come near to describing the atmosphere here. *Massages available.*

Rooms: 8: 5 doubles and 3 twins. All en-suite with bath and shower. Two doubles have bath only.
Price: From R315 – R410 pp sharing. Singles an extra R70.
Meals: Full breakfast included. Light lunch from R20 – R35. Two-course dinners from R75. Three-course dinners from R105. Prices exclude wine.
Directions: From N2 take Stormsvlei turn-off, take McGregor turn-offs for dirt road options or keep on to Robertson, then take McGregor turning. Once in McGregor go up main road, take last turning right which is Smith St, then 1st left into Voortrekker St.

Collins House

Tessa and Sheila Collins
63 Kerk St (Church St), Prince Albert 6930
Tel: 023-541-1786 Fax: 023-541-1786
Cell: 082-377-1340

Collins House stands out on Kerkstraat, unusual as a fine two-storey Victorian townhouse among so many Cape Dutch gable buildings. The open-plan kitchen/sitting room is the warm heart of the house – check out the beautiful tile and wood floor – and when I arrived Tessa was in her 'office', an old desk in the middle of the room, creating wire topiary and listening to the cricket on the radio. There are french doors out to the flower garden, and the very large swimming pool and air-con in all the bedrooms are a blessing during Karoo summers. The town is full of Cape Dutch national monuments and snoozes right at the foot of the spectacular Swartberg pass. You must not fail to experience this and Tessa takes guests up there with evening drinks – or you can hire your own scooter in town. Collins House is long on luxury. Bedrooms are upstairs (almost a rarity in itself in South Africa) and you are mollied and coddled with fine-quality linens and lotions. Tessa herself has been with us from the start, is refreshingly outspoken and likes grown-ups who she can have a drink with and get to know. Luxury is one thing, but character is inimitable... and Tessa, Sheila and Collins House have that in spades. *No children. DSTV is available in the upstairs guest sitting room.*

Rooms: 3: all twins; 1 with en-suite bath, 1 with shower and 1 with bath and shower.
Price: R200 – R400 pp sharing. Single supplement R70.
Meals: Full breakfast included and served till 9.30 am.
Directions: On Kerkstraat in the middle of town.

Map Number: 5

Dennehof Karoo Guest House

Ria and Lindsay Steyn

20 Christina De Witt Street, Prince Albert 6930
Tel: 023-541-1227 Fax: 023-541-1124
Email: steynria@mweb.co.za Web: http://home.intekom.com/dennehof/
Cell: 083-302-5579 / 082-456 8848

New owners, but the same ethos, a genuine Karoo experience. The set-up remains unchanged, an 1835 Cape Dutch farmhouse and outbuildings on the edge of town, infused with personality. An entrance hall, with hand-painted floorboards and bright yellow irises, leads to a beautiful tiled room where a zebra-print sofa strewn with pillows sprawls beneath a gilt mirror. There's more Karoo country chic in the leopard-skin armchairs, upholstered chairs and dairy cabinet with cow-print crockery. Bedrooms are in the house or (erstwhile!) dairy and cow sheds with their whitewashed clay-and-straw walls, green doors and gable ends. Mine was just how I like it, creaking with character: 24-pane window, aged yellowwood shutters, worn wood floors, yawning timber ceiling and iron four-poster. The bathroom was just as big, with claw-foot bath, alcove shelving and shower spilling out a waterfall. On the somnolent stone stoep dozed a collection of chairs, a cushioned daybed and a reclaimed pew. Table settings sparkled in the sunlight, beyond which desert hills appeared through the feathery pepper trees. Then there's the Karoo hospitality. Negotiating the tractor in the road, we all joined the fun at the annual farm show before returning to an Afrikaans dinner of local lamb eaten *en famille*. Truly memorable. *Private, customised tours throughout E. and W. Cape can be arranged.*

Rooms: 4: 3 doubles, 1 with en-suite shower & bath, 1 with bath & 1 with shower; 1 twin with en/s shr. 1 room convertible to self-catering with sitting room & kitchen.
Price: R180 – R250 pp sharing. Single supplement plus 25%.
Meals: Full breakfast included. 3-course dinners by prior arrangement from R70 pp.
Directions: From Oudtshoorn, head north over Swartberg Pass. Turn left at T-junction into Prince Albert, Dennehof signed on right.

Onse Rus

Lisa and Gary Smith

47 Church St, Prince Albert 6930
Tel: 023-541-1380 Fax: 023-541-1064
Email: info@onserus.co.za, Web: www.onserus.co.za
Cell: 083-629-9196

The official pamphlet does a good job of conveying the delights of Onse Rus, but it modestly fails to bear testament to the biggest plus, the Smiths themselves. They fell in love with Prince Albert and the 150-year-old Cape Dutch Onse Rus in 1999 and their enthusiasm for both town and house has not abated since. Guests who have come down over the Swartberg Pass are given a whisky for their nerves and trips to The Hell, a famously isolated community 57km down a dirt track, are easily arranged. Back at the house, the large living room is hung with a permanent exhibition of local artists' work. The four thatched bedrooms all have private entrances, high ceilings, white walls and simple Karoo furnishings. One used to be part of the bakery, another was the printing room for a local newspaper. The house has some history! Lunch is available from Wednesday to Sunday, and if the weather permits – it usually does – you can sit out on the verandah and enjoy fig ice cream in the shade of the Cape ash and Karoo pepper trees. Now there is also a brand-new swimming pool, a thing of particular beauty in such a hot climate. And also a gazebo, a focal point for relaxing in the garden. Here guests are brought food and drink while leisurely hours are whiled away with good books.

Rooms: 4: 2 doubles and 2 twins (one twin sleeps 4). All with en-suite shower.
Price: R220 – R300 pp sharing. Single prices enthusiastically given on request.
Meals: Breakfast included. Pub lunches Wednesdays – Sundays. Dinner on request if restaurants fully booked.
Directions: On the main street (Kerk or Church St) on corner of Church and Bank Sts.

Map Number: 5

Lemoenfontein Game Lodge

Ingrid Köster
Beaufort West 6970
Tel: 023-415-2847 Fax: 023-415-1044
Email: lemoen@mweb.co.za Web: www.lemoenfontein.co.za

Lemoenfontein, in the shadow of the Nuweveld Mountains, is one of those places where whatever your mood on arrival – and after a tiring drive down the N1 mine was ropey – a calmness envelops you like magic vapour. I was suddenly enjoying a cool drink on the vast wooden verandah, gazing over measureless miles of veld and chatting happily to Ingrid about the history of the place. It was built as a hunting lodge in 1850, then became a sanatorium for TB sufferers (the dry Karoo air was beneficial), a farm and finally (and still) a nature reserve. Everything has been done well here, no corners cut and the result is a most relaxing, hassle-free stay. Rooms are stylish and understated with top-quality fabrics and completely comfortable beds. Outside, lawns, a new pool, bar and braai area and the veld are all segregated by high dry-stone walls. You *must* go on a game drive through the reserve before dinner – to look at all the buck and zebra of course, but also to be out in such scenery as the sun goes down. And one final thing: dinner when we got back was at first mouth-watering, then lip-smacking. A real South African experience. *All rooms are air-conditioned.*

Rooms: 12: 7 doubles and 5 twins all en-suite, 7 with baths and 5 with showers.
Price: R280 – R300 pp. Singles on request.
Meals: Full breakfast included. A set dinner is available every night.
Directions: From the N1, 2km north of Beaufort West. Go left at the sign to Lemoenfontein. Go 4km up dirt track, following signs.

Map Number: 5

Eastern Cape

The Cedars Guest House

Linden and Jeanne Booth

Matjiesfontein Farm, Baviaanskloof, Willowmore 6445
Tel: 044-923-1751 Fax: 044-923-1751
Email: jeanne@baviaan.co.za Web: www.baviaan.co.za

Just when I thought I had got to the middle of nowhere I turned off the beaten track into a cul-de-sac! Here you are surrounded by nature reserve mountainous wilderness on all sides. When you go for a hike amongst the stillness, silence and crystal-clear mountain pools you won't bump into another human soul for miles. You are truly 'out there'. On the numerous trails your rewards are bushman paintings in caves, beautiful kloofs and waterfalls, and then a relaxing home to come back to and a swim in the enormous, round, spring-water swimming pool. Linden and Jeanne make this an exceptionally special place with their warmth, calmness and enthusiasm for their piece of paradise. Jeanne insisted on giving me an aromatherapy massage and I certainly didn't object. Her fourteen years as a practising aroma- and massage therapist are manifested in a magical touch and the treatment was heavenly – be gone tense driving forearms! Come evening, I sat under the stars watching Linden turning the organic lamb ribs on the braai and then partook of a finger meal of roasted home-grown vegetables and walnut bread from yonder tree. The Cedars is simply delicious whichever way you look at it. *The guest-house also run a variety of workshops: 6-day body work retreat; exploring how art therapy assists psychological healing processes; indigenous medicinal plant education; skills and methods of bushman rock art paintings.*

Rooms: 4: 2 twins, 2 doubles, 1 bathroom with bath and shower, 1 with bath.
Price: Self-catering R250 – R300 pp.
Meals: Simple organic dinner and breakfasts by prior arrangement.
Directions: From Willowmore on N9 head towards Uniondale. After 2km turn left on R332 to the Baviaanskloof. Stay on this dirt road, following all signs to Baviaanskloof, go through Nuwe Kloof pass and after 8km turn right at sign to Cedars Guest House.

34 Lovemore Crescent

Monica Johnson
PO Box 85, St Francis Bay 6312
Tel: 042-294-0825 Fax: 042-294-0825
Email: dolfinvu@intekom.co.za Web: www.b-b.co.za
Cell: 082-695-3395

34 Lovemore is an unpretentious B&B and an absolute delight. This has everything to do with Monica's warm hospitality and the character of her home, built 20 years ago, though the beachside location is an added bonus. A cuppa appears on arrival and you are then shown up to your quarters, two large rooms under a high thatched roof, with a living area between them, all looking out to sea. The aloe-filled back garden is a bird-watcher's paradise where even the neighbours pop over for the viewing. The front garden has weaver-birds' nests in the trees and possibly Africa's most southerly baobab tree, a tenacious little thing brought down from Zimbabwe by the family in the '80s. And on the other side of the garden there is another separate flat, which can be rented on a B&B basis or as a self-catering unit (but you'd be missing out on an unforgettable breakfast of delicious home-made breads, scones, jams and all…). It lacks the sea views, so Monica feels duty-bound to offer it at give-away prices. With a sweeping vista across St Francis Bay, where southern right whales can be seen in season and dolphins year round, you cannot fail to relax here. Keen surfers will be interested to note (they will in fact salivate over the news) that Bruce's Beauties are at the end of the garden.

Rooms: 2 rooms in the house: 1 double with en/s shower and 1 twin with private shower and bath; 1 flat sleeping up to 6 with 1 bathroom.
Price: Rooms in the house: R250 – R300 pp sharing Flat: R160 pp self-catering, R200 with breakfast.
Meals: Full breakfast included for B&B in the house. Flat, as above.
Directions: From the Humansdorp road take 1st right into Lyme Rd South, then 3rd right onto St Francis Drive, then 5th left onto Lovemore Crescent. 34 Lovemore is sign-posted at each of these turns. 34 is the last house on the left.

Map Number: 6

Duxbury

Sheila Beckett

8 George Rd, St Francis Bay 6312
Tel: 042-294-0514 Fax: 042-294-0514
Email: duxburybb@worldonline.co.za

Duxbury makes no claims to being anything more than a very friendly, dyed-in-the-wool B&B. You stay in Sheila's comfortable, white-walled, thatched cottage in this quaint seaside village where strict planning regulations have ensured that almost all the other houses are thatched and white-walled too. Meet Sheila. She has an impish sense of humour and you are soon settled in, sipping a cup of tea, a co-conspirator in her tales of local, national and international matters. The guest rooms have private entrances and there is also a cottage in the garden. The white-washed walls of the interior contrast with the cheerful décor and this lends the house a fresh and enlivening feel. A leisurely breakfast, made to order by Sheila, is quite a spread and guests have been known to try and cajole Sheila into accepting more money for their stay, refusing to believe that such good value can still be found. Sheila is adamant though, and won't put her prices up. She loves her guests and wants them to experience fantastic SA hospitality. The best B&Bs are places where both owner and guest get as much out of the experience as each other. I give you Duxbury. *Sheila will sort out Kromme River and Marina Canals cruises and golf. The house is just 100 metres from the sea for safe beach bathing.*

Rooms: 2: 1 family suite (1 twin with private bath and shower, 1 king with en-suite bath): 1 cottage (twin with en-suite shower).
Price: R150 – R170 pp sharing.
Meals: Full breakfast included. Restaurants nearby.
Directions: Take Humansdorp off-ramp on N2 freeway from Cape Town 80km short of Port Elizabeth. Proceed down Humansdorp Main Street to T-junction opposite caravan park. Turn L to St. Francis Bay (18km). Take first turning L, 2km after crossing Kromme River Bridge, and follow signs to Duxbury.

Oyster Bay Lodge

Hans and Liesbeth Verstrate-Griffioen

Humansdorp 6300
Tel: 042-297-0150 Fax: 042-297-0150
Email: info@oysterbaylodge.com Web: www.oysterbaylodge.com
Cell: 082-700-0553

Here's yet another film set masquerading as a B&B… this one is for the beach scenes! Hans and Liesbeth have the very envy-inducing run of three and a half kilometres of pristine beach to themselves, the fine white sand of the dunes as pure as it is wind-driven (but for the odd monkey footprint). They have fifteen horses, eight of which are rideable, which roam free on the 235 hectare nature reserve, and the first time I visited there simply wasn't time for a beach ride. So I dreamt hard for two weeks and managed to dream it into reality, returning to experience for real the wind in my hair, salt air in my face and sun shining down… amazing. But there's more: Hans and Liesbeth have made hiking trails from the sand dunes through the fynbos where you'll have a chance to see some of the 140 species of bird on their land and maybe vervet monkeys. I could hear them, but didn't quite catch a glimpse. There are only two guest rooms in the house so your stay is very personable and relaxing with use of the swimming pool and self-catering facilities if you choose. Otherwise, supper could be some Oyster Bay rump steak from their cattle farm or the fresh catch of the day. Come here for the empty beach, the horses and walks along an unspoilt coastline. *Day-tours can be taken to nearby Tsitsikamma Nature Reserve and Baviaanskloof.*

Rooms: 2: 1 self-catering double room and 1 twin both with bath and shower.
Price: R250 - R350 pp sharing, depending on season. Booking advisable, but walk-ins welcome.
Meals: Full breakfast included, lunches by arrangement, 3-course evening dinner R125
Directions: From Cape Town on N2 turn off at exit number 632 Palmietvlei and follow signs to Oyster Bay Lodge. From Port Elizabeth take exit to Humansdorp and then follow signs to Oyster Bay Lodge.

Map Number: 6

Aqua Sands

Richard and Deborah Johnson
No. 7, 11th Avenue, Summerstrand, Port Elizabeth 6001
Tel: 041-583-3159 Fax: 041-583-3187
Email: greenwood@aquasands.co.za Web: www.aquasands.co.za
Cell: 082-462-6774

Aqua Sands is glamorous. Deborah, in red lipstick and a white linen dress, is glamorous. By the time I left, even I felt a bit glamorous too. She is a food stylist and husband Richard is a philatelist (a stamp dealer – but glamorous too!). And their open-plan contemporary home is a repository for an ever-changing, rotating collection of fine art. The guest rooms, with their own separate entrances, are blessed with crushed velvet or silk bedspreads, percale cottons and mohair blankets, red gerberas in fish-bowls and cactus-style soap dishes, an echo of the real cactus garden out there next to the tranquil koi fish pond. On my visit the builders were just completing a full-year visit constructing some unique living areas. Breakfast is served on the architecturally spectacular grey-slate-tiled patio under steel and wood, offset with vibrant splashes of pink, purple and cobalt paint blocks. This is surrounded by a lush garden where palm trees intermingle with indigenous plants and giant aloes… and beyond is the ocean, with safe bathing and sandy beaches a mere two minutes' walk away. If that's too far there's always the large heated saline pool, sauna and steam room within flopping distance of the breakfast table. I met grandpa too – another asset of the house – a champion fly-fisherman with photos to prove it. Come here for a holiday and not just a stopover!

Rooms: 3: 1 queen, 2 king/twin, 2 with en-suite bath and shower, 1 with en-suite shower.
Price: R350 – R450 pp sharing. Singles from R450.
Meals: Full breakfast included. Dinner on request.
Directions: From Cape Town take N2 to Port Elizabeth. Take exit 751B at sign for Settlers Way, follow signs to Summerstrand. Keep left onto Marine Drive along the sea front until 11th Avenue.

Broadlands

Rob Whyte
R336, Kirkwood 6120
Tel: 042 232 0306 Fax: 042 232 0306
Email: Info@broadlandsch.co.za Web: www.broadlandsch.co.za
Cell: 082-445-8837

Broadlands had me won over before I had even negotiated the drive: citrus orchards on either side, an avenue of palm trees, pink, purple and orange bougainvillaea, roses in profusion, an explosion of colour. The sweet aroma of nectar filled the country air. The lake opening out from the house overhung by weeping willows and orange grevillias beyond made my munching of home-made cookies all the more pleasurable. I can imagine the serenity at night, with the lantern lit at the end of the deck and light dancing on the water. The farm here has been in the family since 1885 and apart from the thousands of citrus trees and the pack-house, it looked quite different back then. Today, luxury rooms with chaise-longues, Victorian baths and an anglicized sitting room and fireplaces provide well-appreciated comfort. Freshly-squeezed orange juice for breakfast is, of course, a certainty. The house is just 25 minutes drive from the Addo Elephant Park and for an African bush experience in the real Africa, Rob will take you up to his nearby mountain lodge for a night spent in the wilderness where the sounds of the wild can be heard from the traditional boma. Alternatively he'll take you on a sundowner game drive amongst kudu, nyala and zebra.

Rooms: 4: 2 kings, 2 twins, 3 with en-suite bath and shower, 1 with en-suite bath.
Price: R350 – R450 pp sharing. Singles + 50%.
Meals: Full breakfast included, picnic lunches and dinners on request (2 courses R65).
Directions: From PE take R75 and take second turn off to Kirkwood onto R336. After 10km turn right onto a dirt road for 200 metres.

Map Number: 6 & 7

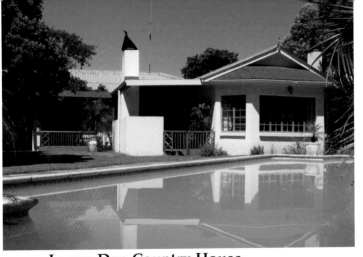

Lupus Den Country House

Priscilla and Noel Walton

Lupus Den Country House, Sunland, Addo, 6115
Tel: 042-234-0447 Fax: 042-234-0447
Email: info@lupusden.co.za Web: www.lupusden.co.za
Cell: 072-1814-750

Priscilla and Noel have not needed to learn any tricks about how to host. They are just naturally hospitable people who make you feel instantly at home and relaxed. When I arrived, lunch was waiting on the table and with a cool drink in hand I already felt part of the furniture. Priscilla and Noel have been living in their farmhouse for 40 years now – although the land it stands on has been in the family's hands since 1894 – and have recently made some adjustments to make the rooms all the more comfortable for their guests. Their citrus and cattle farm is found on the friendly dirt roads between Addo and Kirkwood. And when I say friendly, I mean locals waved hello to me all the way there! The garden, surrounded by citrus groves, blooms with bougainvillaea and an abundance of other flowers and trees. The tiled swimming pool – the type I am particularly fond of – and an enormous tipuanu tree are two of the garden's greatest assets, while vine-shaded terraces are the perfect places of repose after a rendezvous with the elephants in Addo (only half an hour away). You can be guided through Addo and other game parks in their neighbour's very comfortable open-top 4X4. When staying at Lupus Den you can be a tourist by day out in the parks and feel a local when back in the fold. Breakfast includes freshly-baked bread (naturally). A true farm B&B with home cooking – hard to beat.

Rooms: 3: 1 twin and 2 doubles, 2 with en-suite bath and shower, 1 with en-suite shower.
Price: R200 – R250. No single supplements. Children under 10 no charge. 10–12 years 50% of adult rates. Teenagers (13 up) full price.
Meals: Full breakfast included. Dinners (R65) and light lunches (R35), both by arrangement.
Directions: Map can be emailed or faxed.

The Elephant House

Clive and Anne Read

PO Box 82, Addo 6105
Tel: 042-233-2462 Fax: 042-233-0393
Email: elephanthouse@intekom.co.za Web: www.elephanthouse.co.za
Cell: 083-799-5671

The bush telegraph gave advance notice of the many charms at Elephant House. Many tourists and other guest house owners had urged us to visit with a sincerity you could not ignore. It's a stunning house, the brainchild of one night's sleepless pondering by Anne who mapped the whole thing out in her head – a small lawned courtyard surrounded on three sides by thatched and shady verandah. The house is in a sense inside out. The drawing room leads to a dining room outside on the verandah (with antiques and Persian rugs). All the bedrooms open onto the verandah too and dinner (advertised with an African gong) is served there on silver and crystal. Evening meals are lit to stunning effect with lampshades made of Tuareg bowls. Lawns, indigenous trees and the racehorse stud (Clive used to run one in Natal too) surround the house and when I was there the paddocks were full of mares with their foals. The bedrooms are luxurious with antique furniture, carpets, thick duvets and deep beds; and morning tea or coffee is brought to your bed, if so desired. There is also the Stable Cottage, which, separate from the main house, retains the same charm, just a little cosier, and you can prepare your own Continental breakfast under the vines in your private garden. The Elephant House also runs open-vehicle game drives in Addo, a few minutes away, morning and afternoon.

Rooms: 9: 4 twins, 4 doubles, all with en-suite bath and shower; 2 have outdoor showers. Also 1 cottage with en-suite shower.
Price: Seasonal. R800 – R1,200 pp sharing, Stable Cottage R360 – R450 pp sharing.
Meals: Full breakfast included in Elephant House. Self-served Continental for Stable Cottage. Lunch & dinner by arrangem't. 3-course dinners R120 – R150.
Directions: From P.E. R335 through Addo 5km on the road towards the park – you will see a sign off to your left for The Elephant House.

The Safari Lodge at Amakhala

Justine and Mike Weeks
PO Box 9, Paterson 6130
Tel: 042-235-1608 central reservations Fax: 042-235-1041
Email: centralres@telkomsa.net Web: www.amakhala.co.za
Cell: 082-448-2971

As I soaked in my double bath, candles lit, the late sky glowing pink with pleasure, birds twittering, bush buck barking in the surrounding hills and lions roaring from afar (or so I chose to think...), it crossed my mind that this was perhaps not the toughest assignment of my life thus far. Amakhala Safari Lodge is surely the luxurious way to experience the game parks of the Eastern Cape. Beds, equipped with mosquito nets, are super-comfortable and there's a sofa area inside each thatched hut whose canvas fronts and terraces look onto the valley brush and the waterhole below. The bedrooms and the communal hut are decorated with Cape antiques and furniture carved from the wood on Mike's farm. Mike and Justine aren't always at the camp, but Jaco and Rian, their rangers, are sure to take good care of you. After a delicious meal – usually served round the fire outside – and a good night's sleep, an early wake-up call takes you to the Addo Elephant National Park to admire its ponderous pachyderms at close quarters. Game drives to Amakhala Game Reserve follow in the afternoon, with its beautiful and varied scenery of bushveld, savannah, cliffs and animals... lots of animals. Lions should have been introduced into a separate section of the reserve by the time you read this and then the 'big five' will be complete. *Day trips to the neighbouring Shamwari Game Reserve are included in a 3-day package.*

Rooms: 4: 2 twins, 2 king/twins, all with en-suite double baths with shower attachment and outside showers.
Price: Summer R1,980 pp sharing. Winter R1,480 pp sharing. Singles plus 30%. Inc. meals, drinks and 2 safari activities a day (game drives, river cruises, guided walk to discuss indigenous plants with Xhosa game ranger).
Meals: All included.
Directions: From PE take N2 for 60km towards Grahamstown. Turn left on gravel road to Paterson and follow signs.

Leeuwenbosch on the Amakhala Game Reser

Bill and Rosemary Fowlds
Off N2 between Port Elizabeth and Grahamstown
Tel: 042-235-1252 Fax: 042-235-1252
Email: tickbird@mweb.co.za Web: www.amakhala.co.za
Cell: 083-383-2921

Leeuwenbosch has gone from strength to strength since the first edition and remains a real South African find offering an unbeatable colonial safari experience. Firmly established as the senior partner in the Amakhala Game Reserve, it is a place full of zest and character, which has steadily been building its portfolio. There's a whole lot more in the game reserve now and with rhino, cheetah and elephants as new additions the 'big five' is almost complete. Game drives and river cruises for birding and fishing are a must and if you are staying for a few nights a bush dinner is also recommended. Meals are generally served in the Dutch settler's house and remain intimate, convivial and delicious, thanks to Rosemary. For their accommodation, guests can either choose the Victorian mansion with its antique furniture, antique full-sized billiard table and antique photographs of Fowlds ancestors, or the contemporary shearer's lodge. This now houses four luxury rooms each with its own stoep, ideal for lounging in wicker chairs and watching Shamwari game across the way. Bill's tiny cellar pub remains an intimate forum for story-telling and a mini-chapel rounds off the Leeuwenbosch 'village', constructed in time for William Fowlds junior's wedding. All the family chip in to make your stay personable and memorable.

Rooms: 8: 4 rooms in the manor house, 2 twins, 2 doubles all with en-suite bathrooms. 3 twins, 1 double in lodge all with en/s shower and bath.
Price: R1,195 – R1,800 inclusive package of two reserve activities (game drive, river cruise, night drive, canoeing, guided walk) breakfast, lunch & dinner. Dinner B&B from R650. Off-season & last-minute specials.
Meals: Full breakfast included and served until 9.30 am. Dinners are included in the price. Lunches included in package.
Directions: From P.E. take the N2 to Grahamstown (do not take Paterson) for 67km where you'll see signs for Leeuwenbosch on your right only 1.5km beyond Shamwari turn on the left.

Map Number: 7

Witmos Oxwagons

Giles and Jennifer Gush
Paterson 6130
Tel: 042-235-1608 Fax: 042-235-1041
Email: centralres@telkomsa.net Web: www.amakhala.co.za

A Voortrekker would instantly recognize the authentic canvas-covered wagons but perhaps not the giraffe-setting or the trimmings of comfort, even luxury, that have been woven into the camp. Beds are enticing these days with cotton linen and down duvets, which are – like magic – toasty when the night air is cold, but cool on hot nights. In the modern mode of things, each wagon has its own private bathroom down the wooden steps, just a few paces away, lamp-lit. Giles's ancestors were in the oxwagon transport business, so it is perfectly meet and right that the wagons should come to rest on his family land that was once sheep farm, now game reserve. And, yes, what is extra fantastic about the camp is that just a few hundred metres away, yet fenced off, are the giraffes, zebra, rhino, elephant and antelope of the Amakhala Game Reserve. Sitting on the large sundeck, while breakfasting or dining, the savannah-land and its grazing animals are clearly visible and audible – and just a few metres away, I was thrilled to see a vervet monkey with her baby. Game-drives and river-cruises are utterly recommended and also pop in to visit Jennifer at the conservation centre. She has a PhD in zoology and facilitates the monitoring of the game from here. *Dinners are sometimes served at Woodbury Lodge, also located in the reserve.*

Rooms: 3 oxwagons, each with private bathrooms with showers.
Price: R575 pp sharing dinner B&B. In winter cost per night includes a game drive. Game drives R300 pp in summer.
Meals: Breakfast and dinner included. Picnic lunch by arrangement.
Directions: On N2, 80km from PE towards Grahamstown. Woodbury Lodge sign on the right.

Château Blanc

Ann White
32 Westbourne Road, Kenton-on-Sea 6191
Tel: 046-648-1271 Fax: 046-648-1271
Email: annwhite@telkomsa.net
Cell: 083-354-8189

I imagine Ann standing on her balcony, drinking in the Bushman's River opening out onto the Indian Ocean before the house, the fine white sand, the turquoise-blue water, the sand dunes, an intoxicating vision that fills the senses, and thinking, "I really should share this with as many people as I can!" Ergo Château Blanc. She moved here from a farm near the Winterberg Mountains and, as she says, once a farm lass, always a farm lass. She has bought her warm hospitality and baking with her (I had some yummy carrot cake) and she has even secreted a bonsai herb and vegetable garden where you wouldn't have thought one could exist. She has no lawn or vines but just three paces from her house is the beach where blue river meets blue ocean meets blue sky, giving you the best kind of garden you could wish for. In the area you can try out a variety of water-sports (water-skiing, boating, canoeing, surfing, diving), fishing, golfing, horse-riding, or simply enjoy a sunbathe and picnic on the beach. I'm not quite sure why Ann's home is called Château Blanc as it is a camouflaged, sandy-yellow colour and has no castle-like pomp or grandeur. Here you are simply a guest within an unpretentious home with a light-filled room and an ocean view. 100 per cent personable B&B at its best.

Rooms: 2: 1 double with en-suite bath and shower and 1 twin with private bathroom. Single-group bookings only.
Price: R220 pp sharing.
Meals: Full breakfast included. Dinners on request. Restaurants nearby.
Directions: From PE take R72 and turn right into Kenton-on-Sea. Go down Kariega Road until 3-way stop, turn right down River Road, turn left into Westbourne Road.

Map Number: 7

Woodlands Country Cottages

Bev and David Selwyn-Smith

Kenton-on-Sea 6191
Tel: 046-648-2867 Fax: 046-648-2867
Email: woodlands@compuscan.co.za
Web: www.accommodation-kenton.co.za Cell: 082-808-5976

Hidden amidst the woodland surrounds of Bev and David's twelve-acre garden are five brick or wood cottages, isolated, peaceful and brimming with rustic charm. Each has a private deck and braai area, a double wooden hammock swaying enticingly under the trees and its own secret section of the garden, a private haven of indigenous bush, diverse plantlife, expanses of lawn and a wealth of bird life. You can even bird-watch from your private, outside (but enclosed) boma bath; or many like to light candles and soak at night under the stars. The cottages are all kitted-up for self-catering, but Bev's breakfasts are a fully-recommended treat: not only a tempting medley of quiches, omelettes, muffins and pancakes eaten in the garden room, on picnic benches, or anywhere anyhow in the garden; but also an opportunity to meet Bev and David who are charming and unpretentious hosts, and passionate about the Eastern Cape. Unspoiled beaches and game reserves are a ten-minute drive, golf is a chip and a putt away, but shade, verdant surroundings and solace are to be found at Woodlands. Last but not least, David is a self-proclaimed cribbage champion and the on-site pub is the perfect location in which to try and win a free night or two off him.

Rooms: 5 cottages: 2 doubles, 3 twins, all with en-suite bathrooms.
Price: R195 pp sharing B&B, R150 pp sharing self-catering
Meals: Full breakfast included for B&B.
Directions: From PE take R72, past Alexandria, turn left on R343 to Grahamstown and Kariega Game Reserve, go 2km and turn left.

Proctorsfontein Farmhouse and Hermitage

Brian Rippon
PO Box 400, Nr. Grahamstown 6140
Tel: 046-622-2382 Fax: 046-622-2382

Brian Rippon is the perfect host and gentleman (he won't like me saying!): attentive, well-travelled, amusing company and unreasonably humble about all that he, a tri-lingual artist and vet, and Proctorsfontein, his well-loved and lived-in 150-year-old homestead, have to offer. That's why he needs me to blow his trumpet for him… which I think I've just done! You stay as house guests with breakfast, dinner, any drives in the country or out on the cattle farm (when they happen), even drinks (within reason) included in the price. So dump your bags, go for a swim in the pool, take a turn in the garden (the farm has long views over the Assegai River Valley) and join Brian when you're ready for drinks and dinner. Solid country cooking is based on roasts and the like, prepared by housekeeper Poppy, and Brian has many fine wines. Or a braai can be arranged at the family's tented camp in the wilderness. The bedrooms have delightfully faded edges, books everywhere, Brian's accomplished landscapes on the walls and pots of impatience (the flower not the mood) to brighten the day. Hearty farmhouse breakfasts are served on the black slate patio. This is a place where I felt instantly at home. *Dam fishing available. Proctorsfontein is half an hour from Shamwari and Kariega Game Reserve; 1 hour from Addo Elephant Park.*

Rooms: 2: 1 double room with private bathroom; 1 upstairs apartment with twin room and en/s shower.
Price: R350 – R400 pp sharing.
Meals: Full breakfast and dinner included.
Directions: From Port Elizabeth 80km on the National Road to Grahamstown (N2). Turn off to Sidbury on gravel road for 20km to Proctorsfontein.

Map Number: 7

Settlers Hill Cottages

Marthie Hendry
71 Hill Street, Grahamstown 6140
Tel: 046-622-9720 Fax: 046-622-9720
Email: settlershill@imaginet.co.za Web: www.settlershillcottages.co.za
Cell: 082-809-3395

Marthie Hendry's passion for Grahamstown and its history is infectious and will envelop you too, if you stay in one of her delightful cottages, built and originally inhabited by British settlers in the 1820s. Sheblon, an intimate, thatched cottage, is a national monument near the evocatively-named Artificers Square, the city's original artisan quarter. Jasmine, with its separate garden cottage, and Belhambra cottages are larger, but similar in charm and character. Martie's pride and joy is the latest addition to her collection, Settlers Hill Manor. This Victorian house has been recently renovated and has shining yellowwood floors and spacious rooms with en-suite bathrooms, plus a rose garden fronting it despite the trials and tribulations of rose-planting in South Africa. The decoration throughout is a blend of original features and modern where these matter (i.e. in bathrooms and kitchens…), but the notable lack of ostentation only adds to the authenticity. You will be hard-pushed to take any of it in, however, if you attempt everything on Marthie's Things-to-Do-in-Grahamstown list, which is as long as a man's arm. She loves taking people around the imposing Victorian buildings in town or to the witch-doctor shop nearby, where a Xhosa herbalist can mix you up some good luck potions.

Rooms: 4 cottages: 2 are self-catering; Jasmine cottage and Settlers Hill Manor are B&B, and have 7 en-suite bedrooms.
Price: R250 – R300 pp B&B. Self-catering R200 pp.
Meals: Full breakfast included for B&B. There are a number of restaurants within walking distance.
Directions: Marthie meets guests at 71 Hill St, which intersects the High Street at the Cathedral.

The Cock House

Belinda Tudge

10 Market St, Grahamstown 6140
Tel: 046-636-1287 Fax: 046-636-1287
Email: cockhouse@imaginet.co.za Web: www.cockhouse.co.za
Cell: 082-820-5592

The Cock House offers a warm and friendly welcome and fine dining in the setting of a historic old house in downtown Grahamstown. Nelson Mandela has stayed three times and current President Thabo Mbeki has also been a guest (their visits are recorded in photos on the walls of the bar). The recent death of Peter Tudge has been a huge blow to the whole staff, but they have pulled together and it is clear that they enjoy working here. Belinda has taken Peter's place behind the delightful yellowwood bar, a favourite with the locals, and there's always an opportunity to strike up a conversation. The house dates back to 1826 and was one of the first built in Grahamstown. The rooms are named after previous owners, most recently South African author André Brink. A stone-floored verandah stretches along the front of the house (mirrored by a wooden balcony upstairs) and the interior is full of yellowwood beams and broad planked floors. I can recommend the restaurant, which offers an international cuisine with a South African flavour and has its own herb garden, using local and seasonal ingredients wherever possible. The home-made bread is a particular treat. The two large rooms in the main house have glass doors opening onto the balcony and the six converted stables open onto the garden. Personal and fun.

Rooms: 9: 6 doubles, 3 twins, 7 with en-suite bath and shower, 2 with en-suite shower.
Price: R330 – R400 pp sharing. R390 – R480 single.
Meals: Full breakfast included and served anytime. Lunch and dinner available in the restaurant (except Sunday lunch). Dinners from R115.
Directions: From P.E. take 2nd exit from N2 signposted "Business District/George Street". Take off-ramp L, turn L at bridge into George St. Continue down long hill into Grahamstown. At 4-way stop with Market St turn R and you will see the Cock House on the right corner.

Map Number: 7

Coral Guest Cottages

Cynthia and Alf Kleinschmidt

Jack's Close, Port Alfred 6170
Tel: 046-624-2849 Fax: 046-624-2849
Email: cynthia@coralcottages.co.za Web: www.coralcottages.co.za
Cell: 082-692-3911

Staying in Cynthia and Alf's settler's cottage was like being transported back in time, a charming old structure with an unlikely and rather romantic history. Once upon a time, in the mid-1800s, it housed the consulting rooms for a Doctor Jones-Phillipson, having previously been transported to Port Elizabeth from England, then to Grahamstown and then by ox-wagon express to Port Alfred. Our own Alfred, of the Cynthia-Alf variety, discovered the cottage in disrepair and decided to dismantle it, treat the wood and resurrect it body and soul in their front yard. Quite a mission, but well worth the effort! So thank you Alf for your entrepreneurial spirit. Now guests can sleep in a well-travelled Oregon pine cottage, which is quite an exclusive experience. Cynthia's daily and delicious contribution is breakfast, her speciality in both variety and eclectic style. She can cook different breakfasts every day for two weeks, so what you have depends on her creative inspiration on the morning in question. I sampled her eggs benedict africano with cheese sauce and grated biltong, but you may get her crêpe speciality with potatoes, mushroom, bacon and sausage. The beaches nearby are not to be missed so make sure you allow enough time to enjoy them in a relaxed way.

Rooms: 2: 1 twin and 1 double, both with shower.
Price: R185 (in winter) – R245 (in summer) pp sharing.
Meals: Full breakfast included.
Directions: Off the R72 in Port Alfred.

The Loerie Hide

Sue and Nigel Rainer

2B Sheerness Rd, off Beach Rd, Bonnie Doon, East London 5241
Tel: 043-735-3206 Fax: 043-735-3302
Email: info@loeriehide.co.za Web: www.loeriehide.co.za
Cell: 082-458-9825

You would never have guessed that there could be such a garden in the middle of East London. For behind the urban facade lies a densely-forested river valley. The garden plunges down to the Nahoon river and steep paths pick their way down through jungly vegetation full of trees that come straight from Tolkien… dragon trees, num-nums, river euphorbia, sneezewood and quar to name but a few. The trees of the valley are a natural aviary and if you're lucky, the flamboyant and lumbering loerie may be seen hopping around in the branches. Guests sleep in three units (two thatched) around the pool with a fourth self-catering option adjoined to the house. The styles are African (leopard and zebra skin prints, cane furniture) or rustic-cosy (brass bed, thatch, antiques, stone floor). The birds, meanwhile, get busy washing themselves in a bath made from an old grinding stone. Breakfast is served up on a wooden deck attached to the main house, where bougainvillea spills over the balcony and shade is provided by large umbrellas. Nigel and Sue are an extremely hospitable couple, who clearly love their home. I'm not surprised.

Rooms: 4: all doubles with en/s bathrooms, 3 with showers, 1 with a bath and a shower.
Price: R190 – R300 pp sharing and R240 – R350 for single occupancy.
Meals: Full breakfast included.
Directions: Ask for details when you book.

Umngazi River Bungalows

Terry and Tessa Bouwer
PO Box 75, Port St Johns 5120
Tel: 047-564-1115/6/7 Fax: 047-564-1210
Email: umngazi@iafrica.com Web: www.umngazi.co.za
Cell: 082-321-5841

The wild coast may be South Africa's most spectacular and yet least touristy region with its rocky coastline, indigenous forests, secluded coves and many river mouths. And all this is on your doorstep at Umngazi, a lively family holiday resort where the only time you will spend indoors will be to sleep and eat. The relaxed and informal lodge is on the banks of the Umngazi estuary so you can choose between swimming in the pool, the river or the sea, fishing off rocks or boats and walking in the forests. Bird-watching cruises are also organised for sunset. Ferries transport guests over to the beach from a river jetty. Meanwhile, back at home you will be missing out on tennis, snooker and table tennis. I guarantee that a week here, however lazy you are, will see the colour back in your cheeks and a bit of muscle on the arms and legs. And your sense of time will go haywire. Children are well catered for with trampoline, fort, sandpit and designated dining room. You have a choice of sea-, river- or garden-facing cottages and there are three honeymoon suites with working fireplaces, sliding doors onto private patios, sea views, a big spa bath and double outside shower. Weekly fly-in packages are available Friday to Friday from Durban where you fly at 500 feet above sea level along the beautiful coastline – a wonderful experience to start a holiday.

Rooms: 65 bungalows: twin or double on request, all have en/s bathrooms, most with baths and showers.
Price: R350 – R499 pp sharing all-inclusive. Fly-in package R4,500 – R5,050 pp includes flight, 7 nights, all meals & transfers from Virginia Airport. Pick-up/transfer from Durban Int R200 pp.
Meals: All included.
Directions: From the south, Umngazi lies 90km due east of Umtata. From the north, via Flagstaff and Lusikisiki to Port St Johns on a tarred road. There is also a transfer service from Umtata and a private flight service between Durban and Port St Johns.

Map Number: 8

Comfrey Cottage

George, Gerda and Grant Freeme

51 Stephenson Street, Lady Grey 9755
Tel: 051-603-0407 Fax: 051-603-0407
Email: info@comfreycottage.co.za Web: www.comfreycottage.co.za
Cell: 082-576-7224

Spectacular views, passes and geological formations sculpted by volcanic action, such are the Witteberg Mountains on the Maloti route. This is not known as the most scenic route in SA for nothing! Glancing out over magnificent mountains, windy roads, oh and watch out for the goats made me a bit late – sorry about that – but instantly a cup of tea and sandwich sprang forth for a hungry traveller. Hospitality here rules ok. The three G's have recently renovated their hundred year-old cottages into high-comfort Porcupine's Place, with its wooden floors and French door onto the garden; Comfrey Cottage, with its Queen Ann coal fire, old retro fridge and pink-and green stove; Robin's Nest, with its wrap-around balcony and benches on the verandah; Apple Crumble, still to come; and the newly-built, smart-yet-relaxed lounge and dining room. The garden is filled with fifteen different species of fruit trees – pears, figs and walnuts amongst them - and someone was swinging in a hammock contemplating the mountain as I passed. Mountain rambles, bird-watching, visiting the art academy and George's geological tours are favourite activities here. There are unique geological features and alpine flowers at the south-western edge of the Drakensberg and they merit an explanation. What's more, Tiffindell, the only ski resort in SA, is nearby, so be prepared for breathtaking snow-capped mountains come winter.

Rooms: 10: 6 doubles and 4 twins, 2 with en-suite baths, 8 with en-suite showers.
Price: R280 – R300 pp sharing for dinner B&B. Self-catering possible.
Meals: Full breakfast and 3-course dinner included.
Directions: From Jo'burg, take N1 to Bloemfontein, then take N6 to Aliwal North and R58 to Lady Grey. Then follow signs to Comfrey Cottage.

Leliekloof Valley of Art

Dries and Minnie De Klerk
Burgersdorp 9744
Tel: 051-653-1240 Fax: 051-653-1240
Email: sanart@intekom.co.za

What a place! Magnificent Bushman art and high-altitude wilderness to nourish the soul; log fires and home-cooked meals to look after earthier parts. Dries and Minnie have landed on their feet at Leliekloof, a farm adjoining their own property which they acquired a few years ago. The river here has chiselled a tortuous gorge through the sandstone and ironstone hills and the many caves host thirteen remarkable sites of Bushman art, many of the paintings of indeterminable age. Dries took me for an exhilarating morning drive and we visited two of them, Eland and Dog Caves. The quality of the paintings is superb, Dries a full reservoir of information about both the images and their artists. There is also a two-day scenic 19-kilometre hike around the valley, and a large dam for canoeing and trout fishing. Art apart, the countryside will extract from you superlatives you never knew you had. Single guests usually stay, for reasons of sociability, at the De Klerks' farm, while others have the run of Leliekloof House nearer the valley. The magnificent main room is 22 metres long, with sitting area, yellowwood bar, fireplace and huge antique Oregon pine dining table. You can self-cater, but given the stellar quality of Minnie's food (and the variety of things to do), I strongly suggest that you ask her to prepare your meals. Two nights minimum stay recommended.

Rooms: 1 farmhouse with 3 bedrooms (2 dbl and 1 twin, 2 with en-suite bath, 1 en/s shower) plus a loft sleeping 4; also 1 extra bathroom with bath & shower.
Price: Full board rates: R380 – R440 (for three or more). R400 – R460 for 2 people. Single rates on request.
Meals: Breakfast, lunch and dinner included. Dinner is 3 courses including bottle of wine.
Directions: 6km south of Jamestown on N6 turn towards Burgersdorp. Turn right after 10 km. After another 5.5km fork right and Leliekloof is another 1km. Map can be faxed.

Map Number: 7

The Stagger Inn

Robin and Berta Halse & Sean and Ann Bryan

Carnarvon Estate, Sterkstroom 5425
Tel: 045-966-0408 Fax: 045-966-0408
Email: carnarvon@worldonline.co.za Web: www.carnarvon-estate.com
Cell: 082-445-1032

So nice to arrive somewhere and instantly know that the people there will make your stay all the more enjoyable. I wasn't even asked if I'd like lunch… it was assumed and presented. Tea? That came too. Smiling, warm faces are a given at the Stagger Inn and all three generations of the family that help on the estate exude a contagious enthusiasm for it. So here you are in the great outdoors with 25,000 acres of pristine wilderness at your beck and call. You can bird-watch, fish for rainbow trout and large-mouth bass, swim in the weirs of clear spring water, go boating on the dams, do some clay pigeon shooting and spot some of the fifteen species of antelope on game-drives (also lynx, jackal, genets, black eagles, fish eagles and vultures). Or you can just walk among the indigenous shrubs and wild flowers. Ruddy-faced and hungry from the fresh air and activities, guests cosy up by the blazing log fire before a hearty, healthy dinner of home-cooked produce fresh from the farm (cows, sheep, pigs, sawmill and a dairy). And then to bed, hunting-lodge-style in renovated old farmhouses with comfortable (rather than luxurious) rooms for a well-needed night's sleep. As I discovered in the morning, the quality of light up here is a phenomenon, and the views breathtaking. The rolling ridge-country and grassy plains reach as far as the eye can see. Make sure you stay for long enough.

Rooms: 6: 1 double, 4 twins with en-suite bathrooms; 1 double for self-catering with en-suite shower.
Price: R275 – R350 pp dinner B&B.
Meals: Full breakfast and dinner included.
Directions: From Queenstown, take the N6 for 50km and turn right on the R344 towards Dordrecht and follow signs to Stagger Inn (gravel road for 7km).

Redcliffe Guest Farm

Johnnie and Carol Morgan

PO Box 137, Tarkastad 5370
Tel: 045-848-0152
Email: info@dtours.co.za Web: www.dtours.co.za

Johnnie and Carol kindly adopted me for the night when I couldn't – or rather didn't want to – leave their unspoilt country idyll in the depths of the Winterberg Mountains. This is an escape from everything apart from cows, sheep, birds and the natural environment that supports them. The simplest way to enjoy the area is to go for a hike across the rolling grassland hills. The gorge on a neighbouring farm is, I think, the most spectacular spot I have been privy to in South Africa and it goes virtually unvisited. The plateau folds in on itself and plummets hundreds of metres down, waterfalls dropping from terrace to terrace. Or you can go swimming, trout-fishing, mountain-biking, horse-riding, bird-watching, or play tennis back at the house. Carol may cook you her speciality stuffed leg of lamb for dinner and Johnnie will happily show you around his shearing shed. He is especially proud of his merinos whose pure white wool is used to make smart Italian suits. Guests here have all the space they could need both outside and inside the five-bedroom farmhouse, including a light-filled sun room. A real home and the area of highland farms is still to be discovered even by the more adventurous overseas traveller. Surely it is only a matter of time.

Rooms: 1 farmhouse: 1 double and 4 twins, 3 en-suite and 2 with private bathrooms.
Price: R525 pp lunch, dinner, bed and breakfast minimum 2 people, R150 pp self-catering minimum 3 people. Phone to discuss group prices.
Meals: Breakfast, lunch and dinner on request. Self-catering also an option.
Directions: On R344 between Tarkastad and Adelaide. Directions faxed or emailed.

Cavers Country Guest House

Kenneth and Rozanne Ross

R63, Bedford 5780
Tel: 046-685-0619 Fax: 046-685-0619
Email: ckross@intekom.co.za Web: www.cavers.co.za
Cell: 082-579-1807

I can't be the first to call Cavers an oasis, but it is irresistible. There in the distance a stand of tall oaks shimmers unconvincingly in the haze. And then suddenly you are among well-watered and mature gardens, an Eden of lawns and vivid flowers. The fine stone, ivy-encased farmhouse was built in 1840 and has been in Ken's family for four generations. The bedrooms, with wooden floorboards, high ceilings and voluptuously draped windows, are refined and elegant. From one of the upstairs rooms I got an impression of living in the trees with an hadeda nesting at eye level and yellow orioles twittering and fluttering about. Two grand upstairs rooms with pressed-metal ceilings have balconies overlooking the profusion of flowers below. The thatched cottage also has long views over the lawns and up to the Winterberg Mountains. Rozanne is a maestro in the kitchen, cooking with fresh produce from the farm and the surrounding area, and all her meals are mouth-watering feasts. The memory of that salmon cheesecake is even now a Pavlovian trigger that gets the mouth watering. There is a clay tennis court, hiking and riding or even cricket on the magnificent ground nearby. Swimming is in the pool or a big round reservoir. *The guest house is also available as a serviced self-catering unit sleeping 8 – 10 people for the month of December 2004 at a daily rate.*

Rooms: 5: 4 rooms in the manor house: 2 twins & 2 king/twins, 2 en-suite shower, 1 bath, 1 shr & bath; 1 cottage has 1 twin & 1 double sharing bath & shower.
Price: R375 – R500 pp sharing, dinner B&B. The Guest House is available as a serviced self-catering unit sleeping 8 – 10 people for the month of December 2004 at a daily rate.
Meals: Full breakfast and 3-course dinner included. Light lunches on request.
Directions: 8km from Bedford on the R63 towards Adelaide, turn left at the sign and follow the dirt road for 8km.

Map Number: 7

Glen Avon

Bill and Alison Brown

PO Box 154, Somerset East, 5850
Tel: 042-243-3628 Fax: 042-243-3628
Email: glenavon@xsinet.co.za

Glen Avon is the working incarnation of my ideal farm, neatly cosseted in its own valley and hemmed in by mountains. The old homestead - farmed by Bill's family for seven generations - is surrounded by mature gardens and a river which runs through the pastures near the house. There is a preternatural sharpness of definition to both sound and vision… the swish of a cow's tail, the random bleat of a sheep, even the buzz of a bee seemed to ring clear in the morning air. Bill showed me round, including a visit to the historic water mill, which he restored to operational standard 20 years ago. Its watery revolutions have now been stilled, but it is a powerfully nostalgic place to explore. Daily farm business continues unabated, however, and guests can opt to 'help' milk the cows and and shear the sheep and angora goats. Fresh milk, eggs, butter and the peerless lamb that I had for dinner are all home-produced, as are Alison's delicious bread and jams. Activities include fly-fishing, canoeing, tennis, and there are nature trails up to the Glen Avon Falls high in the Bosberg Mountains. Moreover, experts and amateurs alike will feast on the farm's cornucopia of flora and fauna; over 230 species of bird alone can be spotted. When it's time to flop, guests stay in a cosy cottage with stone floors and traditional period pieces.

Rooms: 2: 1 double and twin sharing a bath (can be self-catered); and 1 twin with en-suite shower.
Price: R170 – R200 pp sharing B&B. Self-catering on request.
Meals: Full breakfast included. Dinner on request R60 – R90.
Directions: Turn off N10 at Cookhouse to Somerset East. Go 14.8km and then turn right on gravel road at brown B&B sign. Follow this for 6km to Glen Avon.

Die Tuishuise

Sandra Antrobus
36 Market St, Cradock 5880
Tel: 048-881-1322 Fax: 048-881-5388
Email: tuishuise@eastcape.net Web: www.tuishuise.co.za

Unique accommodation indeed! Sandra has a raptor's eye for historic detail, laced with an antique dealer's nose and the heart of an interior designer – unparalleled in my experience of South Africa. There are 25 houses along Market Street, all antiquely furnished to reflect different styles, eras and professions. The houses were once lived in by bank managers, teachers, wagon makers etc, and you step into their 19th-century shoes when you stay – although the bathrooms, perhaps, retain a little more modernity. Each house is an antique shop in its own right, but modern comforts include fans, heaters and fireplaces. I was lucky enough to visit them all and it is no exaggeration to say I was struck dumb – reason enough for Sandra to have gone to the effort (some might feel). The hotel, a Victorian manor at the end of the street, has a further 19 rooms similarly done out in the style of the time and sherry is served in the drawing room before buffet dinners (my Karoo lamb was delicious). Sandra and her daughter Cherie are dedicated to presenting South African history in a way you can touch and feel. They do cultural performances epitomising the Xhosa and Afrikaner culture - ask in advance. *Closed Christmas Day.*

Rooms: 25 restored 19th-century houses, each rented out as one 'unit'. There is also a hotel.
Price: R250 – R270 pp sharing. No single supplement.
Meals: Breakfast served until 10 am. Traditional dinners available.
Directions: From PE take N10. When you arrive in Cradock at 4-way stop turn left into Market St. Die Tuishuise is 3rd block on left.

Wheatlands

Diana and Arthur Short

Route R75, Graaff-Reinet 6280
Tel: 049-891-0422 Fax: 049-891-0422
Email: wheatlands@wam.co.za
Cell: 082-414-6503

Guests at Wheatlands are thoroughly spoilt. I had read that the main house had been built on the profits of ostrich feathers in 1912 (a so-called 'feather palace'). I'm not sure why, but this led me to expect a humble farmhouse… and to get my shoes muddy finding it! But no. I found instead a gigantic manor house with a façade dominated by three extravagant gables. The house, designed by Charles Bridgeman, mingles Cape Dutch and Edwardian styles with a lovely white-pillared verandah at the back and then a green lake of lush lawn where heritage roses grow like weeds. Park your wagon (or whatever you are driving these days) in the huge sandy courtyard and enter a long, cool, wood-panelled hall, an instant pleasure as you leave the desert heat of the Karoo. It's an appropriate home for the piano, all the antique furniture and the Persian rugs. The corridors are lined with books, there is a snug for reading and guest bedrooms are not converted outhouses, but an integral, lived-in part of the house. There are wonderful wanders to be had in the revelation of a back garden. Diana and Arthur are astoundingly nice people, brimful of the hostly arts. Diana cooks delicious dinners, which are eaten at one large oak table. Arthur, meanwhile, is a serious wool and mohair farmer and cricketer… they even have their own ground.

Rooms: 3: all twins, 2 with en/s bathrooms with baths and showers, 1 with private bathroom with bath.
Price: R250 – R300 pp sharing.
Meals: Full breakfast and dinner included (Karoo lamb a speciality).
Directions: 42km on the R75 south of Graaff-Reinet – Wheatlands turn-off to the left, 8km up a gravel road.

Abbotsbury

Sue and Gordon Scott
PO Box 551, Graaff-Reinet 6280
Tel: 049-840-0201 Fax: 049-840-0201
Email: abbotsbury@cybertrade.co.za Web: www.abbotsbury.co.za
Cell: 072-486-8904

A three-kilometre drive on a dirt track takes you up into the land that time forgot, a small perfectly-formed valley that the Scotts call home. Sue and Gordon are there to greet you in their improbably lush and well-tended garden, which seems immune to the Karoo sun's forbidding glare. An ingenious old water furrow running down from the dam must take some of the credit for this, although a fence has also been added to protect the garden's aloes and roses from midnight-feasting kudus... of which there are plenty despite the privations. Gordon, in fact, has a game-viewing vehicle (a battered old Landcruiser) and will take you in search of the ten species of antelope and other Karoo wildlife on the farm – or you can hike up the mountains yourself. Back at base, guests either stay in a lovely old cottage, circa 1880, or a twin-bedded suite attached to the Scotts' own, even older house. Neither lack for character, with polished yellowwood floors, restored old furniture and photographic prints and artwork on the walls. Sue takes your supper orders when you book so as to have a fresh farm supply at the ready (springbok and Karoo lamb specialities) and you are served in your own private dining room with solid silver cutlery and bone china. Breakfasts are also a royal affair. *Nearby: the sculpture garden of the Owl House, historic Graaff-Reinet, and the awe-inspiring views of the Valley of Desolation.*

Rooms: 2: 1 twin suite with en-suite bath and shower; 1 cottage with double and twin with private bath with shower attachment.
Price: R230 – R270 pp sharing.
Meals: Full breakfast included. Dinner on request R65 – R80.
Directions: 27km north of Graaff-Reinet on N9, turn left onto 3km farm track to Abbotsbury.

Cypress Cottage

Hillary Palmé

80 Donkin St, Graaff-Reinet 6280
Tel: 049-892-3965 Fax: 049-892-3965
Email: info@cypresscottage.co.za Web: www.cypresscottage.co.za
Cell: 083-456-1795

Everyone from Greenwood Guides has now been to stay at Cypress Cottage and it is a pleasure to recommend it to you too. After a hot – and possibly bothersome – drive to this historic Karoo town, it is an immense relief to be welcomed by people as easy-going and instantly likeable as the Palmés… and to be installed in a beautiful early 1800s Cape Dutch cottage… and to find yourself minutes later, cold beer in hand, on a stoep with magnificent mountain views. The bedrooms in the cottage are understatedly decorated with a (highly developed) taste for the natural and comfortable, thus the high reed ceilings, solid pine and slate floors, antique chests, fresh flowers and free-standing baths. Breakfast is laid up outside on the terrace – free-range eggs from house chickens, succulent figs, peaches, prunes and apricots from the orchards. Everything is as fresh and natural as possible. Guests can swim in the bore-hole-fed reservoir, which has been converted into a swimming pool. The garden is an extraordinary feat of will and clever engineering – Hillary has managed to turn desert into lush vegetation despite the difficulties of brackish water. Graaff-Reinet is worth at least two days' stopover in my opinion – Cypress Cottage many more.

Rooms: 3: 2 doubles and 1 twin. All with en-suite bathrooms; 1 with bath, 1 with shower, 1 with both. All with aircon and heating.
Price: R220 – R350 pp sharing. Singles on request.
Meals: Full breakfast included.
Directions: From south: enter the town and pass the police academy on L and go over bridge. Two filling stations on L – take the road between them (West St). Follow to the very end, turn R into Donkin St, guest house first on L. From north: R at T-jct (Caledon St). 4th Left is Donkin St. House last on R.

Map Number: 6

Auberge Caledonia

Johann Swiegelaar and Michael Smit

61 Somerset Street, Graaff-Reinet 6280
Tel: 049-892-3156 Fax: 049-892-3157
Email: caledonia@adsactive.com Web: www.graaffreinet.co.za/auberge
Cell: 082-774-1795

In one of the oldest towns in South Africa, this is the oldest hotel. Built in 1854, it was renovated in 1881 by a hotelier who had it "comfortably fitted up" so that it would "be found cool, clean and comfortable". 123 years later Johann and Michael have embarked on a fresh overhaul that would make that Victorian owner proud. The flat-fronted, wooden-shuttered building sits right on the street and has something of provincial France about it. Double-doors sweep you into a broad and breezy hallway whose smoothed-and-grooved floorboards lead out to a dappled courtyard, its table settings shaded by an ornamental vine. The bedrooms are arranged in adjoined outbuildings, one accessed through the garden, by way of rose parterre and plunge pool, the other from the street. Rooms have honey-coloured wood and whitened walls and are simply furnished with enough space for a film crew to sprawl out in (as they did when I visited). The rooms offer a cooling refuge when the Karoo turns up the heat. One place you won't feel the heat is in the kitchen. That's strictly Johann and Michael's domain. In a Provençal-style dining room that matches the cuisine, they serve up culinary sensations. In 1881 Mr McMurray was determined that the "requirements of the inner man... be strictly attended to"! Johann and Michael espouse this admirable motto as their own.

Rooms: 6: 4 double suites with en-suite shower and bath; 1 double and 1 twin both with en-suite shower.
Price: R210 – R280 pp sharing. A single supplement of 40% may apply in season.
Meals: Full breakfast included. There's an à la carte restaurant on the premises serving dinner daily, mains from R50.
Directions: Faxed when booking.

Map Number: 6

Andries Stockenström

Beatrice and André Barnard

100 Cradock Street, Graaff-Reinet 6280
Tel: 049-892-4575 Fax: 049-892-4575
Email: stockenstrom@elink.co.za Web: www.stockenstrom.co.za
Cell: 082-783-2360

Only those discerning few that choose to stay at Andries Stockenström hold a valid passport to Beatrice's famous dining room. This firmly-upheld house policy keeps it small, atmospheric and intimate, and also means that Beatrice can give her four-course dinners her undivided attention. The food is therefore divine. She selects only the best regional produce to conjure up South African haute cuisine - vegetarians are most welcome, by the way. Here are a few snippets from my menu to get your fingers tapping: de-boned leg of Karoo lamb with potato timbale and Madeira sauce, ostrich fillet with creamy orange sauce, gratin of frozen hazelnut nougat with rum and granadilla sauce. The breakfasts are no less monumental. Andries Stockenström is a Georgian building dating back to 1819 and the high ceiling in the elegant restored dining room is the ideal canopy beneath which to savour Beatrice's feasts. The rooms are cosy, yet refined; upholstered furniture, wooden floors and reed ceilings all making appearances. There is also a brand-new garden room with doors leading onto the patio of the plunge pool. Graaff-Reinet is the fourth oldest town in SA and merits a good look around. But I say again: only if you stay at Andries Stockenström can you eat in Beatrice's dining room!

Rooms: 6: all king/twins, 3 with en-suite bath and shower, 3 with en-suite shower.
Price: R630 – R720 pp sharing dinner B&B.
Meals: Full breakfast and 4-course dinner included.
Directions: Emailed or faxed.

Ganora Guest Farm and Excursions

JP and Hester Steynberg
Nieu-Bethesda, Graaff-Reinet 6280
Tel: 049-841-1302
Email: ganora@xsinet.co.za Web: www.ganora.co.za
Cell: 082-698-0029

JP and Hester, along with visiting palaeontologists and guests, are thrilled with the historic finds on their farm, which together demonstrate a South African heritage spinning back in time from the Boer war to the Bushmen dynasty, to the pre-dinosaur era. 'Give us one day and we will give you 240 million years,' says the brochure. They originally bought their 4000-hectare Karoo property to farm Dohne-Merino sheep, famous for their fine wool (shearing and grading fleeces demonstrated in the shearing shed) and excellent meat. Then JP hit the Jurassic jackpot, so to speak, finding a horde of fossils in an ancient mud slide; and a tip-off from the previous owner led to Louis and Reiner (JP and Hester's teenage sons) finding a cave with not only the engravings from an escapee of the Boer War, but also bushman and Khoi paintings. Hester pointed out the image of a tortoise, the only one found in SA, and explained to me the methods and significance of the art. If history is not your thing (but it will be), you can go horse-riding to the nearby canyon, bundu-hike up the Compassberg Mountain, swim in the Karoo river pools or visit Helen Martins' weird and wonderful Owl House. Guests stay in a tiled-floored, whitewashed, converted kraal (sheep-pen) and, though it is not super-luxurious, after an activity-filled day, a four-course supper and a bout of star-gazing, a good night's sleep is had by all.

Rooms: 1 cottage: 2 twins, 1 bunk-bed, 1 bathroom with shower.
Price: R380 – R420 pp, inc. visits to Boer War engravings, bushman rock shelter, fossil museum/walk & woolshed visit. Self-catering option available. R280 DB&B and lunch from the second day.
Meals: Full breakfast, lunch, tea, dinner included in price.
Directions: Emailed or faxed.

Map Number: 6

KwaZulu Natal

Ivory Beach Lodge "The Cottage"

Massimo and Nicci Negra
379/1 Outlook Road, Southbroom 4277
Tel: 039-316-8411 Fax: 039-316-8411
Email: masniki@venturenet.co.za Web: www.ivorybeachlodge.co.za
Cell: 082-440-9489 or 082-331-3202

Sybarites and nature lovers will find equal delight at Ivory Beach Lodge, the Indo-African style home of Massimo and Nicci Negra. Built on a secluded beach, with vistas of pounding surf and densely-vegetated dunes, guests are accommodated in 'the cottage', a self-contained bungalow which floats in a leafy canopy of trees in the steeply sloping garden. A footpath from the property leads onto seemingly endless golden miles of mostly people-less beach. Organic thatch, wood, rough walls and pigmented floors blend seamlessly with luxurious furnishings. A well-equipped kitchen and decking along the seaboard side make alfresco dining a delight, with whales and dolphins making regular appearances. The property has a salt-water rock-pool and sun deck. This stretch of coast is dubbed the golf coast and Ivory Beach backs onto the fifth tee of one of many excellent golf courses along the coastline. The Negras' award-winning trattoria, La Terrazza, is the obvious place to eat, a 20-minute stroll from the homestead. In July (or so!) billions of breeding sardines come to the coast, trailed by giant flocks of seabirds that dive-bomb the frothing feast. Thousands of dolphins join in too and there are tours out to watch the phenomenon. As for 'the cottage', it remains one of the best beach houses I have ever visited.

Rooms: 1 cottage: 2 bedrooms with bathroom with double shower. Fully equipped kitchen for self-catering and a sitting room.
Price: R350 – R450 pp sharing. Children under 12 half price.
Meals: Fruit, coffee and milk provided. Continental breakfast by arrangement R50 pp. For lunch and evening meals their restaurant is 800m down the road.
Directions: Take the N3 south. Exit at Southbroom South, travel 400 metres, turn first right into Outlook Rd and follow for 2km (approx). Look for number 379/1 down a driveway on your left.

Map Number: 8

Ironwood Lodge

Jim Keightley
7 Figtree Lane, Pennington 1484
Tel: 039-975-1895 Fax: 039-975-3895
Email: info@ironwood.co.za Web: www.ironwood.co.za

As I parked my car below the garden and walked up the steps (old ironwood railway sleepers) to the house, I was met by a barefoot man lightly sprinkled with dust, who introduced himself as Jim. Jim had taken advantage of a few precious moments of guestlessness to finish making a set of chairs, and as a thoroughly impractical person myself, I was drawn to all this hands-on know-how. It turns out that Jim is one of those polymath South Africans with umpteen strings to his bow. He has been in turn a fisherman, geography teacher and cabinet maker. He does most things around Ironwood Lodge himself, from picking mussels off the beach and cooking them (or if not mussels then other fresh seafood), to building irrigation channels taking rainwater to his veggies, and making the furniture for the terrace. This is generally where meals are served, often by Jim and Caron's two children, Clinton and Warren, who clearly enjoy taking turns as head waiter. "Ironwood has a garden of Eden... except you can pick the fruit and you don't get thrown out!" wrote one guest, and Jim likes guests to enjoy the fruits of his labour (you'll get masses at breakfast). The six large, spacious bedrooms share the sea-view and come with their own garden or terrace upstairs. The beach is just over the road and golf courses proliferate in the area. A very relaxed vibe.

Rooms: 6 units: 2 doubles; 1 with shower, 1 with bath. 4 units with a double and twin and kitchette; 3 have showers, 1 has a bath.
Price: R195 – R350 pp sharing. Singles on request.
Meals: Full breakfast included. Dinner by arrangement; 2 courses from R78 (excluding wine).
Directions: From Durban take N2 to Pennington off-ramp. Follow signals to Pennington on R102 going south. Take left into Pennington, drive down to end and shopping complex. Left into Impathie Road about 800m left into Figtree Lane.

Map Number: 14

Rosetta House

Bill and Lee McGaw

126 Rosetta Road, Morningside, Durban 4001
Tel: 031-303-6180 Fax: 031-303-6180
Email: info@rosettahouse.com Web: www.rosettahouse.com
Cell: 082-447-6689

I can't describe Rosetta House as an urban oasis, for all its verdant credentials, as the whole neighbourhood is a symphony in green; but I can certainly give it both thumbs up. Lee used to travel as a medical rep and is therefore expert at second-guessing those small but vital items you have left behind and providing them for you. The house has a big sitting room opening through to the dining area and the kitchen, where Lee prepares her heavenly breakfasts. On fine days you will have it out on the terrace, overlooking the lush, immaculate garden, whose four tall sentinel-like palms are frequently visited by a family of hadedahs, and the sea beyond. I whiled away a few idle moments looking out past King's Park rugby stadium and wondering where that ship in the bay was going (I eventually realised it was anchored, so not far was the answer). There's one room below the terrace, one inside and two others along the railway-sleeper path that crosses the garden. These have their own terrace and kitchen if rented together – but all the rooms are lovely. As a town house you will be grateful for all the convenient extras such as aircon, laundry, phone/fax/internet connection, safety deposit box, secure parking… and for the proximity of Rosetta to shopping, beaches and sports venues.

Rooms: 4: 1 double en/s shower in the house; 2 garden rooms sharing a kitchen (1 twin and 1 double, 1 en/s shower, 1 en/s bath); 1 double en/s shower.
Price: from R285 pp sharing. Singles from R399.
Meals: Full breakfast included. Close to some 30 restaurants for other meals.
Directions: Faxed when booking.

Map Number: 14

Seaforth Farm

Trevor and Sharneen Thompson

Exit 214 off N2, Salt Rock, Umhlali 4390
Tel: 032-525-5217 Fax: 032-525-4495
Email: ttastym@iafrica.com Web: www.seaforth.co.za
Cell: 082-770-8376

Seaforth Farm is a full-blown treat of a guest house. Trevor and Sharneen have many interests, talents and motivations and Seaforth is a constant source of stimulation. Trevor is an official tour guide and will advise you on the 'must-do's' in the area. If you visit in summer there are dolphin tours. Freak numbers are often sighted off the coastline (300 – 500 are normal, but once 3000 were seen, and 11 whales too) and these trips are very popular with guests. Sharneen is a water-colourist and has also won medals for flower-arranging, so the house blooms with extravagant displays and paintings. Trevor is a skilled craftsman and much of the furniture has been made in his workshop (his latest piece, a huge lychee-wood bed) – and it is highly accomplished work. The garden is lush and wild and envelops everything at Seaforth in tropical colour. There are brahman cattle, chickens, pawpaw and pecan trees, and the dam and its abundant bird life. Trevor is coaxing it in with a cunning plantation of pond weed, lilies and islets, and you can bird-watch from a hide overlooking the dam. The guest house provides large, well-equipped bedrooms, a pool and thatched summer-house with dam-view for heavenly breakfasts and candle-lit curry evenings cooked by Mirian Nkhomo, their long-standing housekeeper. Finally, the staff have a stake in the success of their venture. A pioneering guest house indeed…. *Zulu spoken.*

Rooms: 4: 1 family cottage with 2 bedrooms, each with en/s shower; 2 doubles and 1 twin with en/s shower and bath.
Price: R280 pp sharing. Family suite (sleeps 5) from R720.
Meals: Full breakfast included.
Directions: From Durban take the N2 north. Exit on the 214 signed Salt Rock. Go 200m and take the 1st right into Old Fort Road, then 1st left into Seaforth Ave – the house is at the end.

Fairlight B&B

Bruce and Michele Deeb

1 Margaret Bacon Avenue, (Corner South Beach Rd), Umdloti Beach 4350
Tel: 031-568-1835 Fax: 031-568-1835
Email: bdeeb@mweb.co.za Web: www.fairlight.co.za
Cell: 082-775-9971 or 082-443-8529

I got my first taste of Bruce and Michele's laid-back hospitality as soon as I arrived. It was another hot KZN day and I was bustled off for a joyous dip in the sea just across the road – "We can talk later". And we did. This newly-refreshed 'inspector' was soon sipping a cold beer by the pool and tucking into some delicious Lebanese pastries and thoroughly South African boerewors as Bruce tended the braai. The garden behind the house is dominated by two large milkwoods, a great place to shelter from the sun, although there are also sun-loungers around the swimming pool. The front of the house has a wooden deck running all along it, from where you can watch the surfers – all the rooms open onto it. Dolphins love the surf, too, and if you're lucky you can swim with them. Bruce can lend you a boogie board and flippers. Inside, it is effectively a family home and luxury guest house rolled into one – plenty of light and air as befits a beach house, family snaps on the wall and a warm, welcoming vibe to it. Rays of positive energy emanate from Michele and Bruce and their long-standing housekeeper Maria. Soak it up, then go forth and fish, surf or swim with a big smile on your face. Ten miles of heaven, a.k.a. Umdloti Beach, are but 40 paces from the house. *Durban and the airport are both within half an hour's drive.*

Rooms: 6: all sea-facing with en-suite shower (3 with bath and shower).
Price: From R350 – R450 pp sharing. Singles on request from R450.
Meals: Full breakfast included. Meals and picnics by request.
Directions: N2 exit to Umdloti. Follow down to roundabout. Keep right past Total garage and Fairlight is 500 metres along Beach Rd.

Nalson's View

Wendy and Kelvin Nalson
10 Fairway Drive, Salt Rock
Tel: 032-525-5726 Fax: 032-525-5726
Email: nalsonsview@3i.co.za
Cell: 083-303-1533

After a long, long (long, long) day on the road I finally emerged from my car at Nalson's, wild-eyed and mud-besmattered. I couldn't have pitched up anywhere more perfect. Kelvin and Wendy welcomed me as if I had been living there for years. This was my room, these my beers and friends… I owned the place didn't I? A fantastic shower washed off the mud (don't ask) and I was invited to dinner. I couldn't tell who were guests, who were family friends, such is the open-house air of friendship here, and the meal was out of this world. Kelvin and Wendy have an oyster and mussel licence (guests can go with them and pick their own) and these were by FAR the best I've had in SA. Nalson's is one of those places where guests stop over for one night and have to be prised out of the place days later. Breakfast was sensational (both local baker and butcher are true servants of the community!) and, joy oh joy, freshly squeezed fruit juice. Guests who make the correct decision to stay more than one night will get involved in the sea activities – dolphin- and whale-watching on boats, fishing, bird-watching and the ten kilometres of beautiful Christmas Bay Beach. *Ask about children.*

Rooms: 4: 2 doubles, I family and I double/twin; 3 with en-suite shower, I with en-suite bath and shower.
Price: From R240 pp sharing. Singles on request.
Meals: Full breakfast included and served when you want it. Dinners by prior arrangement. Price depends on what you have.
Directions: From Durban take N2 north. Take exit 214 (Salt Rock/Umhlali). Right at T-junction signed to Salt Rock, follow road round to the right past Salt Rock Hotel (on your left). Fairway Drive is next right.

The Chase

Jane and Jonathan Chennells
PO Box 45, Eshowe 3815
Tel: 035-474-5491 Fax: 035-474-1311
Email: thechase@netactive.co.za
Cell: 083-265-9629

Jane and Jonathan have so much to offer their guests that you hardly have to leave the premises. The weather-boarded house is gargantuan (Mrs Chennells senior had a penchant for large, open spaces) with long views of the farm's sugar cane plantations on overlapping mounds of distant hills. On clear days you can even see 90 degrees of sea. (They also have ducks, chickens, horses, cows, sheep and goats like a proper farm should, of course.) The garden is an orgy of barely controllable tropical growth, lush and colourful (check out the tulip tree and the Indian mahogany), its trees often weighed down by parasitic ferns and creepers. Birds are equally irrepressible and there are 70 species in the garden and 280 (!) in the Eshowe area. Kids will love the walled-in swimming pool (13 metres long) where you can swim by floodlight at night too. A hammock swings from a tree, a trampoline is stretched at ground level and there is a hard tennis court. Chennells Chase is an involving, very comfortable, incredibly good-value family home, with huge amounts of space inside and out. Pack a sense of humour and a pair of binoculars.

Rooms: 2: 1 double with en/s bath; 1 twin with private shower. Also a self-contained farm cottage with 5 beds at R400 per night.
Price: R200 – R300 pp sharing. Singles R300 – R400. Self catering in the cottage (sleeps 5) R450 – R550.
Meals: Full breakfast included (except in the cottage – by arrangement only) and served any time.
Directions: From Durban take N2 north for 1 hour. Turn off at Dokodweni off-ramp. Half an hour to Eshowe. Take first left signed to Eshowe, house 1.8km signed on left.

Wendy's Country Lodge

Tony and Wendy Udal

3 Riverview Drive, Mtubatuba
3935
Tel: 035-550-0407
Fax: 035-550-1527
Email: wendybnb@iafrica.com
Web: www.wendybnb.co.za
Cell: 083-628-1601

Tony and Wendy put their hearts into looking after their guests and this is an excellent-value spot from which to visit the nearby St Lucia Wetlands and Umfolozi-Hluhluwe Game Park. The house is safely tucked away in a secure village and surrounded by the Udals' pride and joy, a full acre of tropical garden with pawpaw trees, anthuriums, an orchid collection under cover in a 'cool house' and truly giant snails that love the indigenous mahogany trees. The bedrooms once belonged to children who have grown up and flown the nest and they have been converted, with twists of luxury, for guests. The biggest room was my favourite, with its free-standing bath and shower, but all the rooms have air-con, bathrobes, mosquito nets, duvets in gingham covers and there's plenty of antiquity in the furniture too: old military trunks, early 19th-century Scottish pieces and a particularly nice breakfast table. You can swim in the heated pool, have a braai with the Udals, mingle with other guests round Tony's new bar, or bird-watch in the amazing garden. A new dining room has also been added since our last visit. Wendy and Tony are huge Natal enthusiasts and will make sure you get the most from the nearby beaches and tours that you can do out to the reef, such as kayaking, dolphin-spotting, diving and snorkelling. Tony used to be a tour guide and loves to help.

Rooms: 6: 2 twins and 2 doubles with en-suite bath and shower; 1 twin and 1 double with shower only.
Price: R235 – R350 pp sharing. Singles on request.
Meals: Full breakfast included and served till 9am. Must vacate rooms by 10am. 3-course dinners every night bar Sundays: R100 – R120 (excluding wine).
Directions: From Durban take the N2 north to Mtubatuba turn – follow to the T-junction. Go right where you'll see a sign to Wendy's and follow the signs to the house.

Map Number: 15

Maputaland Lodge

Jorg and Nicola Orban
Kabeljou Ave, No.1, Greater St. Lucia Wetlands Park, Zululand 3936
Tel: 035-590-1041 Fax: 035-590-1041
Email: bookings@maputaland.com Web: www.maputaland.com

Maputaland B&B is great value and a top spot from which to sample the joys of the World Heritage Site, beaches, reefs and big game of the area. Jorg, who is very modest about his talents, is the bird fundi (430 local species live locally!) and his sister Nicola is a dive-master. And they are both registered professional game guides too, so you've got no excuse to laze about! They guide trips out into nearby Hluhluwe-Umfolozi reserve. And, amazingly, Jorg likes to explore the streets of St Lucia itself, taking his guests on night safaris! Hippos, impala and on rare occasion even leopards can be seen wandering about the pavements. Bush babies and chameleons come out during the cicada-hours too. The lodge is recently built, homely, relaxed and comfortable. But you're hardly here to stay indoors! Jorg does a cracking 'bonnet breakfast' (he assures me it's NOT road-kill) for those that go with him on day tours (starting at 4 am and getting back at 6pm – yep – good value alrighty!). Nicola's dive tours are also run on a no-limits basis too and you can dive and snorkel as many times as you like. Ask them about turtle-watching tours (two rare breeds come here), deep-sea fishing and fly-casting for 1.5 metre darga-salmon (which Jorg sometimes also cooks on the braai). Exciting, but very friendly with it.

Rooms: 5: 2 doubles and 3 twins with en-suite bath and shower. 1 double with twin in room and en-suite bath and shower.
Price: R210 pp sharing. Singles R265. Full-day safaris from 4am – 6pm from R375 pp. Half-days from R275 pp.
Meals: Full breakfast included. Dinners by request. Tours include all meals during the day.
Directions: From Jo'burg (7 hrs): take N2 through Bethal, Pongola etc and past Hluhluwe. Turn off to Mtubatuba then left on R618 to St Lucia. From Swaziland (3 hrs): join N2 from Pongola/Mukuzi and head for Mtubatuba. From Durban (3 hrs): N2 towards Mtubatuba, right on R618 to St L. Signs in St L for guest house.

Map Number: 15

Makakatana Bay Lodge

Hugh and Leigh-Ann Morrison
Mtubatuba 3935
Tel: 035-550-4189 Fax: 035-550-4198
Email: maklodge@iafrica.com Web: www.makakatana.co.za
Cell: 082-573-5641

Makakatana Bay Lodge is sensational and I can do little to improve on these photos. If only we had space for ten shots, to show you every aspect of the lodge: the gleaming wooden interiors; the bedrooms (including the wonderful new honeymoon suite), connected by walkways through the forest, with their gargantuan slabs of glass and warm, earthy African colours; the pool encased in decking and raised above the grasses of the wetlands; the lake itself and the extraordinary St Lucia waterways. Guests are taken on pole-driven safaris in mokoro canoes, searching for birds (360 species!), crocodiles and hippos. You can also take a boat trip across the lake for lunch on the beach or a game drive to a nearby reserve before returning to a sumptuous dinner with your hosts in the outdoor boma. The family's old 'Crab House' is the only part of the lodge not raised above the tall grasses. This was once a storeroom for crabs caught in the lake, now a wine cellar with a giant tree growing out of its roof. Huge sliding doors throughout the lodge open onto wooden decks with views over the lake, and the absence of railings just adds to the feeling of openness to nature. From the wooden Swazi tortoise holding open the front door, Hugh and Leigh-Ann will have you hooked. The lodge is beautifully welded to its environment. An absolute treat.

Rooms: 6: 1 honeymoon suite with extra single bed, 2 king suites, 3 twin suites; all with en-suite bath and outside shower.
Price: From R2,150 – R2,750 pp sharing. Singles from R2,800 – R3,000. Prices may change after October 2004.
Meals: Fully inclusive of all meals and safaris.
Directions: Take N2 north from Durban for 250km to Charter's Creek. Follow road for 15km (14km on tar) to fork. Take right fork and follow signs to Makakatana Bay Lodge (4 more km or so).

Hluhluwe River Lodge

Gavin and Bridget Dickson

Greater St Lucia Wetlands Park, Hluhluwe 3960
Tel: 035-562-0246/7
Fax: 035-562-0248
Email: info@hluhluwe.co.za
Web: www.hluhluwe.co.za

A short drive through dense bushveld takes you to this friendly, informal lodge at the end of a sandy track on the shores of beautiful Lake St Lucia. I suggest dropping things off in your wood-and-thatch chalet and making your way to the big deck, the centrepiece of the lodge, for a drink and some orientation. The view is straight across the Hluhluwe River flood plain. There is a pool lost in the trees near the Zulu boma (for evening braais), but most will want to make full use of the all-seeing, all-knowing guides (including Gavin himself) who will take you exploring in this remarkable region. The river is just there for canoe safaris (hippo, croc, birds beyond counting) in the channels and boat trips around the lake (where you can see all sorts of land game coming in to drink). There are game drives through the surrounding sand forests of the Wetland Park, but Hluhluwe Umfolozi Park is not far away either. You can also go on botanical trips or guided walks to old fossil banks and (astounding) bird-watching excursions in the park. Whatever you choose this is an intimate, sociable place, where small numbers and very knowledgeable guides make the experience personal and rewarding. The focus is on the topography, the bird life and the wetland environment as a whole, rather than just the 'Big Five'. *Also a good spot to explore the greater area from.*

Rooms: 12: 8 twins, 2 family rooms, all en/s shower; 2 honeymoon suites (pictured) en/s shr & bath. If you want honeymoon suites, ask when you book.
Price: From R1,095 – R1,675 pp sharing for all meals (except lunch) and all tours. From R785 – R1,495 for dinner, bed and breakfast.
Meals: Full breakfast included. Lunch from R35 – R60.
Directions: From Durban take N2 to Hluhluwe. Turn off & follow through town, down hill to T-junc and turn L. After 1.4km turn R and cross railway. After 3.4km turn R onto D540. Follow 5km signs to lodge. The gate guard will tell you where to go (and follow signs).

Map Number: 15

Kosi Forest Lodge

Brett Gehren

Kosi Bay Nature Reserve, PO Box 1593, Eshowe 3815
Tel: 011-467-1886 Fax: 011-467-4758
Email: info@zulunet.co.za Web: www.zulunet.co.za
Cell: 035-474-1473

Kosi Bay is the sort of place that novelists map out and then construct adventures in. You are picked up by a four-wheel drive, which can negotiate the sand tracks criss-crossing the region. You park up not just your car, but also the modern world you are now leaving. There is no tar and no electricity here. Instead you enter a landscape of raffia palm groves, primary sand forests, mangroves, water meadows, interconnecting lakes (yes, hippo and crocodile like it too and are regularly sighted). And then there is the sea and the mouth of the river for diving, swimming and fishing in 'perfect white sand coves with huge overhanging trees' (says the lodge brochure). The reed-thatched camp itself perfectly balances the wild (your chalet is in the middle of a boisterous forest) with the romantic (candlelit meals and outdoor baths and showers). I loved the deep stillness of the early-morning guided canoe trip and other activities include reef-snorkelling, turtle-tracking, forest walks and bird safaris. I consider Kosi Forest Lodge one of the most rewarding (and therefore best-value) places I have stayed in SA. I recommend a minimum of two or three nights.

Rooms: 8: 1 family 'bush suite'; 6 twins and 1 honeymoon double; all with outdoor bath and shower.
Price: All-inclusive (meals and activities) R1,190 – R1,285 pp sharing. Sing. supp. 30%. Transfer from police station R15 pp. Children under 12 half price.
Meals: All meals and teas included. Also included guided canoeing on the lakes and walk in the raffia forest. 2 nights stay include 1 full-day excursion too.
Directions: From Hluhluwe take N2 north past Mkuze. Turn R signed Jozini. In Jozini thru' town, L over the dam and follow for 37km. Turn R at T-jct and follow for 67km to Kwangwanase. R at Kosi Forest sign and follow tar road round to R and up slope to police station compound. Turn L and park under trees.

Tamboti Ridge

Denise and Brian Blevin
Between Pongola and Mkuze, Golela T-junction, Pongola 3170
Tel: 034-435-1110 Fax: 034-435-1008
Email: shayalodge@saol.com Web: www.shayamoya.co.za
Cell: 083-269-9596

Tamboti Ridge is a wonderful farm-style bed and breakfast found on a sugar and cattle farm. Brian and Denise are great hosts and will fill you in on the masses to do here in the Pongola Nature Reserve: game drives in 10,000 hectares of well-stocked park (everything except lion and cheetah), guided rhino walks, river canoeing, boat cruises, mountain-biking and elephant monitoring (there is a herd of 38 animals). Another highlight is the tiger fishing on the Pongolapoort Lake (sharp teeth, very feisty) in untouched wilderness (hippos, crocodiles, water birds and herds of game at the water's edge). Brian runs the large farm as holistically and organically as possible, producing everything from sugar and vegetables to yoghurt and cheese for the guests… and everyone that comes under the 'home' umbrella. The B&B is set in a peaceful, bird-filled, sub-tropical garden, across the lawn and pool from the main farmhouse. From your room, you look onto a wooden deck, rock pools and up the Pongola River. All activities are arranged through Shayamoya Game Lodge, which is also owned by the Blevins. It is certainly worth a trip up to the lodge for not only the nosh, but also the wild view and an encounter with Nandi, the spotted eagle owl who sometimes pops in.

Rooms: 5: 3 twins and 2 doubles; all en-suite with bath and shower, plus air-conditioning and fans.
Price: R300 – R320 pp sharing B&B. Singles on request. R225 pp for game drives and river safaris. Tiger fishing R600 pp per half-day.
Meals: Full breakfast included. You can also eat lunch and dinners at the main lodge; 3-course meals from R115 (excluding wine).
Directions: When travelling north on the N2, 40km past Mkuze, turn left at the signs directly at the Golela junction. When travelling south on the N2, 30km past Pongola, turn right onto the farm, almost directly opposite the turn to Golela and Swaziland border post.

Map Number: 15

Isibindi Zulu Lodge

Brett Gehren
Rorke's Drift, Dundee 3000
Tel: 011-467 -1886 Fax: 011-467-4758
Email: info@zulunet.co.za or isibindi@iafrica.com Web: www.zulunet.co.za

As I drove up to Isibindi in the early evening, the way ahead was intermittently illuminated by a spectacular thunderstorm. It seemed to be following me. Ignoring the portents, I pressed on Homerically to claim my prize, a night at the wonderful (the first line of my notes just reads 'Wow!') Isibindi Zulu Lodge. It sits on a hill in the middle of a 2000-hectare nature reserve on the Buffalo river, with six secluded chalets looking out over the bush, a modern spin on the traditional Zulu beehive hut. The best view is reserved for the swimming pool, a great place to unwind after an early game drive with lodge manager Dieter. He's a talking bush encyclopaedia and great barman (and it's a great bar – a hunk of polished acacia, with local animal species and a map of the battle of Isandlwana painted on the wall). He also provides an effective foil to resident Zulu historian Prince Sibusiso Zulu, whose cultural evenings combine education with fun (it *is* possible!). Prince also leads tours to the Anglo-Zulu war battlefields, which weave together dramatic tales from both sides. Isibindi has it all, nature, history, culture and even adrenaline sports – the rafting camp in the reserve is one of the best in South Africa.

Rooms: 6: 4 twins, 1 double, 1 honeymoon beehive suite; all with en-suite bath and shower.
Price: R815 – R1075 pp sharing. Single supplement 30%.
Meals: Full board includes breakfast, lunch and dinner, hikes and 1 game drive per day. Rafting, Zulu cultural evening and homestead visits extra.
Directions: Take R33 south from Dundee for 14km, then turn left onto dirt road to Rorke's Drift – 25km or so. Follow signs to Isibindi. 5km beyond the village of Rorke's Drift.

Mawelawela Game and Fishing Lodge

George and Herta Mitchell-Innes

Fodo Farm, PO Box 21, Elandslaagte 2900
Tel: 036-421-1860 Fax: 036-421-1860
Email: mitchellinnes@mweb.co.za Web: www.mawelawela.co.za
Cell: 083-259-6394 or 082-734-3118

George and Herta are a natural, down-to-earth couple whose veins of hospitality run deep… and staying with them is to enjoy a few days awash with incidental pleasures. Herta, a bubbly Austrian, moved out to South Africa twenty-eight years ago and married George, who is a beef farmer – his boerewors is delicious. He is also a keen historian and leads tours out to the site of the battle of Elandslaagte. His study is full of Anglo-Boer war prints and weighty tomes including a collection of the London Illustrated News. (Ask him to show you his father's beautiful collection of bird-eggs too.) If you stay in the main house the rooms are very comfortable and the bungalow across the jacaranda-filled garden is perfect for families or groups. A short drive away from the farm itself you'll find the thatched hunters' cottage on 1500 wild hectares set aside for game. There is a trout dam at the front into which George has built a waterfall, and there are a shower and a plunge pool to one side. The cane-sided shady braai area faces dam-wards and you can watch the eland and kudu come to drink in the evenings. Finally a toast to Herta's cooking which is wonderful! Many of the ingredients are home-grown and all is served on her collection of fine china and family silver. *Bookings essential.*

Rooms: 4: 2 twins (1 with en/s bath, 1 en/s bath & shower); 1 apartment with double, twins & single (self-catering or B&B); 1 self-catering game lodge sleeps 7.
Price: B&B R200 – R250 pp sharing. Singles on request.
Meals: All meals are in the main house. Full breakfast included. 3-course dinners (excluding wine) R80. Main and coffee R50.
Directions: On N11, 35km from Ladysmith, 70km from Newcastle. Also entrance on R602, 35km from Dundee south via Greytown.

Oaklands Country Manor

Jamie and Anna Bruce
PO Box 19, Van Reenen 3372
Tel: 058-671-0067 Fax: 058-671-0077
Email: oaklands@compuserve.com Web: www.oaklands.co.za
Cell: 083-304-2683

Jamie was in the British army for many years and memorabilia pops up at Oaklands in flags and prints. He also runs very popular tours to the nearby Boer War battlefields – but there is no regimentation at Oaklands. The colonial manor, with its original Oregon pine floors and ceilings, is now an intimate country hotel set in 260 acres of heavenly highveld countryside, once home to San tribesmen (see their rock paintings) and still the favoured beat for 185 species of bird. Back at the Manor, kids are well catered for (Jamie and Anna adore them): there's the balustraded pool and a tennis court (with umpire's chair to provoke argument), a games room, mountain bikes… and all that fresh mountain air will put them to sleep should they ever sit down. The stone-walled rooms are fun, converted from old stables and outbuildings. All are different in style, but consistent themes are the colourful duvet covers, bright African art and stunning views from the patios. You are out in the wilds here among mountains, craggy cliffs and paddocks full of galloping horses. The Oaklands pub is renowned for its warm atmosphere and the meals are superb to boot.

Rooms: 13: 7 twins, 6 doubles all with en-suite baths and shower over the bath.
Price: R580 – R780 pp sharing. R610 – R860 for singles.
Meals: Full breakfast and dinner included. Lunch is also available.
Directions: Take the N3 to Van Reenen, turn right at the Caltex garage. Go 7km down a dirt track – Oaklands is signed to the right.

Map Number: 14

Three Tree Hill Lodge

Andrew Ardington
PO Box 3534, Ladysmith 3370
Tel: 036-448-1171 Fax: 036-448-1953
Email: fugdrift@trustnet.co.za Web: www.threetreehill.co.za

This is the comfortable way to experience the Boer War and one of its most famous battlefields, Spionkop Hill. The lodge sits in complete isolation on an opposing hill with views that flood out across the green valley and down to the Spionkop Nature Reserve. You can often see giraffe, zebra, rhino etc from the stoep, although at some distance. There is an all-together feeling at Three Tree Hill. Meals are eaten at one table and the atmosphere is involving on the tours. Andrew knows his potatoes when it comes to the history too – his Boer War tours are engrossing. Meanwhile, back at the lodge you can take time out from all the action in very private cottages, with their own unobserved verandah looking onto the park. They are simple in design with orange oxide floors, hand-embroidered covers on beds – the aloe is the house symbol – wooden wash stands in bathrooms, 100 per cent cotton sheets, down duvets for crisp winter nights. The emphasis is on simple good quality, rather than elaborate decoration. For me the *pièce de résistance* at the lodge was the swimming pool, reached through a gauntlet of dalek-like aloes, and perched precariously on the hip of the valley. Horse riding from the lodge is now available to guests and building on the new library has begun.

Rooms: 6: all twins all with en/s bathrooms with baths and showers.
Price: R750 – R1,000 pp sharing. Single supplement + R300.
Meals: Full breakfast, lunch and 3-course dinner (excluding wine) included. Tours of the battlefield for R350.
Directions: From Durban take the N3 north for 260km – take the R616 left for 19km towards Bergville. Go left onto the D564 for 8km.

Map Number: 14

Spionkop Lodge

Lynette and Raymond Heron

R600, Drakensberg Area, Ladysmith 3370
Tel: 036-488 1404 Fax: 036-488-1404
Email: spionkop@futurenet.co.za Web: www.spionkop.co.za
Cell: 082-573-0224/5

A magnificent storm was exploding over the Drakensberg Mountains when I visited and it was a relief to soon be tucked up in an armchair by the lodge fire with a dog at my feet. Raymond is a convivial Scot who grew up on the far side of the Zambezi. He has plenty of stories to tell. Not least the tragic movements of the pyrrhic Battle of Spionkop, a keystone in the Anglo-Boer war. And you only have to go to the characterful bar and you'll be sitting right where General Buller camped with 27,000 men (Winston Churchill and Mahatma Gandhi among them). The lodge is built on the old Spearman farm and is now a 700-hectare eco-reserve with 270 bird species and a mass of flowering aloes in June and July. You can stay either in bothyish stone cottages, which are comfy and snug with fireplaces for winter and verandahs for summer; or in the colonial farmhouse with its polished floorboards, comfortable rooms, a library full of history books and a sunroom to read them in. But the main heart of the lodge is the 108-year-old stone, converted barn with a massive glass-walled dining room with a sinuous blonde branch growing through the room. Dinner here often relives history and you may find yourself donning a safari suit or maybe a Zulu shield. Game farms, fishing, and horse-riding nearby.

Rooms: 8 doubles, all en-suite with bath and shower. Plus 2 self-catering cottages; Aloe has 2 double beds and a bath; Acacia has 3 bedrooms and 2 bathrooms.
Price: R830 – R930 full board pp sharing. Aloe R690 per night. Acacaia R890 per night.
Meals: All meals included in B&B price. Meals optional for self-caterers: R65 for breakfast, R45 for lunch and R90 for dinner.
Directions: 20 mins off N3 from either Durban or Jo'burg. See web site for map.

Map Number: 14

Montusi Mountain Lodge

Anthony and Jean Carte
Off D119, Alpine Heath, Bergville 3350
Tel: 036-438-6243 Fax: 036-438-6566
Email: montusi@iafrica.com Web: www.montusi.za.net

Montusi feels a bit like a hotel, which just happens to be run by your aunt and uncle. You know... you haven't seen them for years, but no sooner have you stepped from the car than they've got your bed sorted (well, your thatched, Conran-style, country cottage complete with fireplace, selected DSTV and view!) and are fixing you a sundowner on the patio. Yes, the sunsets are every bit as good as the photo suggests. Ant bought wattle-strangled Montusi Farm in the early 1990s. Being a man of X-ray vision, he saw through the undergrowth to a lodge perfectly positioned to catch the surrounding view, he saw fields of galloping horses and he saw lakes to fish in. So he did away with the wattles (via a community project) and a new Montusi emerged. Meals are superb... some examples: lamb with chargrilled lemon and mint, ostrich fillet with garlic and marinated peppers, malva pudding, custard cups. There are many ways to burn off the calories with limitless hiking, horse-riding for all levels of experience, mountain-biking and fishing. But best of all is ex-skiing pro Chris's circus school! It is as professional as they come, with trapezes, bungies, nets, ropes and they sometimes put on shows too. Montusi impressed me because it's a happy family-run place with plenty of style. *Golf and massages available locally. Picnics at waterfall can be arranged.*

Rooms: 14 cottages: 4 are kings with en-suite bath and another twin with en-suite shower next door. 10 are kings with shower and bath.
Price: R600 – R750 pp sharing. Single supplement R100. (Price is inclusive of dinner and breakfast.)
Meals: Full breakfast and 4-course dinner included (wine extra).
Directions: If coming from the south head north through Pietermaritzburg, Estcourt and turn left signed Northern Drakensberg. Continue for 80km through Winterton and Bergville on R74. Follow sign (some small) to Montusi.

Map Number: 14

Ardmore Guest Farm

Paul and Sue Ross

Champagne Valley, Winterton 3340
Tel: 036-468-1314 Fax: 036-468-1241
Email: info@ardmore.co.za Web: www.ardmore.co.za
Cell: 083-789-1314

It was raining caracals and jackals when I visited Ardmore… so to speak. And the deluge didn't lift for a second, so sadly I couldn't experience the stunning views of Champagne Castle (second highest mountain in SA at 3377m) and the Cathkin Peaks which previous GG visitors have enjoyed. The Drakensberg National Park begins just down the road so bring your hiking boots. Ardmore is a super-relaxed, freewheeling sort of place. Sociable and delicious dinners, eaten by lantern light at long tables in the yellowwood dining room, draw on the farm's organic produce – eggs from happy, roaming chickens and fruit, vegetables and herbs from a pesticide-free garden. Paul will tell you all about the art here, all created by the local Zulu community and much from the famous Ardmore Pottery at the end of the garden. There is masses to do: hike to waterfalls and mountain peaks; watch the rare bald ibis that makes its home here; fish, canoe, mountain-bike; the game farm nearby (1/2-hour drive) offers cheap horse-riding to see the rhino, zebra and giraffe; the Drakensberg Boys' Choir performs on Wednesdays at 15h30; and there are 230 rock-art sites in the area too. The small thatched rondavels are sweet and cosy and the bigger ones have fireplaces. Garden furniture is set out under the giant liquid amber tree, an important focal point for the property, where you can take tea and contemplate the mountains.

Rooms: 5 rondavels: 3 large doubles with en/s bath and shower; 2 small with en/s shower. 2 x 2 bedroom cottages: 1 double & 1 twin with en-suite bath & shower.
Price: Dinner, bed and breakfast: R255 – R310 pp sharing. No single supplement.
Meals: Full breakfast and dinner included.
Directions: From the N3 take the R74 to Winterton and go south along the R600 towards the Central Drakensberg for 18km. You'll see a sign on your left, 5km up partly dirt road for Ardmore.

Map Number: 14

The Antbear

Andrew and Conny Attwood

Fernhust Farm, Moor Park –
Giants Castle Road, Estcourt
3310
Tel: 036-352-3143
Fax: 036-352-3143
Email: aattwood@antbear.de
Web: www.antbear.de

Thank goodness Andrew and Conny gave up the corporate rat race in Germany for B&B'ing. They bought and renovated the old farmhouse and, like all the buildings at The Antbear, it is thatched and sits on the top of a hill looking out to the peaks of the Drakensberg. Check out their extraordinary straw-bale house too. Everything here has had the skilled hands of your craftsman host and his father Bruce laid upon it. Andrew is a canny chap. The lodge and rooms are home to his chairs, tables, doors, staircases, towel holders, candle-sticks – the list of working wooden sculptures runs and runs. This is the hallmark of the Antbear. Just across from the lodge's leafy colonnaded front patio an old tractor shed has been converted into four bedrooms. Billowing white curtains frame the view and the rooms have intriguing fireplaces, plenty of humorous sculpture and mosaics in the showers. The first room is superb with a staircase that climbs the right-hand wall, a loft bed-platform in the thatchy peak on the left and a six-foot causeway between the two. Andrew is the chef – Moroccan tajine cooking is his current favourite – and meals will almost be 100% organic if the horses, tortoises, chickens or tame-ish spurwing goose haven't raided Conny's garden. You'd be a fool to stay for only one night. *Birding, rock art sites, river rafting, battlefield tours, local arts and crafts.*

Rooms: 5: 4 en/s doubles in renovated tractor shed; 3 with showers, one with bath. In the main house; 1 dble with bath in room and twin beds next door with e/s bath.

Price: Dinner, bed and breakfast from R350 – R390 pp sharing. Singles add R100.

Meals: Lunch and picnics on request from R40 pp. Dinner usually 3 courses (excluding wine).

Directions: Take exit 152 on the N3 signed Hidcote for 7km. At T-junction turn right towards Giant's Castle. After 14km turn right towards Moor Park onto dirt road. After 5.5km you will see The Antbear sign to the right. The thatched cottages are 2km up the farm road.

Map Number: 14

Sewula Gorge Lodge

Graham and Santie McIntosh and Jacquie Geldart

Off R103, 18km from Estcourt, Estcourt 3310
Tel: 036-352-2485 Fax: 036-352-5986
Email: bookings@sewula.co.za Web: www.sewula.co.za
Cell: 082-824-0329

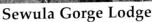

This glorious thatched lodge lives beside a rocky-river gorge filled with cascading waterfalls (the main one is 20 metres high) and swimming pools. As soon as I arrived I realized I had made a significant mistake. I had not organized to stay the night at Sewula and had missed my opportunity to swim under the waterfall looking at the stars (darn and double darn!). The emphasis is on relaxation and seclusion and only one party stays at a time. Staff live away from the lodge and there is absolutely no one about except you, a very rare treat (even by GG standards). For this far-too-low-really price, you can pretend you own this truly heavenly place. It is self-catering, but with any domestic hardship extracted. Not only does nature spoil you, but the staff do too, washing up, servicing the rooms, lighting fires and bringing fresh milk, butter and cream down from the farm. Under the thatched pitch of the main lodge roof are the kitchen, bush-chic sunken sitting room, a giant fireplace, an oversized chess set and much wildly original carpentry and functional sculpture. Similarly lovely are the cottages, which have sleeping lofts for children and face the falls. You can walk to an iron-age settlement, battle memorials and great fishing spots. Jacqui is a stellar host and constantly thoughtful. 100% (as the locals say)!

Rooms: 4 cottages (max 8 adults & 10 children): 3 have en/s shower, 2 of which have outdoor shower too; 1 cottage has en/s shr & bath. One booking at a time.
Price: Min. R600 for the whole place per night self-catering. R300 pp for extra guests, but children half-price if sleeping in loft.
Meals: Restaurants are nearby.
Directions: Exit 143 on N3 from Durban to Mooi River. Take R103 to Estcourt, 20.3km from off-ramp, take right turn onto dirt road to Malanspruit and follow signs to Sewula Gorge Camp (5km from turn-off to reception).

KwaZulu Natal

Sycamore Avenue and Tree Houses

Bruce and Gloria Attwood

11 Hidcote Road, Hidcote,
Mooi River 3300
Tel: 033-263-2875
Fax: 033-263-2875
Email:
sycamore@futurenet.co.za
Web: www.sycamore-ave.com

Tree houses! Bruce is a functional sculptor, once lured to Italy where he restored a barn in Tuscany, but thankfully now back in the fold. There are not many can weave a whole house into the branches of a giant pin oak, but Bruce has done it twice… and no, the first one didn't fall down. There are two such arboreal retreats at Sycamore Avenue. Small staircases lead up and down the tree, up to the bedroom in the highest branches. And there's a neat platform lower down where you can swing gently in a hammock and listen to the golden orioles that sing and nest up here with you. Those who fondly remember *The Folk of the Faraway Tree* by Enid Blyton or *Swiss Family Robinson* will have tears in their eyes! Downstairs you will find a copper autoclave (for heat), a shower with mosaic marble floor, a jacuzzi lit only by candles and more cunning devices than JK Rowling could think up. Below the tree is a magical garden where couples love to get married, with hedges of wisteria sinensis, clematis, groves of silver birch, green lawns, roses, organic veggies. Bruce (short-order fry cook) and Gloria (professor of curries, cakes and crumbles) both twinkle with hostliness, to coin a word, and are great fun. The rooms in their house are lovely too. A 10 out of 10 experience! *Well placed for the arts/crafts region and Giants Castle.*

Rooms: 2 tree houses with 1 double, jacuzzi and shower; also 2 rooms in the main house with en-suite shower and bath.
Price: R300 – R350 pp sharing. No single supplement.
Meals: Full breakfast included. Dinner by arrangement. 3 courses from R90 (excluding wine).
Directions: Take exit 152 off N3. From south turn right, from north turn left onto the R103 Hidcote Rd. Travel for 2km and Sycamore is signed right.

202

Map Number: 14

Old Rearsby Farm Cottages

Jim and Jeannie Parker

Old Rearsby, Hlatikulu Rd, Mooi River 3300
Tel: 033-263-2280, 033-263-1331 or 033-263-2886 Fax: 033-263-2475
Email: parker@parkertours.co.za Web: www.parkertours.co.za
Cell: 082-667-7755

I loomed out of the night – cold, wet and very late (sorry!) – but was still treated to the warmest of welcomes from the Parkers. This, as I understand it from a string of previous visitors, is typical at Old Rearsby (the welcome I mean). My flagging spirits were rekindled by a canny combination of single malt and human kindness, and we were soon chatting away in the drawing room among the water-colours and military prints (Jim was the British defence adviser in Pretoria until 1996, when the Parkers moved here). I eventually ambled back across the lawn to my cottage (one of three set a little apart from the main house), which comes with plenty of books and magazines to read and its own fireplace prepared for lighting. One deep slumber later the rain was a distant memory, and I opened my door to fabulous views across to the central Drakensberg mountains (it's phenomenal hiking country, so bring boots). Breakfast included fruits from the orchard at the back of the garden (peaches, plums and apricots), and I was on my way far too soon. A final smile on the way out – Jim has aligned the driveway to point directly at Giant's Castle peak. *The Parkers can arrange your complete holiday (see their website), by the way.*

Rooms: 4: 3 cottages, all with twin rooms and en/s bathrooms, 2 with showers, 1 with bath; 1 en-suite farmhouse wing with twin beds and en/s shower.
Price: R200 pp sharing. Singles on request.
Meals: The Parkers will direct you to excellent restaurants and pubs locally.
Directions: Take either the Mooi River north or south ramp from the N3 and follow all Giant's Castle signs through and out of village. After climbing straight up Lawrence Rd for 2km, take next left signed 'Hlatikulu 22'. Old Rearsby is another 5km drive on the right.

Map Number: 14

KwaZulu Natal

Stocklands Farm

Eve Mazery
4 Shafton Rd, Howick 3290
Tel: 033-330-5225 Fax: 033-330-5225
Email: edulink@iafrica.com Web: www.stocklandsfarm.co.za
Cell: 082-975-2298

The warm welcome that I received as I tumbled out of my car, late and weary, is undoubtedly typical of Stocklands. As my cognitive faculties jolted back to life over a restorative beverage, it became obvious that Eve and Roland are natural hosts; thoughtful, funny and relaxed. They have put a lot of love and plenty of style into the wonderful old house. The argument goes that half-measures are not really in keeping with Stocklands, and you can see their point. The walls of the original 1850s house, for example, are over 50 centimetres thick and the belhambra tree at the front of the house is no-less-than enormous. Birds come in droves – they love Roland's indigenous trees. I loved the fuchsia tree myself (it flowers in January). Down near the tennis court there is a koi pond and many guests like to savour a slow, hot afternoon in the thick shade on a blanket here after a picnic. The four rooms in the house, like the cottages, are meticulously decorated to individual themes. Eve has found hand-embroidered linen and original works by local artists to decorate and nothing is left out. Choose from a range of breakfasts including the Vegetarian, the Sunrise, the Decadent and… the Sensible! You can't stay in the old armoury, but it's very interesting too. *Game can be viewed right next door, by the way.*

Rooms: 6: 2 suites & 2 bedrooms, 1 with en/s bath, 3 with en/s shower. Also 2 cottages: 1 with 3 bedrooms & 2 bathrooms, 1 with 2 bedrooms, 1 shower.
Price: R180 – R240 pp sharing. Singles on request.
Meals: Full breakfast included or you can self-cater in the cottages. An excellent café next door and more in the area.
Directions: From Jo'burg take N3 to Durban. Take first exit to Howick signed Howick/Tweedie. At Stop sign turn left to Howick. Thru' lights to bottom of hill, turn L to Karkloof. 100m turn R into Shafton Rd. Stocklands is 1km. From Durban take N3 to Jo'burg. Take 3rd Howick turn-off as above.

Map Number: 14

Pleasant Places

John and Linda Hall

PO Box 4, Lidgetton 3270
Tel: 033-234-4396 Fax: 033-234-4396
Email: pleasantplaces@pleasantplaces.co.za Web: www.pleasantplaces.co.za
Cell: 082-456-2717

Pleasant Places perches on a narrow terrace, far above a green valley on a bushy hillside. Massive old trees line the driveway concealing idyllic gardens from everyone but the guests who come to relax here, the eagles and other rare birds that make it their home, and, of course, your caring hosts John and Linda. The property stretches over several levels. The steep slope above is thickly forested with arboreal giants. Liquid ambers, yellowwoods and Caucasian wing-nut trees blanket the slope and seamlessly wrap around the hamlet and its thatched roofs. The main house almost hangs its feet over the edge of the step, a drop of some 80 metres to the river far below the forested lower garden. Sometimes massive gymnogenes cruise past at eye level a mere thirty metres from the breakfast table and you'll see other birds too: malachite kingfishers on John's trout dam, buff-spotted fluff tails, drongos and king sixies. The guest rondavels of course have been built for the view and are surrounded by banks of shrubs and rainbow perennials; one is reached via a roped walkway under its thatched eaves. Each is delightful. You'll want for nothing with the best linens stretched luxuriously over wide beds, while posies of fresh flowers add to the cottagey feel. There is a green hill far away…. *Excellent riding facilities 15 minutes away.*

Rooms: 4 & a family unit: 2 king/twins with en/s bath & shower; 2 queens, one with en/s bath, one with en/s sh; family unit has double and twins, both en/s bath/shower.
Price: R240 pp sharing. R280 for single occupancy.
Meals: Full South African/Continental breakfast incl. 3-course dinner on request, R90. Light lunches by arrangement, cost depends on requirements.
Directions: Join R103 from N3 at exit 132 southbound, or exit 107 northbound. Proceed on R103 for 27.3km southbound or 12.5km northbound to turn-off for Pleasant Places.

Penwarn Country Lodge

Peta Parker

PO Box 253, Southern Drakensberg, Underberg 3257
Tel: 033-701-1777 or 1341 or 1342 Fax: 033-701-1341 or 417
Email: info@penwarn.com Web: www.penwarn.com
Cell: 083-305-3009

Penwarn is simply fantastic. There are two places to stay here (I'm afraid that the cave is no longer an option). The main lodge was converted from an old sandstone dairy and fertilizer shed into colourful sitting rooms, a bar and wonderfully comfortable bedrooms. And then there is magnificent Mthini Lodge complete with wooden deck overlooking the main dam, grazing game, horses, cattle and the mountains beyond. The list of things to do at Penwarn is exhaustive (and exhausting!): trout fishing on dams and rivers (lessons and rods provided); tubing on fast-flowing rivers or swimming in pools fed by waterfalls; bird-watching (lammerguyers may join you at the Vulture Restaurant); mountaineering or abseiling (tricky cliffs everywhere); and game drives where tame eland will approach you, and if you go on a horse you can ride right through the herds of zebra and wildebeest. Some find it all so exciting they get married here! Peta and her staff (or family, I couldn't tell) are great fun. Finally a mention for TV celebrity Nimrod, a (very) tame otter partial to sausages, dog wrestling and baths (close the door or he'll be in yours!). I for one won't forget canoeing by moonlight on the lily-filled dam (not eight metres from my room) with an otter playing beside me. Penwarn is a magical and brilliant place. *All meals included.*

Rooms: 11: 7 suites at Indabushe Lodge, 4 rooms at Mthini lodge. All have en-suite bath and/or shower. (No cave dwelling anymore – sorry!).
Price: Full board is R770 – R850 pp sharing.
Meals: Full breakfast, lunch, 4-course dinner and all snacks are included. Wine is not. Canoeing is free.
Directions: Take Exit 99 off N3 marked Underberg, Howick South and travel 110km west to Underberg, going through Boston and Bulwer en route. Take the Swartberg Road out of Underberg and after 5km turn right onto Bushmansnek Road (dirt track). After 16km turn L to Penwarn (drive is 4km long.)

Free State & Lesotho

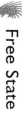

Pula House

Barbara and John von Ahlefeldt

PO Box 88, Smithfield 9966
Tel: 051-683-0032 Fax: 051-683-0032
Email: pula@acenet.co.za Web: www.pula-house.com
Cell: 083-272-3001

Sophistication and jaunty modernity mix eclectically and effectively in this Karoo-style house, which boasts one of the most beautiful drawing rooms I saw on my trip. It was built over 120 years ago for the local magistrate but was sadly neglected before journalists John and Barbara retired from their Devonshire inns in England and got their hands on it. Life has now been breathed back into the old place, and with interest, the exterior of the house revealing little of the drama within. Exotic rugs and pine floors are separated from 15-foot-high pressed metal ceilings by brightly-coloured walls; original South African art and conservative hunting prints hang peaceably next to a highly decorative carpet coat – a relic of '60s London; handsome antique furniture enjoys the presence of modern Africana. 'Juxtaposition' is a word that keeps coming to mind. With precious little water (this is almost the Karoo after all), Barbara has worked a minor miracle in the garden with lush lawns, interesting nooks and crannies to explore, rashes of vivid colour, and the quirky plunge pool is a summer godsend. The sun disappears behind a koppie and sunset on the terrace is a special time at Pula. Finally the von Ahlefeldt recipe of hospitality, humour and style is second to none and the home-made breads and creamy scrambled eggs make breakfasts truly excellent.

Rooms: 4: 2 doubles and 2 twins, all with en-suite bathrooms, 2 with baths, 2 with showers.
Price: R200 – R220 pp sharing. Single supplement on request.
Meals: Full breakfast included.
Directions: Pula House is on Douglas Street which comes off the N6 directly opposite the police station on the Bloemfontein side of town.

Map Number: 13

Smithfield House

Anne and Geoff Montgomery
Brand St, Smithfield 9966
Tel: 051-683-0071 Fax: 051-683-0071
Email: rainbird@futurenet.co.za
Cell: 082-401-0902

Smithfield House is the grandest in town and has been with us from the start. There's now a new team at the helm, but it's still a bastion of stylish living, largely because Anne and Geoff are passed masters at looking after guests. Stints with the Lands Dept. and National Parks saw them work their way south from Rhodesia (as was), until they opened a B&B in the Cape and then another in Natal. Now they've been drawn to the recuperative Free State, and the colonial splendour of Smithfield House, built in 1880. The spine of the house is a pine-floored hallway that floods with afternoon light. High ceilings throughout keep the interior cool in summer while open fires make for cosiness in winter. There's a bright bedroom with yellow trim and wood floor; the larger one at the front is carpeted and painted pastel. Throughout the house you'll find antique furniture, like the grandfather clock in the sitting room and the piano that you might just coax Geoff to play. Seven acres of gardens and grounds are surrounded by tall, shaded, well-tended lawns and neat flower-beds. Sit on the verandah and take in the rose parterre and flowering pomegranate. There's an intriguing L-shaped swimming pool and an all-weather tennis court too. *Golf, sailing on the Gariep Dam, Caledon River fishing and game reserves are all close at hand.*

Rooms: 3: 1 double with en-suite shower; 2 twins, 1 with en-suite shower, 1 with bath and shower.
Price: R200 – R220 pp sharing. Singles R250 – R275.
Meals: Full breakfast included. Good Restaurants in Town.
Directions: There are two huge signs to Smithfield House in town and it's a very small town. You can't miss it.

Springfontein House

Graeme Wedgwood

32 van Riebeeck Street, Springfontein 9917
Tel: 051-783-0076 Fax: 051-783-0425
Email: wedgie@icon.co.za Web: www.springfontein-guest-house.com
Cell: 082-450-6779

Graeme used to run Smithfield House, which he brought to life with cultivated, Epicurean zeal. Well, the same applies here at his new home. Those with a taste for fine living will find a kindred spirit in Graeme, a man whose love of house and garden, countryside, good company, food and wine now sets the tone at Springfontein House. He was once a gallery owner in Johannesburg – a far cry from his first, 26-year career as a London stockbroker – and his personal art collection includes a rather racy Battiss, an inky Sekoto and other originals by South African artists, both established and emerging. African rugs, powdery sofas, bowls of dried rose petals and side tables proffering porcelain complete the sandy-coloured sitting room. Through glass doors is a slate-floored, frond-filled sunroom and an incarnadine dining room, with Georgian tables and silver candelabras. In the bedrooms the curtains are silk, the towels soft and the comfy beds have crisp linen, plump pillows and mohair throws. Outside, white walls dazzle and creepers climb above the stoep; there's a bricked patio and colourful flower-beds, a pool and a series of fishponds. But the reason you come here is to be looked after, and arriving from the biscuity veld, you'll feel lucky indeed. Incidentally, Springfontein holds the rare distinction of being the only town in which I have ever won anything in a lottery. *Graeme will explain about biking, hiking, rare bird-watching, fishing, sailing on Gariep Dam.*

Rooms: 4: 2 twins and 1 double, 1 with en-suite bath and 2 with en-suite shower; 1 family suite of 2 bedrooms (1 dbl and 2/3 singles sharing shower).
Price: R180 pp sharing. Singles on request.
Meals: Full breakfast included. 3-course dinner available on request R70, excluding wine.
Directions: Heading north on the N1 turn off at Springfontein South sign. Follow road, becoming Settler St. Van Riebeeck St is on your left, and Springfontein House is at the end on right.

Bishop's Glen

Ted and Bits Quin
PO Box 9, Glen 9360
Tel: 051-861-2210 Fax: 051-861-2210
Email: bishopsglen@connix.co.za
Cell: 082-374-4986

It's a particular pleasure to stay in a place where the owners give of themselves as unstintingly as Ted and Bits do. I love the fact that they join you (you join them?) for both dinner and breakfast – this is what staying in somebody's home is all about. Nine of us sat down to a sumptuous dinner in the evening and added new resonance to the word 'convivial'. The house dates back to 1813, and the dining room still has some of the original yellowwood timbers. All is lived-in yet elegant, with beautiful wooden furniture and family portraits in abundance. Earlier we had gathered on the plant-encrusted verandah, looking out over the lush garden and its 200-plus bird species, before moving to the sitting room where Ted's 27 (I counted) cattle trophies fill up one wall. My bedroom was impressively large and timbered, with pretty linen and a substantial array of novels. No old travel magazines here! Bits (a childhood friend called Pieces is out there somewhere) does not take last-minute bookings – she likes to be prepared – so make sure you ring well in advance to reserve a night in one of the Free State's finest, homeliest bolt-holes. *There is also a game farm, with many different antelopes.*

Rooms: 3: 1 double and 2 twins; all with en-suite shower, 1 with shower and bath.
Price: Dinner, bed and breakfast: R330 - R350 pp sharing. Singles R400 – R450.
Meals: Full breakfast included. Also dinner: 3 courses with pre-dinner drinks and wine at table.
Directions: Faxed or emailed on booking. Bishop's Glen is 20km north of Bloemfontein off ramp 213 from N1.

Map Number: 13

Malealea Lodge and Pony Trek Centre

Mick and Di Jones
Malealea, Brandhof 9324
Tel: 051-447-3200 Fax: 051-448-3001
Email: malealea@mweb.co.za Web: www.malealea.co.ls
Cell: 082-552-4215

You shouldn't need an excuse to go to the kingdom of Lesotho, but if you do, look no further than Malealea Lodge. Here in the country's heartland – no phones, no mains electricity – Mick and Di have created a fascinating environment through a combination of their own personal warmth, native knowledge and a wealth of natural and cultural attractions. Malealea thrives on its interaction with the neighbouring village, but this is no plasticky 'Cultural Village' experience. The lodge is entered via the area's trading station, horses for treks of up to six days are hired locally (you stay in the villages you visit), and children will guide you on hikes. In the evenings, you listen to a local choir, before a band plays with home-made instruments. It's worth travelling off the high roads to experience moments such as these! Communal suppers are served canteen style – backpackers and ambassadors rub comradely shoulders – before the pub and firelit stoep drag you away. Later your torch guides you back to thatched rondavel or farmhouse-style accommodation – try to stay as near to the front as possible. I arrived in the afternoon rain but woke up to the most stunning of mornings, with the mist lying low down in the valley, and the peacocks crowing arrogantly at everyone. I loved this place. Two nights are an absolute minimum. *Gentle river rafting and abseiling. Best visited between December and May.*

Rooms: 40: 8 doubles and 32 twins all with en-suite shower.
Price: R175 – R220 pp sharing. Single supplement 50%.
Meals: Full breakfast included. Lunch R45. Dinner R65 for as much as you want. Horse treks R200 pp per day. Village accommodation R45 pp.
Directions: Faxed or emailed on booking.

Northern Cape

New Holme Karoo and Mieliefontein

PC and Marisca Ferreira & Ian and Elma Ferreira
Hanover 7005
Tel: 053-643-0193 (New Holme) / 0170 (Miel) Fax: 053-643-0193
Email: karoogariep@mjvn.co.za Web: www.karoogariep.co.za
Cell: 082-567-9211

Ah, life on an African farm! Here amongst the baked hills, shrubs lie like crumbs and inky mountains float on a hazy mirage. A washed-blue sky spins out candyfloss cloud, under which water pumps spin and clank and lime-wash Karoo cottages glint. On a long track, my car kicks up dust causing sheep, springbok, even donkeys to scatter, until I come to planted trees, a stone stable block with bleached-yellow doors, a well-irrigated garden, a colonial homestead and an enthusiastic welcome. PC and Marisca have created the friendliest of homes. There are neatly-fallen Jenga blocks for floors, pine dado boards and hand-painted walls – claret in the hallway, sunflower in the dining room. My room had a canopied bed, dressing table with bales of straw hats, and decorative herds of gawping wooden giraffes. The bathroom – bronzed tiles, gilt mirror, hot shower and fluffy towels – was, like everything here, unimpeachably clean. New Holme is a working farm. Sheep and cattle graze over 12,000 hectares and with neighbouring farms the area's one giant playground. "Next door" there are hippo, rhino and other plains game, and PC will arrange birding drives (250 species nest on his farm) or send you off horse-riding. Kids love the daily livestock feeding and donkey-cart rides. Marisca cooks hearty Karoo dinners, drinks are served in the boma and those mountains spring to life in the evening light.

Rooms: 4: 3 doubles, 2 with en-suite shower, 1 with bath; and 1 family unit with 1 double and 1 twin sharing a bath and shower.
Price: R150 pp sharing. Singles R250.
Meals: Full breakfast included. 3-course dinner R70 excluding wine.
Directions: On the N1 north of Hanover, signed on your west. From Hanover, travel 22km north, to graded dirt road signed on left. Follow road to farmstead at end.

Map Number: 6

Milner House

Leonie and Fires Van Vuuren

31 Milner Street,Kimberley 8301
Tel: 053-831-6405 Fax: 053-831-6407
Email: admin@milnerhouse.co.za Web: www.milnerhouse.co.za
Cell: 082-574-3496

In the world's diamond capital you have to dig for gems. Luckily, GG prospectors travel with spades and sieves and excavated this sparkler: Milner House. On the side of town where mining magnates built their Victorian mansions, the guesthouse sits in a quiet tree-lined street, behind a wall draped with greenery. The double doors of this white-walled, single-storey home open into a tiled living room where you can use the kitchen, snooze on the sofas and tuck into breakfast. The bedrooms are muted in tone, with good-quality linen, hand-made pine furniture and aircon. My favourite had two supine chairs in the light-filled pocket of a bay window. All are clean and comfortable and three have their own stoeps, from which to admire the shady garden. Palms sprout from the lawn, ivy tumbles from green tin roofs and a tree-stump path leads round to a pool. Fires and Leonie, who live next door, know a thing or two about hospitality (they own a couple of hotels in town) and the staff are charming, happily setting you off on your own treasure hunt. Minutes away are the excellent McGregor Museum, collections of contemporary art and colonial Old Masters, the Big Hole – some no-nonsense naming there! – and Rhodes's Kimberley Club. Slightly further afield lie the Kamsferdam flamingos and the Boer trenches at Magersfontein. You can even test your own fossicking skills on a real alluvial diamond dig. Fascinating stuff.

Rooms: 6: 1 twin and 4 doubles with en-suite bath and shower; 1 double with own shower, which can be joined to another double to form a family room.
Price: R200 – R240 pp sharing. Singles R310 – R350.
Meals: Full breakfast included. Local restaurants nearby offering discounts to Milner House guests.
Directions: Ask when booking.

Papkuilsfontein Farmhouse

Willem and Mariëtte van Wyk, Jaco and Alrie

Nieuwoudtville 8180
Tel: 027-218-1246 Fax: 027-218-1246
Email: info@papkuilsfontein.com Web: www.papkuilsfontein.com

I'm going to stick my neck out and say that this is my favourite place to stay in South Africa! And here are my reasons…. You stay in an old stone cottage, surrounded by rock, gum tree and wildlife, not another human in sight. The quality of peace and stillness defeats description. Gas-fired plumbing for baths, hurricane lamps for light – many guests have refused to come back if Willem installs electricity. Then there's the small matter of the gorge and waterfall, which I would have kept secret if I wasn't insistent on your visiting the farm. Your jaw will drop 180 metres into the canyon. Take a picnic to the deep rock pools for swimming above the waterfall and you can climb down into the gorge in an hour and a half. The wild flowers in season are sensational even by Namaqualand standards; the plantlife, divided between Cape fynbos and Karoo succulent, a botanist's dream; steenbok, klipspringer, porcupine and dassie love the terrain and have NOT been specially introduced. Mariëtte is an excellent cook (breakfast a string of surprises). It's a magical place that not many know about and the van Wyks are lovely, friendly people who seem unable to put a proper price on what they have to offer! You should stay *at least* two nights. There's also a restored corrugated-iron cottage for those who need their electricity!

Rooms: 2 stone cottages sleeping 4 and 6: one with bath and one with shower. 1 cottage with one twin and one double both with en/s bath and shower.
Price: R225 – R255 pp sharing. Single rates +R50.
Meals: Full breakfast included. 3-course dinners R100.
Directions: From CT take N1 then N7 to Vanrhynsdorp. Turn off onto R27 to Nieuwoudtville. Turn right into town, and straight through onto dirt road for 22km. The farm signed to the right.

Map Number: 4

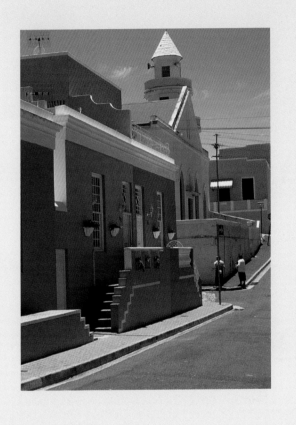

Gauteng

Gauteng

Clouds End

Margaret Berns

93 St Swithins Avenue, Melville (on border of Auckland Park), Johannesburg
2092 Tel: 011-888-1735 Fax: 011-804-5176
Email: margaret@apexcom.co.za Web: www.apexcom.co.za
Cell: 083-379-8526

Clouds End is the ideal location from which to explore Johannesburg and it offers a comfort that is thoroughly welcoming after a day in the city. Just five minutes' walk away are the chic, arty restaurants, bars and cadeaux boutiques of Melville where you can spend a day perusing the second-hand book stores, drinking coffee and watching the beau monde strut by. If you're looking to just chill out in the evening, buy a healthy frozen meal from Wild Olive delicatessen and heat it in your microwave. Then take your meal out into the private courtyard with its tinkling water and a mural wall painted by Margaret's artist daughter. The building is brand new and the finishing touches were just being added when I visited. My favourite was the upstairs Manhattan-style suite, with its wooden floor, orchid in the corner, large, square, engraved headboard, individual sofas and doors leading onto the patio shaded by a parasol. But all the suites are stylish, spacious and well-thought-out, with pristine bathrooms and tasteful contemporary furnishings and pictures on the walls. There is controlled lighting, heating, fans, microwave, mini-oven with hobs, and a fridge. The patios at the back are a little bigger with delicate flowerbeds and the other upstairs room, the only one with no outside area, has a romantic four-poster bed and a red, curvaceous sofa. Breakfasts are served in your rooms.

Rooms: 8: 5 queens and 3 king/twins, all with en-suite bath and shower.
Price: R325 – R399 pp sharing. Singles R450 – R599.
Meals: Full breakfast included.
Directions: Map faxed or emailed.

Elizabeth Manor

Joan Clarke

141 First Street, Cnr Elizabeth Ave, Sandhurst, Sandton 2196
Tel: 011-884-0880 Fax: 011-884-9909
Email: info@elizabethmanor.co.za Web: www.elizabethmanor.co.za
Cell: 082-375-0000

Talk about arriving in style! A man in a suit who seemed to be expecting me led me to a white Rolls Royce. In this soundless carriage I was cocooned from the heat and cars, the traffic-light hawkers, the mines and malls and I felt calm and safe; the perfect acclimatisation between weary flight and bustling city. These streets were built on gold, but it is for the dazzling jacaranda trees that line them that the city is noted. En route to Sandton, we floated over blankets of purple petals to the gates of Elizabeth Manor. I was ushered into the cool of this ochre villa, to a large room with mirrored wall, travertine tiles, vibrant oil paintings, rich wooden furniture and displays of antique curios. Breakfast is served in here or out on the patio. My bedroom was crisp and cushioned, with a large bathroom and access to the garden. There's a pool here too, spanned by a bridge besides which an iron elephant silently trumpets. The lounge boasts no fewer than five sofas and the biggest TV I've seen. Nothing was too much trouble for Joan. She brought me a stream of drinks while I used her computer; she organised car hire and even loaned me the use of her car for the five-minute drive to Sandton City. Breakfast was especially memorable. A great intro to Johannesburg. *Can arrange airport transfers or limousine, helicopter or Ferrari trips to Sun City.*

Rooms: 9: 4 twins with en-suite bath and shower; 1 single with private bath and shower and 4 twin self-catering units.
Price: R200 – R300 pp sharing. Singles R450.
Meals: Full breakfast included. Light lunches and dinners by arrangement from R60.
Directions: Ask when booking. Airport limousine transfers R675.

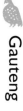

Liliesleaf

Nicholas Wolpe
8 Winston Avenue, Rivonia, Johannesburg 2128
Tel: 011-803-3787 Fax: 011-803-6484
Email: info@liliesleaf.com Web: www.liliesleaf.com
Cell: 083-377-3533

This is the place where Nelson Mandela and senior leaders of the ANC secretly took refuge. It was also from here that the high command of MK, the military wing of the ANC, conducted the struggle for liberation and justice. It was at Liliesleaf Farm that senior leaders of MK were arrested, Walter Sisulu and Govan Mbeki among them. Nelson Mandela, Sisulu, Mbeki and seven others were put on trial (known to the world as the Rivonia trial) for high treason. Photographs, memoirs and documentation in the museum tell the story of Liliesleaf Farm. The 28-acre property is described by Nelson Mandela in his book *A Long Walk to Freedom* as his 'idyllic bubble', his hide-out where he took on a nom de guerre and was known as David, the gardener and cook, dressed in blue labourer's overalls. In the surroundings of this unique historical site guests can eat gourmet meals in the shade of the infamous tree or in the Walter Sisulu dining room hung with photographs of the Rivonia trialists. In this atmosphere of historical and political grandeur, guests are treated to warmth, friendliness and wonderful home-made meals and breakfasts. The Liliesleaf and Rivonia suites come with historic features and stories that will captivate you and keep you spell bound as you soak up the legacy of Liliesleaf. Liliesleaf is a fascinating component of any visit to Johannesburg.

Rooms: 3: 2 kings, 1 twin, all with en-suite bath and shower.
Price: R800 – R1,200 pp sharing. R550 – R850 single.
Meals: Full breakfast included, 3-course lunch R195, 4-course dinner R225.
Directions: Map faxed or emailed.

Ordo Tours

Suzanne and Amos Ordo

PO Box 78220, Sandton, Johannesburg 2146
Tel: 011-883-0050 Fax: 011-883-0049
Email: ordotours@global.co.za Web: www.ordotours.co.za
Cell: 083-252-6776

This is an unusual one for us. But we've sat down to enough breakfasts with glassy-eyed travellers determined to see all that South Africa has to offer in as few days as possible to know that some of us – particularly first-time visitors – could do with a little help when it comes to planning. Let's face it, if you're rushing off to catch a plane or to drive five hours to tick off the next sight before the last crumb of toast has hit the breakfast table, you're not really giving yourself enough time to savour South Africa. The key to an enjoyable holiday is to make it manageable. Which is where Ordo Tours come in. Of all the tour operators we've seen, they come closest to our philosophy in their selection of places to stay and will happily help plan your holiday, exclusively using the places in the book. Suzi and Amos will put together a personalised itinerary that will suit your budget and pace, based on your preferences and their local knowledge. They'll take care of as little or as much as you want, be it booking the odd night or commission-free flight-arranging, car and mobile phone hire or piecing together guided tours that usher you round the country in air-conditioned micro-buses. Off-the-shelf packages cover Cape Town and the Winelands, the Garden Route, Johannesburg and Pretoria, Kruger National Park and Vic Falls.

Rooms: n/a
Price: Prices according to itinerary. Package tours from R3,810 for 3-day Kruger Park Tour to R12,925 for 9-day South Africa Highlights excursion. Prices are pp sharing.
Meals: n/a.
Directions: n/a.

Liz at Lancaster

Liz Delmont

79 Lancaster Ave, Craighall Park 2196
Tel: 011-442-8083 Fax: 011-880-5969
Email: lizdel@megaweb.co.za Web: www.lizatlancaster.co.za
Cell: 083-229-4223

Liz's place on its own is our idea of a B&B (more on that later), but throw in Liz as well and you get something special. In my limited experience she is an anomaly among South Africans, having no great interest in rugby, football or cricket, and this despite being surrounded by a sports-mad family. Liz teaches art history and post-graduate tourism development at Witwatersrand University, and is a fascinating person to speak to about South Africa both past and future… and about Jo'burg. She will point you in all the right directions for a genuine, heartfelt and hard-to-come-by insight into her home city. But guests at Liz's also have plenty of space in which to do their own thing. The big comfy rooms are either side of the main house, with their own entrances and parking spaces. Two more have been added since our last book; that is to say, Liz has given over even more of her home to her guests. A separate cottage has its own kitchen and sitting room. They all open up onto a private patio, where breakfast is generally served, with potted plants climbing up the walls and plenty of shade. Between them is a rose-filled garden, while at the front of the house is yet more green space around the pool. Finally, a mention for the friendly staff, who have a stake in the venture.

Rooms: 4: 3 doubles (1 with kitchen) with en/s bath and shower, plus 1 cottage with kitchen and sitting room.
Price: R270 – R350 pp sharing. Singles R400 – R540.
Meals: Full breakfast included. Dinners on request but very close to Parkhurst and many restaurants.
Directions: Jan Smuts Ave runs down the middle of the city and Lancaster Ave is off it. Directions on web site.

Melrose Place Guest Lodge

Sue Truter

12a North St, Melrose 2196
Tel: 011-442-5231 Fax: 011-880-2371
Email: melroseplace@global.co.za Web: www.melroseplace.co.za
Cell: 083-457-4021

Once ensconced behind the electric gates at Melrose you have entered an Eden-in-the-city. The verandah overlooks a large flower garden and enormous swimming pool, all shaded by trees. Eight new rooms don't crowd it at all. It is such a pleasant environment that you may find yourself shelving projected tasks for a day's lounging about. My room was a suite attached to the main house, with mounted TV, huge bed (built up with cushions and pillows), a big bathroom and double doors onto the garden. The high levels of luxury in all the rooms are not reflected in the rates. Sue is the sweetest of hostesses, quick to smiles and reacting sensitively to the mood and wishes of each guest. On the night I stayed we had a braai with an amazing array of meat dishes and salads which appeared from nowhere, and Sue's team will cook dinner for anyone who wants it every evening. Her aim is to maximise the number of happy campers staying. This is her home after all, complete with kids, dachshund and a parrot in its forties. While guest contentment is running at 100 per cent, it's difficult to see what else she can do. *Laundry provided on request. Nearby: Wanderers cricket ground, Rosebank and Sandton shopping precincts and many restaurants. Airport transfers arranged by Sue.*

Rooms: 14: all en-suite (1 bath only, 4 bath and shower, 9 shower only); includes two cottages.
Price: R325 – R375 pp sharing. Singles R505 – R595.
Meals: Full breakfast included. Lunches or dinners by arrangement: R45 - R85.
Directions: Ask for a map when booking. Or a map is on the web site.

Whistletree Lodge

Kobus Farrell

1267 Whistletree Drive,
Queenswood, Pretoria 0121
Tel: 012-333-9915 or 6
Fax: 012-333-9917
Email: wtree@icon.co.za
Web:
www.whistletreelodge.com

Here's a house with a tale to tell, the Victorian setting for the scandalous and ultimately tragic love affair between Lt. Brown and Lady Sumnerville. Throughout the house, military portraits, excavated horseshoes and news clippings serve as the story's historical props. Kobus tells me that the interior is Scottish baronial, but really he's a cultural magpie with an eclectic mix of colonial pieces. Impressive staircases and landings provide new perspectives on the lofty rooms. In secluded nooks and crannies, magazines spill from baskets at the foot of comfy armchairs. There's an Art Deco cigar-room, reference library and yellowwood boardroom where Kobus's Pretorian family photos can be traced back five generations. A sleek jazz bar looks out to the pool, lawns and tennis court, and the newer bedrooms (modern comforts and antique furniture) have views across the jacaranda trees or the floodlit koppie at the back of the house. You can stroll here in the evenings, before returning to a dinner prepared fresh to your tastes. The service is distinctly old-school, attentive, discreet and instant. If you have been before, you are likely to be remembered. The building has been designed as a modern take on the pyramids, its sloping walls and ecclesiastic fenestration exalting sun and sky. Of course this contrast between old and new is somewhat blurred, and that's half the fun. *Closed 15th December to 5th January.*

Rooms: 12: 6 queens, 1 double, 3 singles and 2 twins, all with en-suite bath and shower.
Price: R550 – R975 pp sharing. Singles R535 – R1,050.
Meals: Full breakfast included. Lunch by arrangement. 3-course dinner R160 excluding wine.
Directions: From JHB airport, follow the R21. Turn onto the N1 motorway. Turn off at the N4. At the 2nd traffic light turn right into Duncan St which leads into Gordon Rd. Look out for signs to WTL.

Ipe Tombe Guest Lodge

Pat and Bob Gold

63 Kingwillow Crescent,
Ranjiesfontein, Midrand 1685
Tel: 011-314-5829
Fax: 011-314-2260
Email: isavingo@mweb.co.za
Cell: 082-875-5526

They said I'd find gold in Johannesburg, and I did. Pat and Bob Gold, to be precise. There's a village feel to Ranjiesfontein, and Ipe Tombe sits in its leafy crescent. Uniquely for Johannesburg, there are no high walls here, making a welcome change. Instead, the Golds are fenced in by the horsey crowd ("neigh-bores"?) – Harry Oppenheimer's stables are here – and the guesthouse's name is taken from a Durban Cup winner. Midrand itself is now the new commercial centre of Johannesburg, and Ipe Tombe is popular with business guests. It's not hard to see why. Pat and Bob have a knack for making their guests feel right at home (even those poor businessfolk who wish they were). They loan mobile phones and organise picnics and game-viewing. When I visited Bob was busy fetching and ferrying guests around the city, and I had a drink with Pat in their small bar which spills into a patio with wildlife mural and pool area. Meals are tailored to your liking and timing, including even the wee small hours. And the breakfast! Having had an enormous dinner the night before, I was presented with the world's second biggest omelette (I couldn't face a 12-egg monster). Rather embarrassingly, I devoured it quickly enough for the chef to remark that I had quite an appetite. Which I took to be a compliment. *Well positioned for airport, Pretoria and routes west to Magaliesburg and Madikwe and east to Kruger.*

Rooms: 6: 3 queens and 3 twins, all with en-suite bath and shower.
Price: R250 – R300 pp sharing. Singles R350 – R400.
Meals: Full breakfast included. Lunch, 3-course dinner (and midnight feasts) available. Prices R65 – R85, excluding wine.
Directions: N1 north, take exit to R652 heading east. At first lights, turn left onto R101. Pass garage on right and another up on left. Ahead at lights and look for turning on right signed Ranjiesfontein.

North West Province

Hideaway at the Farm

Mike and Sabine Manegold

Pelindaba Road 10, Broederstroom, Hartbeespoort 0240
Tel: 073-302-9422 Fax: 012-205-1309
Email: info@hideawayatthefarm.com Web: www.hideawayatthefarm.com
Cell: 073-302-9422

I couldn't imagine a less contrived and more relaxing place. Mike is a laid-back, nurturing soul (and reformed advertising executive) with a real commitment to and passion for South Africa and this spirit reigns at the farm. With views to the Hartbeespoort Dam and magical Magaliesberg – Johannesburg's playground and natural magnets for water-sport and hiking enthusiasts – the farm consists of a two-bedroom farmhouse and two conjoined rondavels backed by a koppie. The farmhouse has an open-plan kitchen and a large comfortable lounge whose sliding glass doors lead to a pool. Across the drive are the rondavels: slate floors, fleshy walls and towering, thatched ceilings. Though the farm no longer yields produce, it "farms people" instead. Charming Benjamin runs the place and chef Edwin will serve you breakfast on your patio. There's a braai area marked out by Sabine's dream symbols while lower down Benjamin is busy building a bar and café, which will showcase Edwin's fabulous fare. But the real reason to come to the farm is because it is filled with the optimism of the new South Africa. Swiss-born Mike has a wealth of knowledge about his adopted country but to listen to Benjamin's balanced tales of the Apartheid years is to witness the new hope for South Africa first hand. An enriching experience.

Rooms: 3: in the farmhouse: 1 double with en-suite bath/shower and 1 twin with en/s shower; 2 rondavels each with double and en/s bath/shower plus cooking facilities.
Price: From R210 pp sharing. Singles on request. Weekly and monthly rates available.
Meals: Full breakfast included. Café restaurant on site for other meals and a good number of restaurants within a ten-minute drive.
Directions: From Johannesburg follow signs to Randburg and N1 heading north-west. Take R512 past Lanseria Airport toward Hartbeespoort Dam. At T-junction turn left and the farm is signed on the left.

Map Number: 13 & 17

Dodona

Beresford Jobling

Dodona Farm, Hh 8-9, Hartebeesthoek, Skeerpoort, Magaliesberg 0232
Tel: 012-207-1320 Fax: 012-207-1351
Email: dodona@worldonline.co.za
Web: www.hartbeespoortdam.com/dodona Cell: 082-494-7568

I found the moments that slipped away sitting with Beres and his dog, in the shadow of the world's oldest mountains, listening to him recount local histories and call out the name of birds in the garden, amongst the most peaceful I've spent in Africa. Amonst other things Beres is an illuminating art historian, a vellophile and a direct descendant of Andries Pretorius, the Boer commander who led the massacre of the Zulus at Blood River, and who made his home on this farm. Battle has left an indelible mark on this area, and on Dodona. Beres's doughty grandmother built (with her own hands!) the thatched chapel here to commemorate family caught in conflict. A stone path leads to the Boathouse, a blushing colonial-style cottage housing two old-fashioned apartments, coir-carpeted, with delicate windows, Victorian furniture, fireplace and bookshelves. Days can be filled with ballooning, biking, hiking, riding and water-sports on Hartbeespoort Dam. Battlefields, game farms and the Cradle of Mankind are close by, too. But you may prefer to sit by the lake and spot high- and lowveld birdlife or wander round the sun-dappled garden. There's a freshwater plunge pool, a croquet lawn and a variety of conifers and gums, one of which Beres assures me becomes quite sensuous under moonlight. There's so much to recommend here… "except the nightlife," says Beres. But even so you can always dosi-do at the local square dance. *The Magaliesberg is a World Heritage site. Closed between Christmas and New Year.*

Rooms: 2 self-contained apartments, 1 king and 1 twin, both with en-suite bath and shower.
Price: R390 pp sharing.
Meals: Full breakfast included, eaten at the main house or brought to you.
Directions: From Jo'burg, take R512 north, past N14 and Lanseria Airport. Turn left at T-jct, through Broederstroom and left, signed Cradle of Mankind, towards Hartebeesthoek.

The Mountain Country House

Tessa Fleischer

Plot 94, Kalkhaeuwel, Broederstroom 2021
Tel: 012-205-1268 Fax: 012-205-1268
Email: tfleischer@iafrica.com Web: www.sa-venues.com/nwp/mountain.htm
Cell: 083-236-7431

In the birthplace of modern man, perched on a rocky koppie, there's a Spanish castle where a willowy woman lives with a wolf. No word of a lie: amongst the wheat-coloured hills of the Cradle of Humankind sits a castellated hilltop hacienda with curling white walls, tilted terracotta tiles and rounded beams that peek out like portholes. Inside, parquetry flows beneath cathedral ceilings to rooms decorated with sculptural pieces. Railway sleepers sweep up to a billowy bedroom overlooking the Magaliesberg and across the courtyard there's a stone-floor cottage with iron bed and kitchenette. It turns out that what I took to be Moorish is actually "a sculpture with holes in it". Designed by Tessa's late husband it's something of an artel, complete with gallery and studio. Tessa's a silversmith; she's well-travelled, graceful and great fun. She readily cracked open a bottle of chilled wine which we drank on a cushioned terrace, one of a series (terraces, not bottles) cascading to the hilltop pool, while fellow artisans Godfrey and Lazarus wrangled with wrought-iron. They're very much involved here, as is Tessa's daughter, who built a timber cabin entirely out of recycled material. You can stay there and enjoy an alfresco, lamp-lit, kloof-edge bath. It's close to Jo'burg, whose horizon lights Tessa sees as a glittering necklace. I liked this place so much, I still kick myself for not staying longer. It's moreish after all.

Rooms: 3: 1 double in-house with en-suite bath and shower; 1 double cottage and 1 cabin (sleeps 6), both self-catering with bath and shower.
Price: B&B R260 pp. Self-catering from R200 pp to R650 for 6 pax.
Meals: Full breakfast included for in-house guests. Nearby restaurants and cafés for meals throughout the day.
Directions: From Johannesburg take R512 north. Look out for turning to Lanseria Airport. Continue on R512 for 12km, then turn left to gates of Cradle of Humankind Reserve. Guard will guide you to Mountain Country House.

Mosetlha Bush Camp

Chris and June Lucas
Madikwe Game Reserve
Tel: 011-444-9345 Fax: 011-444-9345
Email: info@thebushcamp.com Web: www.thebushcamp.com
Cell: 083-653-9869

Mosetlha puts the wild into wilderness; no doors or glass here as they would hinder the feel and dust of Africa permeating your very core; no electric fences surround the camp as there is no electricity; no worries either as you leave them at the gate. Facilities are basic but real; guests draw their own hot water from a donkey-boiler before proceeding to the shower. Recently the kitchen was extended and a new thatch and stone lapa has been added for guests to read, relax and compare sightings, but the authenticity remains untainted. The wooden cabins are comfortable, but used only for sleeping – you are here for the wilderness experience of the outdoors. Chris's passion for conservation and his environment shines through and is contagious (which reminds me to say that the area is malaria-free). His guests depart much the wiser, not only because of the game drives, but also because of the superb guided wilderness walks. Yes, the Madikwe Game Reserve (70,000 hectares) has the so-called 'Big Five', but a game lodge worth its salt (such as this) will fire your imagination about the whole food chain. Even the camp itself is an education – all sorts of birds, small mammals and antelopes venture in. Come for a genuine and memorable bush experience.

Rooms: 8 twins sharing 3 shower/toilet complexes.
Price: All-inclusive from R895 per person. Drinks (beer, wine, fizzy drinks, mineral water) extra.
Meals: All meals and some refreshments (coffee, tea, fruit juice) included.
Directions: Detailed written directions supplied on request.

Map Number: 16

Jaci's Tree Lodge

Jan and Jaci van Heteren
Madikwe Game Reserve, Derdepoort 2876
Tel: 014-533-3834 Fax: 014-533-2521
Email: jaci@madikwe.com Web: www.madikwe.com
Cell: 083-447-7929 or reservations on 083-700-2071

"Hold on!" Joe Ranger hollers above walkie-talkie crackle and engine rattle. We're gunning through bush, bouncing along a sandy track, leaning in to avoid being whipped by thicket. Lion spoor's been spotted – a pride on the hunt – and we're in an adrenaline-pumping race to find them first. When we do, we watch in breathless awe as they saunter by less than a metre from us, senses fixed on their prey: an elephant, who charges and they scatter. We're still abuzz when we return to our already-run baths and chat animatedly around the boma fire at dinner. Jaci's has this effect on you. Wonderfully indulgent, this is one of Tatler's favourites. Beyond the foyer's tree-pierced, blonde-thatch roof lies an expansive restaurant overlooking riverine forest and separated from the chic bar by a four-sided open fire, which together keep you in long cocktails and gourmet food. Relax the excess off in a hammock; alternatively there's a pool and gym. Save your gasps of delight for the tree houses. Sitting six metres above ground and linked by a rosewood walkway, their glass doors concertina open onto private decks. Vibrant colours form a backdrop for a bed festooned with silk cushions, burnt-orange suede beanbag and swollen stone bath with handmade copper pipes. But Jaci's trump card is the rangers whose enthusiasm creates a wonderful, wild adventure. What a job they have – daily taking breath away. *Further along the river bank you'll also find Jaci's Safari Lodge with its opulent canvas and stone suites.*

Rooms: 8 tree houses each with king-size bed and bath and outdoor "jungle" shower.
Price: R2,695 – R4,000 pppn sharing.
Meals: All meals and game drives included.
Directions: Directions faxed or emailed on booking. Transfer from Jo'burg and flights to Madikwe airstrip also available; ask when booking.

Mpumalanga

Something out of Nothing

Sarah Mahlangu
Middleburg 1050
Tel: 013-242-2113
Fax: 013-242-2113
Email: somenot@lantic.net
Cell: 082-939-5492

Sarah is a remarkable woman. Her job creation project has literally been built from nothing, but is now a flourishing restaurant of South African cuisine and a craft shop, displaying arts from various African regions – I was delighted by the jewellery, beaded dolls and traditional Venda, Shangani and Siswati clothes. Sarah not only has a special gift and warmth with people, but is also a skilled craftswoman and teaches her staff and guests – in particular Ndebele painting. Tourists initially came to eat at Sarah's restaurant for a cultural experience and would beg her for an extension of that exposure by staying in her house; she moved out of her small, bricked, thatched home to make rooms available for those who would like to experience her hospitality and lifestyle. She takes visitors on township tours and has even accompanied tourists to the local jazz session and night-vision church for a song and a clap. She wishes to present the tourist with a genuine experience. Her house is not glamorous… many of the dividing walls don't reach the ceilings. She is purposefully chipping away at the white enamel on the bath to expose the raw metal. However, the sitting room is filled with African trinkets and furnishings and there is a small back yard for breakfast under a pear-tree. Come and meet Sarah and embrace a rich side to South African culture rarely experienced by overseas tourists.

Rooms: 2: 1 double with en-suite bath, 1 twin and 1 double with shared bathroom with raw bath.
Price: R125 pp sharing.
Meals: Full English breakfast included. R15 for a traditional meal and Sarah also cooks westernised food.
Directions: Directions faxed when booking.

Five Assegais Country Estate

Francis Darvall

PO Box 593, Machadodorp 1170
Tel: 013-256-9263 Fax: 013-256-9190
Email: francis@lando.co.za Web: www.fiveassegais.co.za
Cell: 082-889-6757

Paul Kruger himself had this original stone house built in 1850 as an Uitspanplek (way station) en route to the gold mines of Barberton. Ox-wagons would pass by on the dirt track over the Swurweberg Mountains from where you have a spread of undulating green hills with a view that stretches to Swaziland. We walked in the remarkable landscape with its sandstone outcrops stemming from the ancient seabed of the Gondwanaland period. The stones shelter a wonderland of stunted yellowwood trees and aloes which lead to the second highest falls in Mpumalanga, Brides Leap Falls, a painting of which, by Bertha Everard, hangs in the South African Houses of Parliament. You can come here to fish trout, ride horses and stretch those legs or simply recline under the pergola next to the pool. Francis has renovated the house beautifully. He is an artist by profession and his aesthetic 'eye' never sleeps! There are tambooti wood surfaces in the kitchen, grey slate floors in the kitchen and bathrooms, while original Oregon pine floorboards deck the light-filled, open-plan lounge. Francis's oil paintings hang on the walls and I particularly admired the green granite chopping-board cut from the stones outside. The house feels like a real home with its vast library of books and National Geographics, satellite TV and laid-back atmosphere. Breathe in the fresh mountain air and relax.

Rooms: 1 booking only: 2 doubles with en-suite bath and shower, 1 double with private bath and shower; 1 kids room with 4 single beds.
Price: R200 – R250 pp sharing.
Meals: Self-catering only, but on request you can have food stocked and cooked for you under your supervision.
Directions: N4 past Belfast and take second turning into Machadodorp. Turn left onto R541 to Badplaas. After 17.5km take Bloemfontein turn off to the right. This becomes a gravel road, go for 3km to T-junction, turn left and continue for 3km.

Cranes Nest

Wilfred and Rosemarie' Middleton & Mark and Lynne Hughes

Wilgekraal, PO Box 389, Lydenburg 1120
Tel: 013-256-9055 Fax: 013-256-9048
Email: cranesnest@mweb.co.za Web: www.crane.co.za Cell: 082-330-2155

'Malapeng' at Cranes Nest was named by the locals and means 'place of the old walls'. Foundation walls dating back to 700 AD indicate habitation by indigenous people and later the Boers. Up in the mountain yonder, which forms part of the Mpumalanga Drakensberg range, you will find remains of walls used by the rainmaker for initiation ceremonies. At the bottom of this mountain are four bush-chalets. The walls are semi-concrete, semi-canvas with dinky, en-suite, thatched-roof bathrooms. A sofa and table outside under a canopy overlook the mountain. These are compact, fun cottage-tents with colourful mirrors, sinks and Ndebele designs and colours painted on walls. All have private gardens. Guinea Fowl cottage is built in rock with a big open-plan kitchen, lounge and dining area and Eagle Owl is a thatched cottage surrounded by red canna flowers and indigenous trees. Guests commune in the high-ceilinged thatched dining room, cool with large tiles on the floor. Evenings are also spent around the fire in the boma where braais are popular in summer. Rosemarie' and Lynne cook according to wants and needs and treat guests to home-made bread and muffins. There are three trout dams where you will also spot the rare southern kneria – fish with ears! Blimey! Enjoy the tranquillity, serenity and the beautiful verdant surrounds.

Rooms: 6: 4 chalets, all kings/twins with en-suite showers and outside showers; 2 self-catering cottages.
Price: R520 pp sharing catered. Self-catering: R325 pp per night.
Meals: Full breakfast and 3-course dinner included (vegetarians welcome).
Directions: Emailed or faxed when booking.

Map Number: 18

Hops Hollow Country House

Theo and Sarie de Beer

PO Box 430, Lydenburg 1120
Tel: 013-235-2275 or 083-627-6940 Fax: 083-118-627-6940
Email: hops@hopshollow.com Web: www.hopshollow.com
Cell: 084-526-2721

The highest brewery in South Africa, Hops Hollow combines the warmest of welcomes with home-made beers, scrumptious meals and a picturesque setting. There is something rather Scottish about the scenery surrounding this guest-house high on the Long Tom Pass, with its mountains, mist and crisp air. The area has many Boer War and gold-rush connections and Theo will tell you about both historical and natural wonders. Following a Damascene conversion one moonlit night he gave up clerical work for life in conservation and has never looked back. When not at his day job with the Mpumalanga Parks Board he's a proper microbrewer (supply your own 'De Beer' pun) and loves showing guests around his brewery. A rather baronial pub with vast columns made from old railway sleepers should be complete by the time this book is published. Sarie, meanwhile, is the force behind the guest house whose bedrooms have thick duvets and large cushions and, in some cases, views best appreciated from the pillow. She is also a wonderful cook (lots of beer in the recipes) and her breakfasts are super special, a 3-course meal in themselves. I defy you to leave Hops Hollow with your belt on the same notch. This small twin-pronged business is a delight, for ale-lovers and otherwise.

Rooms: 3: all twin/doubles with en-suite showers.
Price: R250 – R300 pp sharing. Singles R275 – R315.
Meals: Full breakfast included. Dinner by prior arrangement: 3 courses R85 – R95.
Directions: On R37 between Sabie and Lydenburg, opposite milestone 22.2 on the Long Tom Pass (distance from Lydenburg).

Kavinga Guest House

Stuart and Ros Hulley-Miller

R37 Nelspruit/Sabie Rd, Nelspruit 1200
Tel: 013-755-3193 Fax: 013-755-3161
Email: kavinga@mpu.co.za
Cell: 083-625-7162

Thick orchards of avocados buffer Kavinga farmhouse and its green lake of lawn from the outside world. Ros assembles a country breakfast on the stone-tiled verandah, which is latticed with rare jade vine and camouflaged by plants and flowers. If you are like the majority of the Hulley-Millers' guests you will spend a good deal of time there, lying on wicker furniture and deck chairs or flopping indolently in the pool while Ros dispenses indispensable drinks. Spacious bedrooms dotted around the grounds are classily decorated and pander to the 21st century with satellite TV, bar fridges and sumptuous bathrooms (with both shower and free-standing bath). The family unit has its own sitting room with a sofa bed to unravel for extra bodies. French windows open onto small covered patios with broad views over the Lowveld. I think it was Walt Disney's Baloo the Bear who said: 'Float downstream, fall apart in my backyard'.... *Just 45km to the Kruger National Park.*

Rooms: 5: 3 twins, 1 double and 1 family unit with 1 double and 1 twin – all with en-suite baths and showers.
Price: R235 – R250 pp sharing. Singles R295 – R325.
Meals: Full breakfast included. Dinner by arrangement: R85 for 3 courses
Directions: 14.5km north from Nelspruit on R37 towards Sabie. Sign to right.

Map Number: 18

Chez Vincent Restaurant and Guesthouse

Vincent and Sara Martinez

56 Ferreira Street, Nelspruit 1200
Tel: 013-744-1146 Fax: 013-744-1147
Email: chezvincent_sa@yahoo.com Web: www.chezvincent.co.za
Cell: 082-331-1054

What wonderful hosts! And I certainly picked a good night to stay. On Sundays the restaurant is closed, but Sara (English) and Vincent (French) invited me and their other paying guests to a private dinner party for friends. Dinner parties aren't usually on the menu! One of the other guests is a regular and told me over dinner that he appreciated the proximity of the guest house to the airport and town amenities and enjoys the delicious food and friendly, relaxed atmosphere. Well, I can vouch for that. Nelspruit is a hub town, gateway to Mozambique and Swaziland, and also the Kruger National Park. Some guests come over from Maputo for shopping and others are international visitors stopping over before entering the park. All enjoy Vincent's South-African-influenced French cuisine in his cosy, intimate restaurant and breakfasts of scrambled eggs and smoked salmon are also a winner. Rooms here are brand-new, light-filled, air-conditioned and six of them have doors opening out onto either side of the swimming pool. Each has Sara's choice of a funky splash of colour: lime green, turquoise, yellow, pink and orange. She has enjoyed building up the guest house little by little and they both seem thoroughly happy in their South African family set-up, far from France and northern England. Chez Vincent's is the only non-chain restaurant in town and is a comfortable, very friendly stopover before the next leg of your journey.

Rooms: 11: 7 doubles with en/s showers and bath, 4 family rooms each with 1 double, bathroom with shower, sofa-bed, lounge and fully-equipped kitchen.
Price: R220 – R250 pp sharing. Singles R270 – R300.
Meals: Full breakfast included. A la carte restaurant on premises.
Directions: Take N4 to Nelspruit and turn right into Paul Kruger Street at Absa Square. This leads into Ferreira Street. At end turn right (still Ferreira St) and immediately left into service road, Chez Vincent is 4th house on the left.

Map Number: 18

Ambience Inn

Johan Lubbe and Issy de Lira

28 Wally Scott St, White River 1240
Tel: 013-751-1951 Fax: 013-751-1951
Email: ambience@lantic.net Web: www.ambienceinn.co.za
Cell: 082-928-0461

Lost again, I stopped at some traffic lights where I asked police officers in the car next to me for directions. Helpful police fellows in this town! I was escorted through a canopy of flamboyant trees – in full red-blossom livery – to the end of a quiet cul-de-sac where guinea fowl roam between properties. Johan is a fashion designer and has fashioned his house, brand-new and built from scratch, into an Aztec-style palladium. Terracotta-coloured columns and walls provide the entrance into a sub-tropical, indigenous garden of clivias, gingers, macadamias… and a colossal kapok tree with cotton-wool 'flowers' which Victorians apparently used to stuff their pillows. There is a refreshing and get-fit-worthy, fifteen-metre-long, narrow, lap swimming pool bordered by blue mosaic tiles. On the guests' stoep is a manicured garden of mosses, tropical staghorn ferns and orchids clinging to old tree stumps. The bedrooms are comfortable with cool-for-the-summer screed floors, high ceilings and African bedspreads. All of the rooms have private outdoor courtyards with alfresco showers and breakfasts are served on the stoep with hessian curtains hanging from the high mantle and wind chimes singing in the breeze. Johan makes breakfasts to suit your preference and can also create a take-out picnic for early starts into the nearby Kruger Park.

Rooms: 6: 4 doubles and 2 twins, all with en-suite showers and outside shower.
Price: R195 – R220 pp sharing.
Meals: Full breakfast or picnic basket. Dinners on request and restaurants nearby.
Directions: From Jo'burg take N4 to Nelspruit and turn left onto R40. When in White River turn first left after first traffic light into Henry Morey Rd, then right into Frank Townsend Rd, then left into Wally Scott St.

Jatinga Guest House

John and Lyn Davis
Jatinga Road, Plaston, White River 1240
Tel: 013-751-5059 /013-751-5199 Fax: 013-751-5119
Email: info@jatinga.co.za Web: www.jatinga.co.za
Cell: 082-259-4118

You know from the smile at the boom-gate and the cheerful greeting at the end of the gravel drive that all will be well at Jatinga. From the tiled foyer, you're led through an atrium hallway to a terracotta-tiled lounge. This is bathed in sunlight flooding through open French doors that lead onto a somnolent verandah. Here couples on cushioned wicker chairs take tea overlooking a glassy croquet lawn and sub-tropical garden strewn with jacaranda petals. The large bedrooms, some modelled as modern rondavels, radiate from the 1920s homestead. Victorian rooms have outdoor showers, the Provençal house concrete baths so big they should come with a lifeguard. I stayed in the Colonial Suite and, clothes despatched for laundering, found I could enjoy my mini-bar ministrations from any number of positions: the oversized bed, the sofa, the claw-foot bath, the patio…. But the choices don't end there. You can browse safari journals in sofas like quicksand; perfect your heliotropic posturing by a pool shielded by ramrod palms; or sip sundowners on the deck above the White River. In the light-filled dining room with its cellar of top-notch wines I gleefully tackled the crab curry, my clean clothes preserved by a bib, the battle-scarred tablecloth not so lucky. You are so well looked after here you may forget that your safari adventure awaits.

Rooms: 14: 4 luxury suites and 10 superior rooms, all with en-suite bath and shower.
Price: R835 – R1,095 pp sharing. Singles R1,095 – R1,395.
Meals: Full breakfast included. A la carte restaurant serves lunch and dinner daily. Light meals available 24 hrs. Gourmet picnic hampers on request.
Directions: From Nelspruit head to White River (approx. 20km) and proceed through town. Continue straight along the R538 to Karino/Plaston for 4.3km from last traffic light, crossing over two railway lines. Turn right onto the Jatinga Road (dirt road). Travel for 1.9km to the Jatinga Gate.

Numbela Exclusive Riverside Accommodation

Michael and Tamasine Johnson
White River 1240
Tel: 013-751-3356
Email: relax@numbela.co.za Web www.numbela.co.za
Cell: 082-335-9528

I happened upon Numbela by chance on a day off and got lucky. Upon arrival I was met by a happy group of guests bringing the remnants of a picnic up from the river beach, and was soon joining them on the sandy bank for a drink. Just outside White River, the lodge is on a 200-acre wet-and-woodland wonderland that teems with bird life and which you are free to explore. Two cottages are separated by a converted mill-house. One has a raised stoep with a swing-seat piled with pillows and the interior is all about flair. The main room is enlivened by earthy red and orange paint-work, the bedroom is dressed with blushing fabrics and the washed-blue bathroom comes with an outdoor shower. The smaller thatched cottage near the river has chalky walls and claret-coloured floor with high ceilings, an Oregon pine kitchen, stable doors and an open fire. The bedroom is decorated with African artefacts, their origins explained in a thoughtful pamphlet. There's a welcome attention to detail, from the faultless design to the touches like refreshingly complimentary spirits and mixers and the delicious breakfast delivered to my patio. And you couldn't ask for more affable hosts than Michael and Tamasine. They are on hand to help with tasks great or small: organising Mozambique visas, balloon trips or spa treatments. These are people doing their own thing well. *Close to Casterbridge Farm shops and restaurants, golf courses and the Kruger gates.*

Rooms: 2 self-catering cottages: 1 double with en-suite shower plus mezzanine single; 1 double & twin with en-suite bath & outdoor shower.
Price: B&B: from R380 pp sharing. Self-catering: from R660 for 2 people, R1,000 for 4. Singles on request.
Meals: Full breakfast included in B&B rate. Kitchen stocked with essentials including spirits and mixers (B&B only).
Directions: 20km north of White River on R40 Hazyview road. The oval sign is clearly visible on left. Turn left and follow the signs down a dirt road for approximately 1km to the gate.

Map Number: 18

Tanamera

Craig and Liz McFadyen

Sabie Road, Hazyview 1242
Tel: 013-764-2900
Fax: 013-764-3517
Email: tanamera@tanamera.co.za
Web: www.tanamera.co.za
Cell: 082-456-9799

The view plunges into the Sabie River Valley with indigenous bush massed on sloping mountains either side of the tumbling water. The lodge has been positioned with punctilious accuracy to make the absolute most of this spectacular view and some unforgettable sunsets. Each room has its own private sundeck with unobstructed views, giving a tree-canopy sensation. Despite the heat of the day, there was a cool breeze flowing up through the valley and the thatched suites with their double doors onto the deck remained cool, yet were still sun-filled. The bedrooms, with their hand-made clay wood-burners and stylish furniture, are open-plan, a screen separating the bedroom zone from the bathroom. This comes complete with oval stone bath, view and waterfall shower – you sit among the 'rocks' and water pours down over you. For the real thing, you can go on a guided walk with Craig down to the deep pools of the river below where you can also fly-fish. Flop-worthy sofas and chairs fill the communal area around the large stone fireplace with the bar in the corner and beautifully embroidered drapes on the walls. There is also a 'home' behind the lodge, which sleeps ten, with a two-storey-high thatched ceiling, a gallery at mezzanine level leading to the bedrooms and a covered wooden deck with wicker furniture. A hammock hanging from the beams provides an ideal lounging area. High-class, yet super-friendly-relaxed!

Rooms: 4: 3 kings and 1 twin, all with en-suite bath and shower.
Price: R790 pp.
Meals: Full breakfast and dinner included. Lunches on request.
Directions: From Jo'burg take N4. Turn off at Belfast Dullstroom on R36 to Lydenberg. Go along the Long Tom pass on R37 to Sabie. Tanamera is on the R536, 26km from Sabie on the left.

Böhms Zeederberg Guest House

Marlene, Tina and Andrea Böhm
R536, Sabie 1260
Tel: 013-737-8101 Fax: 013-737-8193
Email: bohms@mweb.co.za Web: www.bohms.co.za
Cell: 083-29-3342

Böhms Zeederberg is a real institution in this part of the world, a large country house (in physical proportions rather than number of rooms), sitting pretty on one side of the Sabie River Valley. Your hosts are the extremely welcoming Böhms, mother Marlene and her daughters Tina and Andrea, and a cornucopia of exotic birdlife. The large swimming pool, sauna, lapa and jacuzzi are pure indulgence and the temptation to slip into the latter with a glass (or bottle) of champagne overwhelming. The chalets are dotted around neatly clipped lawns and each has its verandah, great view and own personality. My favourite has an intricate wrought-iron bed-head and yellow painted walls. A walking trail to the river below guarantees many sightings of wildlife and birds including the purple-crested loerie, a fan of the huge fig trees that dot the farm. You can admire the sunsets from the large stone verandah before hearty and delicious dinners in the main house. Also on the property is the Windmill Wine Shop, run by other members of the Böhm family, Thomas and his wife-chef Jacqui, who is a source of gastronomic delights. Come for luxury, pampering and peace. *20 mins to Kruger National Park, Blyde River Canyon et al. Hot-air ballooning, river rafting, game drives, riding and fishing all within easy reach.*

Rooms: 10: 5 doubles and 5 twins, 8 with bath and shower, 2 with shower only.
Price: R370 – R420 pp sharing. Singles R420 – R470.
Meals: Full breakfast included. 4-course evening meal R100.
Directions: From Jo'burg take N4. At Belfast take R540 to Dullstroom and then to Lydenburg. Take R37 to Sabie and then turn left after 26.6km from the R536 towards Hazyview.

Map Number: 18

Rissington Inn

Chris Harvie
PO Box 650, Hazyview 1242
Tel: 013-737-7700 Fax: 013-737-7112
Email: info@rissington.co.za Web: www.rissington.co.za

Informality and relaxation dictate at the Rissington Inn; you feel this even as you mount the broad steps to the verandah for the first time. Sun-lounging guests dazily contemplate the flower garden full of frangipani; the swimming pool is a rectangle of cool aquamarine; the hazy valley shimmers beyond. In the evenings gourmet, incredibly good-value candlelit dinners are served by friendly staff. We have eaten with Chris on four separate occasions and never been disappointed, despite much creativity and daring in the dishes. High ceilings put the lid on well-designed rooms. The one I had was enormous with a Victorian bathroom and its own sitting area. But Rissington isn't the sort of place where you feel like hiding away or watching TV. Owner/mover/shaker Chris actually seems to LIKE seeing his guests doing what they want, dressed how they feel and making friends. When you arrive there is usually a gaggle of guests lined up at his wooden bar and you could easily mistake them for Chris's personal friends. They probably only arrived a few minutes before you. *Hazyview sits at the portals of the Kruger National Park.*

Rooms: 14: 2 queens, 3 with 2 queen beds, 3 queens with an extra single, 6 king/twins, all en-suite bathrooms. Garden rooms have outside showers.
Price: R270 – R495 pp sharing. Single supplement + 50%.
Meals: Full breakfast included and served till noon. Restaurant on-site for à la carte lunch and dinner.
Directions: 2km south of Hazyview on R40 White River Numbi Gate (KNP) Rd. On right coming from main Hazyview 4-way stop – see signs for Rissington and Kiaat Park.

Map Number: 18

Destination Kruger Park

Hennie Van Deventer
PO Box 1705, Kruger National Park, Hoedspruit 1380
Tel: 015-793-0457 Fax: 015-793-2587
Email: reservations@destinationkrugerpark.co.za
Web: www.destinationkrugerpark.co.za

I was picked up and driven to a temporary encampment of khaki tents gathered on a sandy flat – the start of a real Boy's Own adventure. By the time you read this, they may have de-camped to an even better location. An evening game drive took us for sundowners to a spot where predators roam – down the hatch and back into the truck as quick as dignity would allow. Safely around the boma fire later, of course, I (well, we all) denied any such nerves! The traditional lamplight supper is where tomorrow is planned. Despite my excitement, I slept soundly till I was woken to listen to a territorial lion and to join the early morning walk. In bleary sunlight, zebra glowed gold as the dry grass and Marais and Chris, our reassuringly large guides, displayed a fathomless knowledge of local fauna and flora. We came across the small – army ants and dung beetles – and the not-so-small – a heavily-tusked elephant, who later found us when he wandered into camp. By then the temperature had soared and a hot wind was flapping at the tents, so we took turns to cool off under the shower. It's what I've been searching for. Whether walking with elephant, listening to lions or simply standing in the grandeur of the park, this place speaks to the soul. *Hennie can organise white-water rafting, ballooning and microlight flights.*

Rooms: 5 tents, all twins with en-suite camping loo and basin. Shared outdoor shower.
Price: R1,980 pp sharing. This includes all meals, game drives, guided bushwalks, mineral water, table wine, transfer from Hoedspruit or Eastgate airport and park entrance/conservation fees.
Meals: All meals and games activities (game drive, bush walk and picnic) included.
Directions: Will be provided with confirmation of booking.

Plains Camp

Nikki and Gerrit Mayer

Rhino Walking Safaris, Kruger National Park, Skukuza 1350
Tel: 011-467-4704 Fax: 011-467-4758
Email: kruger@isibindiafrica.co.za Web: www.zulunet.co.za
Cell: 083-631-4956 or 083-953-8580

This is where I fell for Africa: sitting outside my tent in the Kruger, sipping G&T (for the quinine, you understand) and watching game serenely traverse Timbitene plain. This is the only private lodge where you can walk in pristine wilderness – nothing short of a privilege. From Rhino Post, the fabulous sister lodge on the Mutlumuvi river bank (where you can stay) you walk to Plains Camp. Here the refined, pioneer tents have dark wood furniture with brass hinges and leather straps, and bathrooms with copper taps protruding from tree stumps and the largest, softest towels. During the day, you can doze on the chocolate-leather sofa or sip highball cocktails in the plunge pool. Pith helmets, surveying tools, maps and a gramophone add to the bygone feel and, to cap it all, the head ranger Gerrit is the sort over whom Karen Blixen might have swooned. Walking on rhino footpaths, the trails let you soak up both the scale and detail of the bush. No mad rush to tick off half-glimpsed Big Five, this – it's all about the quality of the sightings. That said, we encountered glowering buffalo, rampant rhino, lionesses on a hunt and had a pulse-quickening showdown with a bull elephant that I'll dine out on for ages. Afterwards we sent the sun down the sky and, wrapped in rugs, headed toward gas-lamp beacons for a never-ending feast. A safari fantasy come true.

Rooms: 4 twin-bed African-explorer-style tents, each with en-suite shower and overhead fan.
Price: R1,900 – R2,375 pp sharing. 'Sleep outs' are R2,200 – R2,650 pp. Ask about 3-, 4- or 5-night packages and single supplements.
Meals: All meals, activities, game drives and walks included.
Directions: From the Paul Kruger Gate follow signs to Skukuza Rest Camp. Drive through Skukuza on H1-2 towards Tshokwane and Satara. Cross Sabie and Sand rivers and after second turning to Maroela Loop, turn left signed Rhino Walking Safaris.

Lion Sands Private Game Reserve

Robert More

Sabi Sand Game Reserve 1240
Tel: 013-735-5000 Fax: 013-735-5330
Email: res@lionsands.com Web: www.lionsands.com
Cell: 011-646-4890

Set in 3,700 thrilling hectares in the Sabi Sand Game Reserve, Lion Sands is a family-run operation that provides a luxurious safari experience without ever forgetting to be friendly, welcoming and enormous fun. Owned by the same family since 1932, it's the only property in the reserve with substantial access to the Sabie River and you can sit by room or pool and applaud the wildlife show that the river stages day and night. There are two camps, the more informal River Lodge and the new, ultra-luxurious Ivory lodge. Opulence abounds and the rooms in both camps are thatched and spacious with a contemporary Afro-European elegance. All have river-facing decks and supremely comfortable mattresses and most else that the heart could desire. Ivory Lodge bedrooms even have private plunge pools, zen gardens and courtyards! Evening meals – and the food is first-class – happen in any one of myriad locations: dining room, boma, bush, river-bed braai or privately and romantically overlooking the river bed. And to top it all off, they have some superb game viewing. Mine started early as a young lioness chased my car, and at dawn the next day we saw a leopard within a minute of leaving camp. A wonderful place with tremendous staff and atmosphere – get there soon.

Rooms: 26: River Lodge has 16 king/twins, 4 doubles; Ivory Lodge has 6 king/twins. All rooms have en-suite bath and shower and outside shower.
Price: R.L: low season R3,000 pp sharing, singles R4,050, high season R3,850 pp sharing, singles R5,500. I.L: R7,000 pp sharing, singles R9,500.
Meals: All meals and 2 game drives and drinks on game drives included. Other drinks excl. for R.L guests. Local spirits and wine incl. for I.L guests.
Directions: Map can be faxed. From Hazyview follow signs to Kruger Gate. Turn left at Lion Sands sign and follow signs to River Lodge or Ivory Lodge.

Idube Private Game Reserve

Sally Kernick
Sabi Sand Game Reserve 1242
Tel: 011-888-3713 Fax: 011-888-2181
Email: info@idube.com Web: www.idube.com

There are few establishments where the staff seem to have as much fun working together as at Idube. Be they guides, trackers, managers or chefs, the Idube crew exude a delightful sense of goodwill to each other and to all mankind. And it's not difficult to see why. Warthog roam through the camp, elephants pass nearby; there is space and greenery, beauty and beast. The land was bought in 1983 by Louis and Marilyn Marais and Louis sensibly built the swimming pool before designing and constructing the rest of the camp himself. Guests sleep in chalets dotted around the sloping grounds, while the thatched seating and dining areas look out over the Sabi Sand Game Reserve. A rope bridge over the river bed takes you to a hide where you can admire the Shadulu dam and its regulars without being admired yourself. Two game drives per day plus guided walks give you the chance to see what's happening elsewhere in the reserve and tracker Titus amazed us with his ability to read bent grasses and droppings. We took time out for sundowners by a dam, accompanied by a bull elephant and a bull hippo. There was much posturing and manliness, not least from me, before a return to camp for dinner and conviviality under the stars.

Rooms: 11: 2 kings and 9 doubles all with en/s bathrooms and outdoor shower.
Price: Winter (May to end Sept) R1,950 pp sharing. Summer (October to end April) R2,800. Single supplement +35%.
Meals: All 3 meals plus morning and evening drives and a guided walk included. Drinks and transfers extra.
Directions: 34.4km from Hazyview along R536 towards Kruger Gate. Follow signs off to the left. 19.5km along a dirt road.

Map Number: 18

Nkorho Bush Lodge

Dirk and Jacqui Becker
Hluvukani 1363
Tel: 013-735-5367 Fax: 013-735-5585
Email: nkorho@mweb.co.za Web: www.nkorho.com

When I arrived, Dirk was up a ladder, one of the rangers was varnishing some wood, the school teacher (for Jacqui and Dirk's children) still hadn't gone home despite being on holiday leave, and there was just a generally friendly and involving bustle about the place. Guests come back here year after year because this family-run lodge is so welcoming and personable. The lodge has been in Dirk's family since 1950. While he was growing up he spent his holidays visiting the lions and elephants and the spirit of the bush was stamped indelibly upon him. Now he, Jackie and their rangers share this enthusiasm with their guests. The camp is under a kilometre away from the Kruger Park's unfenced boundary and game roam freely between the Kruger and Sabi Sands – a breeding herd of buffalo passed just in front of the camp while I was there. Brick-walled rooms are thatched and interiors have a tree theme, tree branches as the posts of the beds, tree-trunk tables and sleeper wood cupboards. Dinner (vegetarians are catered for) is usually served in the boma under the canopy of the night sky. If you make enough fuss, the staff perform the local dance, or you may be lucky enough to have a lantern-lit bush braai to sample some traditional South African cuisine. And then there are the game drives....

Rooms: 6: all queens with en-suite bath and shower.
Price: R1,095 – R1,260 pp sharing, all inclusive (3 meals, 2 game drives, optional bush walk).
Meals: All-inclusive.
Directions: Upper Sabi Sands. Map emailed or faxed.

Swaziland

Phophonyane Lodge

Lungile de Vletter
PO Box 199, Pigg's Peak
Tel: +268-437-1429 Fax: +268-437-1319
Email: lungile@phophonyane.co.sz Web: www.phophonyane.co.sz
Cell: +268-604-2802

A South African visa is enough to see you popping over the border into the Kingdom of Swaziland and immersing yourself in 500 hectares of pristine nature. Phophonyane Lodge is perched high on a valleyside in thick indigenous forest with the constant background music of a thousand birds (230 species) and the rushing white water of the Phophonyane River cascading down the kloof below (waterfall-viewing walks are a must). You move between the main lodge and the various tents and cottages on cobbles and wooden walkways, past murals and rough wood sculptures, natural materials blending easily into the landscape. Some of the cottages have sitting rooms, private gardens, narrow wooden staircases up to bedrooms and balconies, big showers, kitchens et al. The safari tents with their private decks are simpler but more romantic. You are lost in the trees and I stayed in one of the two right down by the rushing water's edge, the best sleeping draught imaginable. The reserve is criss-crossed with hiking paths leading to natural rock pools for swimming, and guests congregate at the bar in the evenings to watch the sun go down. Family-owned and run, Phophonyane is perfect for outdoorsy nature lovers. Since the last edition a new salt-water swimming pool has been added in front of their newly-built restaurant. This has a small library and sitting area too. *4x4 drives to mountains and Bushman paintings available.*

Rooms: 4 cottages (2 sleep 5, 1 sleeps 2); 2 with shower, 1 with b, 1 with b and sh. 5 tents (4 sleep 3, 1 sleeps 2); 1 has en/s sh, others have nearby private b'room.
Price: Safari tents R300 - R330 pp sharing, singles R420 - R460; Cottages R420 - R520, singles R600 - R760.
Meals: Each unit is self-catering, except some tents. A la carte restaurant available and picnic lunches can be prepared.
Directions: 14km north of Pigg's Peak Town or 35km from Jeppe's Reef border post to sign posts then approx 4km of dirt road following the signs to the entrance.

Map Number: 18

Limpopo Province

Tangala Safari Camp

Eugene and Nici Potgieter
Thornybush Nature Reserve
Tel: Res: 015-793-0321 Fax: Res: 015-793-0296 (h): 015-793-0543
Email: reservations@tangala.co.za Web: www.tangala.co.za

"Just nip around the rhino – he's somewhere up ahead – and we'll see you back at the lodge in a few minutes." Such was my introduction to Tangala as I drove past the other guests on their evening game drive. Situated in the middle of the Thornybush Game Reserve, the camp offers a true bush experience and Eugene is its king. A cross between Errol Flynn and David Attenborough, he's a mine of swash-buckling wisdom who knows pretty much every darn thing about the wild. He spent years working for the Department of Nature Conservation before turning the Potgieter family holiday home into a safari camp. There is a kind of rugged luxury here. No wooden masks adorn the walls, but sherry greets your evening return and drums call you to eat. There is no electricity to remind you of home, but the thatched huts provide ample delights: voluminous mozzie nets, hurricane lamps, thick towels and a choir of cicadas combine to lull you to sleep. Game viewing is generally excellent – I was lucky enough to see all the 'Big 5' inside 24 hours – and not necessarily that far away. Two days before my arrival, guests had watched a lion take down a wildebeest right opposite the bar. All *is*, of course, entirely safe, but half the fun is to believe otherwise.

Rooms: 5: 4 twins with en/s shower and private verandah; 1 honeymoon double with en/s bath, private verandah and viewing deck.
Price: R990 (low season) – R1,495 (high season) pp sharing.
Meals: Brunch, tea, 3-course supper, game drive snacks, 2 game drives and bush walk included.
Directions: From Nelspruit, north on R40. Turn R towards Hoedspruit (still on R40) & turn R after almost 2km onto the Guernsey Rd. Road becomes dirt after about 5km. Continue on dirt to T-junction. Turn R and 200m on L is Tangala gate behind a green building. Gate guard will open gate. From here it is 7.2km to camp.

Map Number: 18

Pezulu Tree House Lodge

Gilly and West Mathewson

Guernsey, Hoedspruit 1380
Tel: 015-793-2724
Fax: 015-793-2253
Email: pezlodge@mweb.co.za
Web: www.pezulu.co.za
Cell: 083-376-3048

The sorry victim of a tree-house-free childhood, I was intrigued by the concept of Pezulu – six different reed-and-thatch constructions spread among the trees surrounding the central building, which is itself entwined around a large amarula. They are all hidden from view behind branch and leaf, and many have bits of tree growing up through the floor to provide the most natural of towel rails, stools and loo paper holders. The 'houses' are named after the trees in which they sit: 'False Thorn' has a magnificent shower with views over the Thornybush Reserve – be prepared for inquisitive giraffe; while 'Huilboerboom' is a honeymoon suite set eight metres above ground (privacy even from the giraffe). Gilly's husband West conjured Pezulu out of the Guernsey Conservancy on the edge of the Kruger Park. There are no predators in this area, only plains game, so you and the buck can wander around the property in perfect safety. Activities on offer include the usual two game drives a day and/or guided hikes. They can also arrange microlight flights and visits to rehabilitation centres and the white lion breeding project... assuming they can persuade you down from the trees.

Rooms: 6: 1 family unit (1 double and 1 twin) and 5 doubles; 1 with en/s shower, 2 with separate bath, 3 with separate shower.
Price: All-inclusive rate: R950 – R1,500 pp sharing. Single supplement R100.
Meals: Fully inclusive of all meals, game activities, microlight flights, guided day trips to Kruger and tours of the Panoramic Route. No drinks included.
Directions: Ask when booking.

Gomo Gomo Game Lodge

Van Zyl Manktelow & Ryan Ashton

Timbavati Game Reserve, Nelspruit 1200
Tel: 013-752-3954 (reservations) Fax: 013-752-3002 (reservations)
Email: gomo@netactive.co.za Web: www.gomogomo.co.za
Cell: 082-454-2571

When Simon visited Gomo Gomo two years ago, he edged heroically past four male lions, sighted wart hogs, elephant and zebra, and all before he had been welcomed into camp. On arriving this time round, I learnt that one of the gardeners had just slain a spitting cobra with a slingshot and a leopard had killed an impala in camp. This bush is not for taming! Electricity has been added, but fans and bedside lamps complement, rather than compromise, the bush atmosphere. You sleep in rondavels or safari tents (I prefer the latter), some of which are river-facing and have private decks. A day in camp usually contains morning and evening game drives and a bush walk before guests gather for dinner in the boma and sit round a fire in as much of a circle as numbers allow. Want to or not, you will find yourself telling big-game stories (or at least big stories about game). The camp sits right by the Nhlaralumi River (swimming is a mite hazardous – fewer crocs and hippos in the pool) and the sounds of the night will stay with you (in a good way) for a long time. To top it all, managers Rudi and Ancabé are an impressively enthusiastic couple, a vital element, which makes the camp stand taller than others.

Rooms: 9: 5 brick-and-thatch rondavels (3 with 2 bedrooms), 4 with shower, 1 with bath; 4 luxury safari tents all with en/s shower.
Price: R700 – R1,250 pp sharing. Single supplement R350.
Meals: Full breakfast, lunch, dinner and game drives included. Extras are your bar bill and any curio purchases.
Directions: From Hoedspruit take the R40 south for 7km. Go left at Eastgate Airport sign. Follow to the gates – signed Gomo Gomo in the park.

Map Number: 18

Umlani Bushcamp

Marco Schiess
Timbavati Nature Reserve
Tel: 012-346-4028 Fax: 012-346-4023
Email: info@umlani.com Web: www.umlani.com
Cell: 083-468-2041

Rhino-tracking on foot; a rather exciting experience with a couple of bull elephants; sun-downers as the bush settles for the night... this is what safaris are supposed to be about, and Umlani delivers. The camp is set on a gentle slope above a dry river course (wet in spring) and no fence separates you from the Timbavati Nature Reserve's more feral inhabitants – you do not, for example, leave your hut at night to investigate snuffling noises! You sleep in comfortable reed-walled rondavels with thatched roofs (no bricks here) and no electricity, and you shower *au naturel,* in complete privacy, looking out over the greenery. Umlani also has the best pool in the bush, which you sometimes share with the elephants. Marco and his wife Marie ran the camp by themselves for a decade until the demands of a young family compelled them to find some help in the form of managers Don and Nina, a wonderfully welcoming couple who ensure you're looked after. After the evening game drive everyone sits out on the deck by the bar, mulling over what's just been seen before sitting down for dinner and mulling over the affairs of the world. Thoughtful hosts and knowledgeable rangers provide the charming, human face of a full-on bush experience. Civilisation in the midst of the wild. *A minimum of three nights is recommended.*

Rooms: 8 doubles (2 sleeping 4); all with en-suite outside showers.
Price: R1,700 pp sharing. Singles R1,950. Three-night special: R4,350 pp sharing or R5,100 for singles.
Meals: All meals, drinks and 2-3 game activities included.
Directions: You will get a map when you book.

Tshukudu Game Lodge

Lolly and Ala Sussens
Hoedspruit 1380
Tel: 015-793-2476 Fax: 015-793-2078
Email: tshukudu@iafrica.com Web: www.tshukudulodge.co.za
Cell: 083-626-4916

You snooze, you lose," goes up the cry on Tshukudu's unique morning walking safari. It is just as well to listen to the ranger's advice unless you want the accompanying lion leaping onto your back or an elephant knocking you over. There is true adventure here and not only for the children for whom Tshukudu is paradise. This is an active reserve where orphaned animals are reared and re-introduced to the wild, and it is possible to encounter animals that have made the successful transition. Guests are encouraged to share in the process, meeting the animals close up and walking through the bush with them. There are two game drives a day too, but plenty of opportunity to relax at the pool or the thatched bar. Dinner is a group affair, usually in the circular reed boma under the stars, where only the delicious buffet interrupts excited chatter. There are many game lodges in the Kruger area, but precious few are family-built, -owned and -managed. A warm, involving and edifying experience. Great for kids.

Rooms: 13: all doubles or twins with shower en-suite.
Price: R1,150 pp sharing. Singles R1,400. Includes all meals, game drives and walks.
Meals: All meals are included, but not drinks.
Directions: R40 north from Nelspruit. 4km north from Hoedspruit turn right at the Tshukudu sign – 6km down dirt road.

Mfubu Lodge & Gallery

Olga Kühnel and Jack Colenso
Balule Nature Reserve, Phalaborwa 1390
Tel: 015-769-6252 Fax: 015-769-6252
Email: olina@telkomsa.net Web: http://travel.to/mfubu
Cell: 083-635-0646

I've been deeper into the bush, but rarely has it seemed so penetrating. There are no fences here, just the guarantee of hot water, cold beer and animals that come to you. At dinner we ate the best Jansson's Temptation this side of the North Sea and awaited curtain-up. Silently hippos trotted onto centre stage, a brilliant moon silhouetting them against the white canvas of an alluvial beach. Nowadays the Olifants River eases like oil, so in the morning we ran the gauntlet, wading through its crocodile-infested waters. (Well, someone knew someone who thought they heard one here once). Safely on the other side, we clambered aboard a Land Rover, mingled with rhino, buffalo and giraffe and watched birds from a hide. On longer drives, Jack has been known to cook eggs on a shovel. Easy for a WW2 flying ace who's building himself a plane. "I've got all the parts," he says, "all I need is a miracle." The lodge itself sits on the riverbank, a trio of thatched cabins with fans, electric lights and tented fronts, connected by a walkway which weaves amongst trees. Further off, there are two cottages with kitchens, game-viewing platform and art gallery – Olga collects local art and encourages guests to paint, pen or ponder. It's not so much "shamrackle" (one of Olga's spoonerisms) as delightfully unrushed. Our friends in the bush.

Rooms: 5: 3 twin cabins sharing two showers; 1 twin timber cottage and 1 double stone cottage, both with own bath and showers.
Price: R490 pp. Single supplement R100.
Meals: Full breakfast and 3-course dinner included. Drinks not included. 3-hour game drive R120 pp including snacks and sundowners.
Directions: From Jo'burg N12, from Pretoria N4, through Witbank to Belfast. Left on R540 to Lydenberg, then R36 through Strijdom Tunnel following signs to Phalaborwa. Turn right onto R526 to Mica. 22km from Mica on R530 turn R on dirt road following Mfubu signs (about 9km).

Map Number: 18

Zuleika Country House

Altie Adendorff
R531, Hoedspruit 1380
Tel: 015-795-5064 Fax: 015-795-5063
Email: zuleika@tiscali.co.za Web: www.zuleika.co.za
Cell: 082-823-0609

The Drakensberg mountain range errupts magnificently from the horizon forming the lip of the Blyde River Canyon, the third largest in the world. The mountains are just a few kilometres past the end of Zuleika's garden and the view warrants a good glug of wine at sunset while you are seated on the wooden deck - meals are also served out here. You can either venture off to the dam at the base of the canyon (a twenty-minute drive) where you will feel insignificant in the lea of so much towering rock; or just less than an hour's drive will put you on top of the world overlooking the vast green-filled chasm. Zuleika is a new venture for Altie and Lucas, and their wonderful nature ideally suits having guests. The building is brand new, thatched, with built-in beds and earth-coat concrete floors, slate bathrooms in earthy hues and wooden-stick towel rails. Colours are rich and dusky; smoked blue, sand yellow and terracotta red. The best room is an open-plan suite with private balcony with view for romantic quiet evenings and listening to fish eagles in the mornings. Altie has converted an old farm dam into an elevated swimming pool and next to it is a thatched lapa for braais and shade under the indigenous marula tree. There are also two self-catering units with wooden ceilings, tiled floors, cherry-wood blinds and a kitchenette. Zuleika's next-door neighbour is an organizer of hot-air ballooning expeditions, microlighting and white-water rafting.

Rooms: 7: all king/twins, 2 with en-suite bath and shower, 1 with en-suite bath, 4 with en-suite shower.
Price: R275 – R550 pp.
Meals: Full breakfast included. 3-course fixed dinner of African cuisine by arrangement. Tea garden is open to public for light à la carte lunches.
Directions: On the R531. Map faxed or emailed.

Map Number: 18

Blue Cottages Country House

Calli and John Williams
Olifants River Estate, Hoedspruit 1380
Tel: 015-795-5114/5750 Fax: 015-795-5931/5062
Email: info@countryhouse.co.za Web: www.countryhouse.co.za and
www.kruger2canyons.com

Serendipity rules! Hungry as ever, I stopped off at a friendly-looking, afro-chic restaurant on my way to the Blyde River Canyon (truly magnificent!). After a delicious salad and a browse in the craft gallery, I spied some cottages nearby and immediately had a good feeling about them. It is immensely satisfying to find gold at the end of a scented trail. Luckily, Calli and John seemed as enthusiastic about our book as I was about their individually-wrapped rondavels set amidst a lush jungle of indigenous and tropical trees. Crane and Quail are small, round and thatched, whitewashed on the outside with blue doors and smothered in Virginia creeper. Inside, delphinium-blue walls, quaint cottage furniture and just enough space for a bed – sweet as pie. The private bathroom is in a separate hut just a few steps away. Crane and Garden Cottage come replete with delightful sitting rooms and kitchen(ette)s. Bedrooms, sitting rooms and the terrace are decorated with a showcase of superb African artefacts, the best pieces from their well-established Monsoon Gallery. Food is another bonus, the guest book riddled with rapturous references to Calli's culinary wizardry. Dinners are served on the verandah by lamplight and a traditional or 'health' breakfast will greet you in the morning. A delightful discovery and a good base for the Blyde River Canyon and Kruger Park. *All rooms have air-con or overhead fans.*

Rooms: 4: 2 rondavels (1 dble & 1 twin with private outside bath/shower); Garden Cottage (1 dble, en/s shower); Farmhouse Suite (sleeps 5, en/s bath & sh).
Price: Crane: R185 pp sharing; Quail: R135 pp sharing; Garden: R275 pp sharing; Farmhouse: R230 pp sharing. Singles + R50.
Meals: Breakfast included. Dinner R79 for 3-course meal.
Directions: On the Hoedspruit to Lydenberg road (R527) 28km from Hoedspruit.

Garonga Safari Camp

Bernardo Smith

Greater Makalali Game Reserve, Hoedspruit 1380
Tel: Res: 011-537-4620 Fax: Res: 011-447-0993 Camp: 015-793-0160
Email: reservations@garonga.com Web: www.garonga.com
Cell: Camp: 082-440-3522

Garonga is as close to heaven as most of us ever get. Bernardo has succeeded in creating a luxurious, yet completely relaxed, North African oasis in the middle of the South African bush: terracotta colours, thick earthen walls, cushions on low beds and billowing white fabrics. The pace is slow and unpressurised, the perfect relaxed environment for honeymooners, couples celebrating anniversaries – or for just about anyone who needs to make it up to someone else. Game drives are always available, but you may prefer to lie in under the high, white-tented canopy of your amazing room, dreaming of the candlelit bath taken under the stars on the previous evening with a bottle of wine; or of the sensational food you have enjoyed and hope still to enjoy. Alternately you can choose a more solitary, more exotic night's sleep twenty minutes from camp on a platform high above the water. Still stressed? Then return to Garonga and fall asleep in one of the hammocks or be pampered by the resident aromatherapist while gazing languidly over the nearby waterhole. Probably the most romantic place to stay in this book.

Rooms: 7: 4 king/twins and 2 doubles with indoor and outdoor shower; 1 bush suite with bath, shower, outdoor shower and air-conditioning.
Price: R2,375 – R7,200 per room.
Meals: Breakfast, lunch and dinner included, as well as picnics, sleep-outs and bush bath, house wines and beers, soft drinks.
Directions: Directions will be given to you when you book.

Coach House Hotel and Spa

Guy Matthews

Old Coach Rd, Agatha, near
Tzaneen 0850
Tel: 015-306-8000,
reservations: 015-306-8027
Fax: 015-306-8008
Email:
info@coachhouse.co.za,
reservations@coachhouse.co.
za
Web: www.coachhouse.co.za
Cell: 083-627-9999

The Coach House *is* a hotel, but it is a rare achievement in the genre to retain such a friendly and personal atmosphere; this is down to a dynamic Guy Matthews and his attentive team. You are encouraged to slow down, switch off, breathe in the air and maybe take a snooze on your own patio. The setting is spectacular, although the Drakensberg hid coyly behind the mist when I stayed. The food is also delicious and comes mostly from the surrounding farms. There is a floodlit croquet lawn (if you can muster the energy), a keyhole-shaped pool, a new spa with heated pool number two, a substantial gym and a variety of treatment rooms. You can also go hiking in the grounds (560 hectares, mostly dedicated to macadamia and pecan nut plantations) or sample the joys of the little nougat factory, the snooker room with views of the lowveld, the sitting room with roaring fires, and the oldest (109 years!) money jukebox in the world. Since the first edition people have continued to speak highly of the Coach House and it deserves its excellent reputation. *No children under 14. Kruger National Park is 100km away. Close to the Coach House: Rooikat Forest Trail, Debegeni waterfalls and township and cultural tours.*

Rooms: 41 rooms, all with en-suite bathrooms.
Price: R638 – R975 pp sharing (B&B). Single room R850 – R1,300 (B&B). Includes use of the sensorium.
Meals: All meals available in the restaurant. Casual breakfasts R120. 3-course set-menu dinners R250 (wine extra) or à la carte. Dress smart-casual.
Directions: Ask when booking.

Kings Walden Lodge

David and Tana Hilton-Barber
Agatha, Tzaneen 0850
Tel: 015-307-3262 Fax: 015-307-1548
Email: info@kingswalden.co.za Web: www.kingswalden.co.za
Cell: 083-380-3262

The famous garden at Kings Walden has been designed like a ship with terraces descending towards the prow – full of secret nooks and crannies. You never know what's round the next corner: a mirrored rose garden perhaps; a herb garden; an ornamental pond; lavender walks; bare-breasted sphinxes guarding a staircase leading to the next terrace up; a huge swimming pool or maybe Tana pottering in her straw hat? Found in the foothills of the northern Drakensberg Mountains, the three-acre garden is a series of flower and foliage compositions each chosen for colour, texture and shape on land that's been in Tana's family since the turn of the last century. The house sits at the stern of the imaginary boat atop a plateau that drops away on three sides affording long and spectacular views across the lowveld Letsitele Valley to the Drakensberg escarpment. As morning mist clears you'll think you're on the roof of Africa. Decorated in the style of an English colonial homestead, rooms are full of antiques and feel homely – all with open fireplaces in their sitting rooms. You will eat well here too, by the way. Tana's *cordon bleu* cooking is delicious. From Kings Walden you can drive or hike in mountains or forests, visit waterfalls, go boating and fishing on dams, play golf or tennis. And it's one hour to the Kruger National Park.

Rooms: 5: 4 double suites and 1 family unit with double and bunk beds and its own kitchen.
Price: R295 pp. Single supplement R95.
Meals: Full breakfast included. Lunches, picnics, scones and tea and 4-course dinner by arrangement.
Directions: From Johannesburg: N1 to Pietersburg then R71 to Tzaneen. Turn right onto the R36 just before Tzaneen. Stay on the R36; at first stop street, turn right to Agatha and sign to Kings Walden – approx 15km from Tzaneen – on the same road as the Coach House Hotel.

Indexes

Index by town name

For our rural properties, we have listed the nearest town.

Index by house name

THE GREENWOOD GUIDE TO

AUSTRALIA

special hand-picked accommodation

Second Edition, 2004/5

Following advanced and extremely delicate surgical procedures, we have managed to split Australia and New Zealand into two completely separate books. Both are alive and doing very well. The Greenwood Guide to Australia (2nd edition) contains 120 lodges, B&Bs, small hotels, inns and self-catering cottages.

For more information or to order any of our guides see our web site at
www.greenwoodguides.com
or email us at
editor@greenwoodguides.com.

THE GREENWOOD GUIDE TO
NEW ZEALAND

special hand-picked accommodation

Second Edition, 2004/5

The Greenwood Guide to New Zealand (2nd edition) contains
100 B&Bs, lodges, farms and self-catering cottages.

For more information or to order any
of our guides see our web site at
www.greenwoodguides.com
or email us at
editor@greenwoodguides.com

THE GREENWOOD GUIDE TO
CANADA

special hand-picked accommodation

First Edition

This is the latest addition to the Greenwood Guides series. 87 great B&Bs, inns, lodges, self-catering cottages... and even lighthouses and boats.

For more information or to order any of our guides see our web site at **www.greenwoodguides.com** or email us at **editor@greenwoodguides.com.**

Notes

Notes

Notes